African Drumming

The Harriet Tubman Series on the African Diaspora

Harriet Tubman Series

African Drumming

The History and Continuity of African Drumming Traditions

Modesto Amegago

AFRICA WORLD PRESS
TRENTON | LONDON | CAPE TOWN | NAIROBI | ADDIS ABABA | ASMARA | IBADAN | NEW DELHI

AFRICA WORLD PRESS
541 West Ingham Avenue | Suite B
Trenton, New Jersey 08638

Book and Cover design: Saverance Publishing Services

Library of Congress Cataloging-in-Publication Data

Amegago, Modesto Mawulolo Kwaku.
  African drumming : the history and continuity of African drumming traditions / Modesto Amegago.
     p. cm.
  Includes bibliographical references and index.
   ISBN 978-1-59221-934-6 (hard cover) -- ISBN 978-1-59221-935-3 (pbk.) 1. Drum--Performance--Africa. 2. Drum--Africa--Social aspects. 3. Drummers (Musicians)--Africa. I. Title.
  ML1035.A52 2013
  786.9096--dc23
                                        2013000921

Harriet Tubman Series

Table of Contents

Acknowledgements

I would like to thank our predecessors who have passed on the drumming, music and dance and cultural knowledge to us. I would also like to pay tribute to my father Atifose Amegago who handed over the baton of the music/dance to me and my mother Esiga Lodonu whose enthusiasm in music and dance performance and support had nurtured my artistic endeavours. My special thanks go out to all drummers of the Aŋlɔga Dɔnɔgbɔ, Dzelukɔfe and the entire Aŋlɔ state and Ewe nation, particularly, Kofi Eda Agɔvi, Klu Agbonotsi Vloefe, Emmanuel Ahiabor, Detsi-Kwasi Kugblenu, and the instructors and staff of the Ghanaian School of Performing Arts, particularly, Johnson Kemeh, Foli Adade, Salomon Amankwando, and the international communities for passing on the musical knowledge unto us. I also thank my informants including Professor Nketia, Darte Kumordzi, Emmanuel Agbeli, Zablong Abdallah, Christopher Ametefee, Wisdom Kpedor, and Godwin Korku Gati for giving me further insight into the art of drumming. My thanks also go out to William Diku, S. K. Kakraba, Aaron Bebe, and Piarrette Aboagye for teaching me how to play the gyil, xylophone, and nmani gourd percussion and songs. I would also like to thank Katrina Keefer for reading my work and giving me the necessary feedback. My special thanks go out to Professor Pablo Idahosa, Paul Lovejoy, Brenda Spotton Visano and Brenda Hart of York University for giving me the necessary support and opportunity to write this book, and to the members of the Nutifafa Afrikan Performance Ensemble for all their collaboration and support. To my family members at home and abroad whose moral supports and sacrifices have enabled me to accomplish this work, I owe much indebtedness.

Preface

This book has been inspired by the desire to preserve, disseminate and sustain African drumming/music and dance traditions. It is the result of the writer's cumulative experiences as a performing artist who was born and trained within the Ewe and Ghanaian drumming/music and dance and cultural traditions, and who continues to investigate the African and world music and dance practices, and share them with the world's peoples. In this book, the author attempts to highlight the essential elements of African drumming which would serve as a basis for understanding the cultural contexts and practices of African drumming/music and dance. The book is written in such a way as to be understood by readers of various levels.

Drumming is integrated with the social, occupational, religious, and political lives of the African peoples. For many years, the art of African drumming had been transmitted from one generation to the other through oral and practical means. These modes of transmission had been very effective in the past. However, the introduction of the Western educational system, new modes of documentation and communication on the African continent continue to pose a major challenge to the African traditional educational and communication systems. In addition, the relegation of African performing arts and other cultural practices to a status of heathenism, barbarism and primitivism by the West has contributed to their marginalization from the new educational system and their continuing decline in the African societies.

After independence, many African countries began to revive their cultures through research, documentation and preservation of African performing arts; music, dance and drama and introducing them into some of the new educational and cultural institutions (as curricular and extra-curricular activities). These institutions continue to train new generations of African Performing Artists, who together with the African Diaspora and Africanist artists and scholars continue to investigate, document and disseminate African performing arts and cultural values at local, urban and global settings. Recently, many of the world societies have begun to reconsider the cultural significance of drumming - hence its introduction into some of the world's institutions and communities in and outside of schools. However, Westernization and Christianization continue to threaten the survival of the traditional contexts of African drumming and education. These situations prevail while many of the older drummers/musicians are passing away at a faster rate. These issues necessitate further research into the contexts and processes of African drumming in order to document and share them with the global communities and posterity.

This book seeks to augment the prevailing literature on world drumming/music, dance and cultures, and to serve as a source of reference and inspiration for drummers/musicians, artists, arts educators and other interested people.

The author pays tribute to all the predecessors and fellow drummers, informants and scholars/researchers whose works provide valuable sources of inspiration, reference and a solid foundation for the book. He acknowledges the integrated and multidimensional nature of African drumming and will refer to the various components, related activities and contexts of African drumming where appropriate. He also admits the fact that, as the field of African drumming/music is very broad, he will draw from his experiences and the prevailing knowledge to shed light on the essential concepts, contexts and processes of African drumming in an effort to illuminate important aspects of this little-known topic.

The book is organized into eight main chapters: Chapter one provides an overview of the origin of drums and drumming in African cultures. Chapter two provides a discussion and examples of drums used in African cultures while chapter three discusses the uses and functions of drums in African cultures. Chapter four discusses the role of drummers in African societies; drummers' training, status and remuneration while chapter five discusses the organization of African drumming/performing groups. Chapter six provides a discussion of the drum making processes while chapter seven discusses the techniques, structure and processes of African drumming, factors that contribute to good or successful drumming and modes of appreciating African drumming. Finally, chapter eight elucidates the linguistic/textual basis of African drumming and the basis of expressing African drumming patterns, beats or sounds, followed by a summary and conclusion. Also included in the book are some photographs of African drums, drummers, dancers and various cultural producers.

Orthography

The letter ɔ which is inserted from the font Lucida san Unicode sounds like "or".

The letter ʋ which is inserted from Lucida san Unicode stands for a bilabial fricative letter, pronounced as if one is blowing air over the lower lip.

The letter ƒ which is inserted from Lucida san Unicode is also pronounced as if one is blowing air over the lower lip.

The letter ŋ which is inserted from Lucida san Unicode is pronounced by exerting some tension in an area of the throat closer to the soft palate and sounds like the suffix "ng" of "going"

Chapter One

Concerning the Origins of African Drums

Over the years, the various African societies have preserved a variety of instruments and repertoires of music/dance forms, which together constitute part of the African cultural heritage. One of such instruments is the drum, which forms the focus of this book. I will now provide a brief review of the definitions and origins of African drums before proceeding to other topics.

A drum is usually defined as a musical percussion, made of a hollowed out (usually cylindrical) body, covered at one or both ends with tightly stretched membrane(s) or head(s) with tuning devices or pegs which tighten or loosen the membrane to achieve different tones, which produces a booming, tapping or hollow sound when played (*The Random House College Dictionary Revised Edition*, 1988, p. 406).

Drums are broadly categorized (by musicologists such as Curt Sachs and Von Hornbostel) under membranophones because of the use of animals' hides in covering the heads of most of them (see Nettl, 1972, pp. 90-93). However, the concept of a drum in the African context may extend beyond membranophones to include percussion logs, xylophones and some other instruments that are categorized as idiophones. In reality, the instruments categorized under idiophones or self-sounding also have to be played or struck or set in motion in order for them to resonate. In addition, drums covered with membranes, xylophones and other instruments need wind or air in order to resonate properly, although they may not require human beings to blow the air directly or indirectly into them. Viewed from these perspectives, the (musicologists') distinction between aerophones (wind instruments) and other instruments becomes blurry. The African conception of drum may also encompass accompanying instruments, such as bells, clappers, voices and movements or the entire performance as will be elucidated later.

Information about the origin of drums in general and African drums in particular is lacking. Part of this information is in the form of oral narratives, some of which seem to have been based on empirical facts while others might have been based on speculations. This information may be of interest to researchers or scholars who would like to investigate further into the origin of drum(s). Drums are said to have been in existence since the beginning of human civilization. Some historians date the origin of drums to as far back as 6000 BC. Some small drums are said to have been discovered in Mesopotamian excavation around 3000 B.C. (Destefano, http://wwwpendz4.tripod.com/historyofdrums.htm). In the 1956 archaeological expedition to the Sahara, Henri Lhote and a team of explorers discovered in the Tassili n'Ajjer at Sefar, a rock painting featuring eight dancers; five women and three men) which has been attributed to the Sahara period of the "Neolithic hunters" (ca, 6000- 4000 B.C.) (Agawu, 2003, p. 3). According to Gerhard Kubik, the painting is probably one of the oldest testimonies of music/dance in Africa. It is characterized by rich dance decorations and clothing style, painted in white on a dark brown skin. The flexible athletic bodies of the men have markedly flare-shape leg dressing. Kubik who cites this and other evidence in a discussion of African music history draws on a theory of Helmut Gunther to suggest an affinity between the dance depicted on the rock painting and a contemporary Zulu stamping dance known as indlamu (Kubik, 1994, pp. 22-23; Agawu, p. 3).

Further, Frank Willet (1977) who opened up archaeological source material on Nigerian music by examining representations of musical instruments on stone terracotta from Ife (Yorubaland) concludes as to the history of Yoruba music that, during the classical Ife times, approximately the 10th to 14th centuries A.D., *igbin* drums were used, probably for Ogboni and Obatala, among others, although talking drums were not (Kubik, p. 28).

Investigations about the origin of drum(s), drumming or music and dance within African traditional societies would assist in understanding the origin of drums and related instruments. Many African societies have stories that refer to the origin of particular drums, or music/dance, or music/dance in general. For example, almost all my Ewe informants in Ghana (including oral historians, drum makers and drummers) attribute the origin of Ewe drums and music/dance to hunters. An informant would say "my grandfather or this person... told me that a hunter went to hunt and came across a group of animals (such as monkeys and dwarfs, playing drums and dancing. Being impressed by their performance, the hunter disguised or hid himself and observed the performance for some time. On his return, he re-enacted or shared this experience with the community and since then, the drum or drumming or music/dance has become part of the community."

A similar account about the origin of African drum/music/dance has been preserved in a text of Kpɔli or Orisha, divinity Letemedzi or Oretemedji in Afa or Ifa divination corpus of the Ewe and Yoruba respectively. This text was narrated to me by an Afa priest Atifose Amegago (at Aŋlɔga in 1999) as follows: "In the beginning, there was no drum or drumming in human society. A hunter went afield one day and came across a group of dwarfs performing music/dance. He disguised himself and observed the performance for some time, and later lured the dwarfs to human community where they taught human beings how to make drums". The event is said to be commemorated in a divine song of Letemedzi which states,

> *"Letemedzi Adza do go miva misi kpoyokpoyo,*
> *adziehe, anyiehe, miva misi kpoyokpoyo,"*

Meaning

> "Letemedzi Adza has put on new attire (life begins),
> come let us dance and twirl,

3

people in the north and south, come let us dance and twirl."

An informant (Kpedɔ 2010) states, "…the drum is a tree cut from the forest; its inside is hollowed out and its head has been covered with animal skin. But human beings learned drum making and drumming from animals through hunters". Another informant (Emmanuel Agbeli, 2010), states, "most Ewe drums or drumming styles that we perform today originated among our ancestors; some were borrowed from other people. In the past, drum making was not a specialized profession. Any smart or crafty person could go into the forest and cut a tree or log whose inside was partially eaten by insects or hollowed out, to make a drum. As years passed by, drumming had become beneficial to the society and specialist drum carvers had emerged. I know one drum-maker at Abɔ called Anani who started carving the *gboba*."

Some drums were reported to have been inspired by the sounds of other environmental creatures. For example, the origin of the Akan *aburukuwa*, a small and closed-ended supporting drum (used in *kete* orchestra) is traced to a singing bird called *aburukuwa*, whose sounds the drum was designed to imitate and whose name it came to bear. Also, the *etwie* drum of the Akan is said to have been inspired by the snarl of the leopard that the drum was designed to imitate (Kebede. p. 66). Similarly, the *laklevu* (wolf or sly-fox drum), a friction drum used by the Like clan of the Aŋlɔ-Ewe seems to have been inspired by the sounds of the wolf or sly-fox that the drum was made to imitate. The origin of the Congolese *ngoma* drum is said to have been inspired by the sound of the leopard that the drum was made to imitate The leopard is said to be a totemic animal of the region, "co ngo" which according to Dr. Fu-Kiau Bunseki, an expert on Congo culture, means 'land of the leopard' (see Kebede, p. 55; 64).

Similar accounts pertaining to the origin of African musical instruments may be heard in the African xylophone cultures. For example, according to the Dagara, the *gyil* (xylophone) originated from a man or a great hunter who went into the forest to hunt for a game and heard a pleasing sound. As he moved towards the direction of the sound, he saw the *kotombile*, a dwarf playing the *gyil*. Being fascinated by the music, he went home and called a friend to accompany him into the forest in order to catch the fairy and learn the music. As they went back into the forest, they were able to catch the fairy who taught them how to play and construct the *gyil*, xylophone. They then took the instrument to their community which they would play on various occasions, and to which women would dance (see also Vercelli, internet: musicweb.ucsd.edu/~/percussion-papers/rr_mvercelli[1]pdf. A similar account has been documented by Trevor Wiggins and Joseph Kobom (1992) which concluded that the men killed the *kotombile*, (dwarf), set fire, roasted its meat and ate it, after it had taught them how to make and play the *gyil*. According to Wiggins and Kobom, some Dagara people continue to believe the blood of the Kotombile still remains with the xylophone, hence it cannot be played by women since their blood would not mix with that of the fairy when they menstruate (Wiggins and Kobom, 1992, p. 3). Another narrative recounts how a village had been raided in the Upper-West region of Ghana and its inhabitants fled and scattered in the wood. In search of a way to bring the villagers back together, one man came across a piece of wood which he suspended over a ditch and played. The man found the sound very pleasing and, therefore, gathered additional wood and summoned his fellow villagers together by playing them. From then on, the instrument has been retained and modified.

Another story was narrated to Julie Strand by Fiye-Sine Konate (Kokolikan, Burkina Faso in 2009). The story goes that a very long time ago a Tusia hunter went into the bush and climbed a tree to wait for animals to come by. While he was waiting in the tree, a *jinn* or mythological being/spirit that lived in the bush, came along and pulled out a xylophone it had hidden in the grasses. After playing it a while, the *jinn* put it back and left, after which the hunter descended from the tree to examine the instrument. Once he started playing the instrument, the *jinns* knew he was touching their instrument and came back, and asked the hunter how he found the xylophone. The hunter responded that he saw the *jinn* and that he wanted to learn how to play the instrument, so the *jinns* taught him how to play and construct it, and showed him the specific types of tools needed to construct it (Strand, 2009, p. 177). The Sambla for example, claim that the *baan*, (xylophone) was brought to them by the Tusia (Strand, p. 177).

Further, the Susu (Sosso) oral tradition traces the origin of their *bala*, (xylophone) to a Susu king Sumaoro Kante who reigned around the 13th century. He was reported to have received the instrument from *jinna Maghan*, the king of the *jinns* (supernatural forces), and this instrument made him a powerful figure, and nobody else was allowed to touch it. One day, a *jeli* or griot called Bala Faseke Kouyate sneaked into the king's palace and started playing his *bala*. The king caught him in the act and he improvised a song in praise of him. Being impressed by the playing/singing of Faseke Kouyate, the king spared him from punishment. From then on the king made Bala Faseke his *bala* musician. It is further maitained that when Sunjata Keita defeated Sumaoro in 1236, and founded the Mali empire, he took the *bala* or *balafon* as war trophy and made Faseke Kouyate his musician and a guardian of the instrument. Since then, this musical role continues to be passed unto the descendants of Bala-Faseke Kouyate. The original instrument is said to have been preserved in the Guinean town of Niagassola (African music safari.com: http://www.african-music-safari.com/african-balafon-history.html). Related narratives about the origin of the xylophone may be heard among the Senufo and other African peoples. The *bala* xylophone is called by different names in various Mande cultures, such as *balo* (among the Mandinka of Gambia), *baluga* or *balant* (in Senegal, Guinea Bissau and Gambia) and *balugui* or *balangi* (among the Susu of Sierra Leone) (African music safari.com). The popular name, *balafon* derived from a two Malinke words, *bala* which is the name of the instrument, and *fo*, which means to play). The word *balafon* thus refers to the act of playing the *bala*.

The attribution of the origin of African drums or drumming/music and dance to animals, birds, hunters and mythological beings points to the connection between human beings and other environmental creatures and features. There seems to be some logic in such narratives. Empirically, most African drums/instruments are made from logs or wood of plants/trees and skins of animals that live in the trees or forest. One may say that the animals (who live in the forest and whose parts are used in making the drums) are more knowledgeable about their own environment and the functioning of parts of their bodies. A hunter, by virtue of his profession, is someone who explores the environment and who would have become familiar with the various species of flora and fauna over time. The hunting profession demands special knowledge and skills, and a hunter may be regarded as an explorer, geographer, scientist, biologist, physicist, craftsperson, an artist and a warrior (Amegago, 2000, pp.110-111).

Further, the origin of the *djembe* drum (also called *yembe* or *sangbanyi* among the Susu) is traced to blacksmiths. According to the Bamana (Bambara), the first *djembe* was invented by Numu, a Mandinka/Susu) blacksmith, from the skin of a mythical cross giraffe and zebra. The word, *djembe* is said to have derived from the saying: *anke dje, anke be* which means "everyone gather in peace". The word, *dje* is the verb for gather and *be* translates as peace. These words point to the primary function of the drum as a means of summoning people together in peace (Doumbia and Wirzbicki, 2005). It is worth noting that since the environmental sources reflect the true origin of African instruments and other artistic elements, an African may attribute the origin of the drum he had invented to such sources in order to pay tribute to the sources.

Other historical narratives attribute the origin of the drum or music/dance to metaphysical sources. According to his highness Oba Adetoyese Laoye 1 (former king of Ode), an authority on Yoruba music (also stated by Akin Euba, 1988), when Obatala, (the Yoruba divinity responsible for creativity) lived on earth, he had four wives and whenever he wished to dance, his wives would provide hand clapping for him. After some time, Obatala became bored with hand clapping and decided to make four drums for his wives to play. The drums were named after the wives: Iyanla, Iya Agan, Keke and Afeere; they are single-headed fixed-pitch drums which form the *igbin* drum ensemble, which is still used by the devotees of Obatala (Euba, 1988, p. 6).

Similarly, the *bata* drums of the Yoruba are reported to have evolved around Shango, a Yoruba king who reigned between 500-800 years ago and was deified as the God of thunder and lightning. Another legend from Ifa literary corpus (as narrated to Euba by Ifa scholar Wande Abimbola) recounts how Shango during his life time used to dance to all kinds of music without discrimination. In an ensemble at which different drums were present, he would move from one ensemble to the other. The people of Oyo felt that there should be one specific ensemble which would be associated with their king (Shango). Hence, they persuaded Shango to hold a competition for all the Yoruba drum ensembles, at which would be chosen one ensemble which would be identified with him. At the competition, the ensembles took turn to play and were eliminated one by one until there remained only the *bata*, which came to be associated with Shango (Euba, 1990, p. 42). The *bata* drums are still used by Shango's devotees. Akin Euba notes further that the music and other artistic symbols used by the devotees of Oya, the river goddess and the wife of Shango, are similar to those used for Shango (Euba, 1988, p. 6). The origin of *ijala*, (the hunters' music/chants of the Yoruba) is often attributed to Ogun, the divinity responsible for metal, iron or technological works (Euba p. 6).

The Yoruba consider Ayan as the patron God of drumming. As reported by Oba Laoye (to Euba, 1959), Ayan once lived on earth and came to the Yorubaland from Saworo (located in the region of Borgu in Kwara state) in Ibaribaland, where the Bariba people live today. He was the first drummer in the Yorubaland who taught the Yoruba the art of drumming, and is regarded as the ultimate ancestor of all drummers (Euba, 1988, p.7). Yoruba drummers also believe that Ayan is the spirit which resides in the drum and dictates everything they play on the drum. One of the praise names of Ayan is "Ayanagalu Asoro gi": "Ayan of Agalu, one who speaks through the medium of wood". All Yoruba drummers are said to have personal drumming names, prefixed by the word, Ayan, such as Ayantunji, Ayandele, Ayankolade (Euba, p. 7). Ayan is also regarded as the provider of all benefits for the drummer: drummer's house and other worldly belongings (as stated by Laisi Ayansola, an exponent of the *dundun* drum). He is also the power that gives the drummer the necessary confidence to enter an ensemble of dignitaries and perform his music. At least once a year, members of the drumming family make a joint sacrifice to Ayanagalu. Individual drummers may now and then make minor sacrifices on their own, either because the Ifa oracle recommends them, or because the drummers wish to show gratitude to Ayanagalu after a lucrative engagement (Euba, p.7). Ayan is honoured in the following *oriki* for *dundun* (as narrated by Ayankule to Akin Euba):

Ayanagalu asorogi	Ayanagalu, speaker through wood.
Amuni jeun olodi	He that compels one to eat the food that is contrary to one's tastes.
Amuni wo korokoro oloja	He that leads one into the innermost reaches of the market (Euba. 1990, p. 90).

A review of some oral and written accounts concerning the origin of the *dundun* drum is also provided by Euba (1990). A version of the accounts states that the *dundun* was first used by Ayan. Another version of the narrative (recounted by Ile Ife drummers) states that the *dundun* drum was brought to Ile Ife from heaven by the founders of Ile Ife. Yet, another account states that the *gudugudu* and *iyaalu* came to Ile Ife from Mecca, while an Ijebu Ode drummer states that his father brought the *dundun* to Ijebu-Ode from Oyo (Euba, 1990. p. 12). In addition, Salami Ladokun, one of the drummers of the Alaafin of Oyo maintains that it was Alaafin Atiba who introduced the *dundun* to Oyo and other Yoruba towns. The Oyo people were dissatisfied with the music being played for them and Atiba instructed his messenger to look for *dundun* which existed where they used to live and which they used to amuse themselves. The Mecca origin of the *dundun* was reiterated by Adenji who maintained that God created the *gudugudu* and *iyaalu* for Prophet Mohammed, which were placed in a mosque and guarded by two spirits. One day, as Mohammed and his followers were praying, some enemies approached to devastate the mosque. The spirits immediately began sounding the drums and so alerted the worshippers (Euba, 1990, p.39)

Another account (as published by Thieme and obtained by Euba in a personal interview with Oba Laoye I) dates the origin of the *dundun* to the Yoruba's migration into their present homeland, prior to the founding of Ile Ife, their migratory route having crossed the territory of the Ibariba (Euba, p.39).

Other legends relate to the order of appearance of individual *dundun* instruments: some hold that of all the *dundun* drums, the *gudugudu* (kettle drum) was created first, followed by *iyaalu*, *gangan, isaaju, kanango* and *kerikeri*. Yet, another account holds that *iyaalu, kanango, gudugudu, isaaju*, and *ikehin* were created together at the beginning and *kerikeri* was later created. Another informant suggests that *iyaalu* developed from *gangan* and *kanango* and that *gudugudu* was created before *iyaalu* while King suggested that the *koso* may be the first of the Yoruba drums (Euba, 1990, p. 40). Other oral and written accounts refer to the use of the *dundun* during *ijaiye* war (1860-65), leading to the defeat and capture of Adediran, the leader of *ijaiye* and the *dundun* drum (ibid, pp.40- 42). The hourglass tension drum was also depicted on a plaque of Benin thought to have been cast around 1550 and 1650 (ibid, p. 43).

A lexicographical work of Helen Hause (as reviewed by Euba 1990) contains extensive evidence pertaining to the origin of the *dundun* and names of musical instruments. Hause traces the etymology of the names of some of the *dundun* and other instruments of the Yoruba to show that they derived from the same source with tension drums found in other parts of West Africa. Her work points to the diffusions of musical terms originating from common roots over wide areas of West Africa as well as the north and south, and east and west migration patterns of West African peoples. The work also indicates that terms for musical instruments originating from the same linguistic roots sometimes refer to different instruments that emerged from different areas. Hause thought that the hourglass drum might have originated from Asia and was later introduced to Africa by the Arabs (Euba, p. 43).

The hourglass drum was also depicted in one of the Bharahat reliefs from India dancing from 2nd century B.C. which showed an instrument which Sachs described as hourglass drum (Euba, p. 45). The drum was also reported to have existed in Celon and Japan during the middle ages, to where it was imported from East Turkestan in the 4th century A.D. There were also reliefs in Central Java, containing illustrations of the hourglass drum dating from 8th century A.D. which is presumed to have gone to Central Java from India through Sumatra. Sachs also reported the excavation of earthen-ware objects or drums having an hourglass shape in Costa Rica (Euba, p. 45). He further referred to the similarities between the modern Indian hourglass drum and the ordinary Far Eastern hourglass drum in their construction, and provided a description of coiled drum sticks illustrated on the Indian relief of 2nd century B.C. and the hook form of the oldest kettle drum sticks of the near east (Euba, pp. 45-46).

Based on the analysis of the available data, Euba concludes that the development of the *dundun* is inevitably tied to the history of the Yoruba; their migration from Near East under Arabs and Jewish influences, in two major waves between 700 and 10th century AD (Oduduwa migration) around Bida and settlement at Ile Ife, from where they spread out in two phases: The first, during the 11th century and the founding of the kingdom of Ketu and Shabe in the West, Oyo in the Savannah and Benin in the East and the second phase, which was characterized by the formation of the Oyo empire (which reached its peak in the 17th and 18th centuries). Euba's analysis supports the view that the tension drum was introduced to the Yoruba after their settlement in their present home, and that the *igbin*, single-headed fixed pitched drums (used in ritual contexts and credited to Obatala) might have been older than the tension drum (Euba, p. 48). He also suggests that *kanango* was the first Yoruba tension drum, from which the *gangan* developed, followed by *isaaju*, front guard and *ikehin*, rear guard (Euba, pp. 54-55). However, these suggestions may be liable to further investigation.

Referring to the origin of the hourglass drum among the Dagbamba (also known as Dagomba) of Northern Ghana, Zablong Zakaria Abdallah (2010) states that the first *lung* or *donno* (hourglass drum) is traced to Bizun, the first *lunga*, drummer and founder of the drummers' lineage in Dagbon state. Bizun was reported to be a motherless child of one of the wives of Naa Nyaglsi, the king of Dagbon state (ca. 1353) and was often taunted by his half brothers. He would dress in rags and beg for left over food and take consolation in beating rhythms on a broken calabash. His music fascinated Naa Nyaglsi, who eventually chose him to succeed him (sit on the Yendi skin of the Dagbon state). But Bizun refused and instead, asked for the right to beat the calabash in peace. In response to this, Naa Nyaglsi declared that henceforth, the children of Bizun should be the official drummers of the state/court and be responsible for documenting the history of the nation and advising the kings/

chiefs. Thus, the *Lunsi* are perceived to have held the keys to the gates of Dagbon (Abdallah, 2010, p. 51). Although the above narrative does not provide detailed information on how the first *lung* was constructed by Bizun, one may assume that his playing of the calabash and his assigned role would have necessitated the invention or adoption of a more suitable instrument: the *lung*. Judging from their appearances and similarities, it is likely that *lung, lunka, tama* and *dundun* hourglass drums of the Dagbamba, Sambla and various Mande sub groups, and the Yoruba had originated from a common source.

The *udu,* (meaning pottery and peace), or *abang mbre*, pot for playing or pot drum of the Igbo of south-eastern Nigeria is said to have been invented by Igbo women from clays collected from sacred locations. One story holds that a potter once made an opening in a water vessel or pot and discovered its pleasing sound. Since then, the Igbo women continue to mold the *udu* based on the original model. The *udu* drums were later popularised in the United States and Western world by Frank Georgini an artist, designer and master ceramicist, and teacher who was introduced to the drum in 1974 by Abbass M. Ahuwan Akaji, a potter, artist and Professor at Amadu Bello University, Zaria, Nigeria. Since then, Frank Georgini has continued to mold hand-made *udu* drums and has developed a new technique called slip casting, to mold new types of *udu* referred to as claytone series (which have the same or similar tonal qualities with the original *udu*). The claytone series consist of four sizes of the molded version of the traditional *udu,* called claytone no. 1, 2, 3 and 4: the *kim kim, tambuta,* which creates very bright tones with short to medium decays; *utar,* which creates low bass tones with medium to long natural decays; *udongo,* which creates very rich and extreme textures between chambers, ranging from mellow, round, dry sound to bright, sharp, angular and wet sounds; *mbwata,* which creates rich textures between the chambers: the lower rounder chamber produces mellow, round, dry bass tones; the smaller flat chamber produces bright, sharp and wet tones; and *hadgini* which Georgini developed in collaboration with Jamie Haddad, produces brighter and transparent sounds like *tabla*. The new technique was aimed at producing good quality *udus* which are accessible to the wider audience at affordable prices. In 1998, the *udu* production rights were licensed to LP (Latin Percussion)

Music Group, the world leading hand percussion company (Mads Bischoff Abyhoj, 2011; dealney.com).

Patricia Tang (2007) has also shed light on the origin of the Wolof *sabar* drums. She reported (as narrated to her by Armadou, Mapate Daigne) how a long time ago, two brothers were sent to collect firewood, and a fight broke out concerning a brand of firewood each of them wanted to collect, which resulted in the untimely death of the younger brother. Not knowing what to do, the elder brother carried his brother's corpse home. On his return, his parents chased him away with the corpse, as he went and sat behind the house in a shade of a large tree (with the corpse). At meal times, the family would bring him his share. At a time, when a strong wind blew, his voice could not be heard loud enough. Therefore, he obtained two sticks and struck them against each other. During one night, one of the sticks was hollowed out by termites. The next day, the boy realised that the hollowed out stick was sounding louder than the other one. He then obtained a hollowed log on which he struck the two sticks to produce melodious sounds. On the seventh day of his exile, two crows which were fighting landed on his head. One had killed the other and scrapped a hole in the ground with its claws and buried the corpse in it. The boy imitated the crow by burying his deceased brother and returned to the house with the hollowed tree trunk that he held dear. Subsequently, the neighbours would come and ask him to make drums/music for them in return for gifts. Since then, his accidental killing of the brother was overlooked or repressed (Hale 1998, p. 61 as cited in Tang 2007. pp. 30-31).

Tang further narrates how the Wolof traced their drumming to neighbouring Serer who also claim to have learnt it from the Soose. The story also refers to Maysa Waalay Jon, an exiled king of Kaabu, who came to settle in Saloum with his family and griots and brought with them some percussion called *sarouba ndend*, one of the *sabar* drums. The Serer were inspired by this instrument and constructed other drums and rhythms called the *pitam*. The story also refers to how people from Dakar learnt the art of drumming from Serer and how drumming travelled from the Soose (people) to Sine, from Sine to Saloum and then to Dakar (Tang, 2007, p. 31). The account legitimizes Kaolack as the centre and birth place of *sabar*. Mbaye's explanation dates the origin of the *sabar* to the time of Maysa Waalay Jon in the fourteenth century (Tang, p. 31).

It is worth noting that some of the above cultural narratives actually refer to the early period of the groups' cultural formation and have been transmitted across generations due to their continuing relevance to the people's historical and cultural experiences. The significance of the drums or drumming/music/dance would have necessitated constant reflections on their origins.

Investigation of the concepts of drum in African languages may also shed light on the meaning, purpose, usage and origin of certain drums. It is worth noting that many African languages are said to lack words that refer to music and rhythm alone; and terms associated with performance usually have multiple meanings. Many of the African languages are referred to as tonal languages because the same word, when expressed in different tonal range may mean different things. For example, among the Fɔn and Ewe of Benin, Togo and Ghana, the words *hu* and *vu,* when expressed in the mid tonal range, would mean drum. The same words refer to music/dance, performance and vehicle. The words *hu* and *vu,* when prolonged as *huu...* or *vuu...*, may serve as human's imitation of the sounds of the wind (eya), moving vehicle, drum and other environmental creatures and features. The word *vuu* (a bilabial fricative), pronounced like blowing air over the lower lip), when expressed in low tonal range, may serve as a description of the duration of an utterance, action or phenomenon. In addition, the word, *hu,* when expressed in low tonal range, refers to divinity. Similarly, the Akan word, *twene,* refers to drum while the word, agorɔ, refers to a range of behaviours associated with play, drumming, music making, dancing and performance. The Igbo term, *egwu,* which means play, also refers to music; songs, dance and visual design (see also Agawu, p. 21).

Judging from the Ewe's perspective, the words *hu* and *vu,* both refer to drum, vehicle and their sounds and some sounds of human beings and other environmental creatures and features. The analysis also points to the function of the drum as an instrument for imitating, or projecting human and other environmental sounds. Human beings express themselves by using their vocal organs to utter intelligible and unintelligible sounds. An African may also use his/

her hands to tap the torso, chest and thighs, or stamp the feet on the ground to generate sounds. A potential African instrumentalist may express him/herself by experimenting with environmental objects and features, such as trees, logs, sticks and rocks. For example, an Ewe child living in the coastal area of Ghana, may be seen playing the side of a coconut tree whose stem has been partially hollowed out (due to ageing, decay, insect bites or accident) to satisfy his/her expressive desires. Also, as noted earlier, a Dagbamba child may be seen playing a broken calabash to express his desire for drumming/ music making. Another child may be seen beating pots, bowls and other utilitarian objects for the same reason. Such expressions usually involve the uttering of verbal sounds and the movement of other parts of the body. In can be inferred from the above analysis that the human's desire to express or experience sounds that appeal to him/her would have led to the invention of drums and related instruments in the original home of humanity. The drum may then be viewed as a medium of expressing or projecting the sounds, feelings and thoughts of human beings, or sounds desired by humans. It may also be regarded as a symbol of living, human, animal, spirit, and sounds of the universe. In response to the question about the origin of African drum, Dr. Date-Kumordzi states,

> The whole universe is sound. We call God Hatɔ Kpanli, or Atompani, male and female. The whole creation and existence is meant to become out of sound. Drums create rhythms and sound, and it is rhythm that is controlling the universe. Drums represent aspect of creation where things are set in motion. Dances are used to keep the rhythm and motion together. Drums become the fundamental principle through which we keep the rhythm and motion together. Drumming is the very foundation controlling the rhythm and motion of creation (personal conversation with Date-Kumɔdzi, August 26, 2010).

Other historical accounts (as documented by Nketia, 1971) attribute the origin and development, preservation and revival of certain drums, drumming, or music and dance types to some African kings and chiefs. For example, King Wegbadja or Akaba of Dahume, who reigned between 1679 and 1708 was associated with the creation and adoption of *kpanliga* poetry, recited with the accompaniment of double bells, the orchestra *abindondon*, or *hounga* (big drums, which were played behind the king to proclaim the victory of the royal army), the *gohoun, ako hounvla, adjakpete, dogba* and *ado* orchestras (Nketia in Wachsmann, 1971, pp. 12-13). King Tegbouessou of Dahume (1732-1775) was associated with the creation or revival of *agbadja, hanye, gokoe* and *gbolo* orchestras while King Guezo of Dahume (who reigned from 1818-1858) was associated with *agbessissohoun, bloukpete, kantato* and the revival of the gohoun orchestras (Nketia in Wachsmann, p. 14. The *ntahera* horn ensemble and *kete* drum orchestra were associated with Osei Tutu, the founder of the Ashanti Kingdom; the *mpebi* and *nkwawiri* drums of the Akan were attributed to Opoku Ware (1712), (successor of Osei Tutu) (Nketia in Wachsmann, p. 14). The Ashanti oral history also attributes the *apirede* orchestra (used at the courts of paramount chiefs in the Akan area of Ghana in connection with stool house ceremonies) to Apea Bosompem Boaban (Nketia in Wachsmann, pp. 15-16).

Some theorists propose an independent origin of the xylophones while others propose a diffusionist theory by tracing its origin to Asian sources. Some of the early anthropologists, musicologists and scholars speculate about the settlement of Indonesians in Mozambique around 500 C.E., based upon evidence of their settlement in other large river valleys in Africa (Mozambique, 2004) thus making a strong case for the infuence of Indonesian musical practices and resources in Mozambique.

The distribution of the xylophone in Africa was first mapped and discussed by Olga Boon (1936), and this map was used as a basis for examination of African xylophones distribution by later anthropologists and scholars - notably, Kurt Sachs (1940), Von Hornbostel, A. M Jones (1964/65), Lois Anderson (1968), Nettl Bruno (1972) and Roger Blench (1982) (see also Strand, p.154). Sachs proposed the Asian theory in his treatise, "The History of Musical Instruments" by claiming that the xylophone was invented in Indonesia and brought to Madagascar through migration, then to East Africa (Mozambique) and from there was distributed in Central and West Africa. Sachs further maintained that the advanced xylophones of the African primitives was borrowed from higher civilization of the Malays (cited in Blades, p. 74; http://ww.wiki. answers.com/Q/was_the_xylophone_invented_in_west_africa). A. M. Jones contends that the xylophone was brought from Asia to Africa by invading settlers about 2000 years ago. It has also been suggested that the Portuguese trade ships may have transported the concept of xylophones from Indonesia (Jones, 1964, p. 168). Nettl in referring to the origin of the African xylophones) states, "...it evidently originated from southeast Asia, and it has spread almost entirely around the world. Approximately 1500 years ago, a group of Malayo-Polynesians speaking peoples migrated to Africa, probably to Madagascar, and carried it with them. The fact has been generally accepted since certain tribes in Madagascar speak Malayo-Polynesian language and since Kunst has found some correspondences in the tuning of Indonesian and African xylophone" (Nettl, 1972, p. 100). These theories were also extended by Blench (1982) in an article about Indonesian influences on African music and Culture (see Kaptain, 1992, p. 10). Theories about the Indonesian origin of the African xylophone had been accepted by some scholars while others consider it to be harsh and absurd. For example, Hornbostel and Kunst believed that the Javenese slendo and pelong scales were exactly reproduced in Africa (Blades, p. 74). Other scholars such as Bernhard Ankermann and Siegfried Nadel disagreed with Sachs and Hornbostel while Boon felt more research along ethnological lines is needed before any conclusion is reached (cited in Blades, pp. 74-76).

In particular, the *timbila*, xylophones (of the Chopi of Mozambique) along with their highly orchestrated *ngodo* dance dramas which bear some similarities to the Gamelan shadow puppet dramas is often attributed to Indonesian sources. But, as Hogan notes, it is important to distinguish between influences and origin since the latter is difficult to pin down (Hogan: http://ww.ethnomusic.ucla. edu/pre/vol11html/Hogan.html). Hogan goes on to state that while xylophone practices in southern and eastern Africa have almost certainly been influenced by Indonesian travelers and settlers, they may have originated on the continent and have undoubtedly been developed according to a deeply African musical sensibility (Hogan: http://ww.ethnomusic.ucla.edu/pre/vol11html/Hogan. html).

Records of the *balafon* based on empirical evidence date back to at least 12 century CE before the arrival of the Portuguese in Africa (as noted earlier). In 1352, a Morroccan traveller, Ibn Battutta, reported the existence of the *ngoni* and *balafon* at the court of Malian ruler Mansa Musa (Hogan, http://ww.ethnomusic.ucla.edu/pre/vol11html/Hogan.html). Lois Ann Anderson, who corroborated the evidence about the existence of the African xylophone prior to the 13th century in Mali, also included in her account information on the many types of xylophones seen and heard in Africa and southeast Asia (New Grove Dictionary of Music and Musicians; Kaptain, 1992, p. 9). Claims about Indonesian origin of the African xylophones need to be substantiated by proper methodology and truth. Such claims are fraught with ethnocentric biases. Given the prevalence of the xylophone in its variety and uniqueness accross the West, Central, Eastern and southern part of the African continent, including areas that did not appear to have had any contacts with Indonesia nor had been influenced by its xylophone, it is plausible to state that the African xylophone might have originated independently of the Asian xylophone, and the instrument might have existed among certain African peoples long before it gained recognition in the 12th and 13th centuries.

Intercultural contacts through mutual friendship, trade, territorial expansion, conflict and conquest also culminated in the borrowing, adaptation and invention of certain drums. For example, the *fɔntɔmfrɔm* (drum) orchestra is said to have been captured by the Ashanti from the Denkyira and incorporated into the Akan political system. The (male and female) *atumpan* drums of the Akan were said to have been captured by Opoku Kwabon of Bekwai in a war against Akroma Apim of Nyame Duaso (during the reign of Opoku Ware (1712-50) (Nketia in Wachsmann, p.19). A suite of *kete* drumming called *adinkra* was reported to have been created by the Akan to commemorate the capturing of Adinkra, the king of Jama, a sub-group of the Akan (Opoku, 1987, p. 194).

The contact between the Ashanti and some northern Ghanaian groups led to the adoption of *mpintintoa*, gourd vessel drums by the Ashanti from their northern neighbors (Nketia in Wachsmann, p. 18). These drums had been incorporated into the Akan political paraphernalia. Similarly, the contacts between the northern and southern Ghanaian groups led to the widespread adoption of the *lung* or *donno*, (hourglass drum) and *gun-gon* or *brekete*, (double-headed drum) by many southern Ghanaian ethnic groups. According to Nketia, the hourglass drum was introduced to the Asante by Atakora of Mampong Beretuo clan, and was later incorporated into the dirges of Beretuo of Mampong and Ahensa (one of the places in Adanse where the Biretuo people of Mampong migrated from).

Further contacts between the Akan and various Ghanaian groups led to the widespread adoption of the Akan *atumpan* (male and female drums) by many Ghanaian ethnic groups (such as the Ewe, Ga, Dagbamba and Gonja). Also, according to Nketia, the contact between the Akan and Fon-Ewe of Dahume reflected in the existence of the musical types called *bloukpete* and *ketehoun* in Dahume. Further interaction between the Akan and Ewe of southern Ghana reflected in the creation of *asafo* or *vuga*, *aflui* and *kufade* by the Ewes of southern Ghana. These musical genres form part of the Ewe military organizations. The Arabs' contact with Sub-Saharan Africans groups may be seen in the presence of double-headed cylindrical and hourglass types of drums among the Arab, Berbers and many West African groups. In addition, the West's contact with African peoples is reflected in the presence of the marching band, particularly in the colonial African educational institutions, churches, military, police and prison services.

The European contacts with the Africans, and the Trans-Atlantic Slavery and subsequent movement of African peoples to the Diaspora, culminated in the emergence of many African derived drums, such as the *bomba* in Puerto Rico, *congas* in Cuba and the United States, and the *marimba* and other instruments in Guatemala and other Diaspora settings. There is a wide agreement about the African origin of the Latin American *marimba* although some writers have attempted to trace it to their local cultures. Some writers claim that the original *marimba* was brought to the Americas by Africans from Congo (Kaptain, p. 8). George List and Linda O'Brien for example, maintain that the African xylophone was a model upon which the Guatemala *marimba de tecomates* was developed. They also point to the fact that the word *marimba* is African derived and there was lack of archeological evidence of any pre-Columbian *marimba*. Gerhard Kubik cites this in his new

Grove Dictionary of Musical Instruments article about the *marimba* as does Garfias (1982 and Fenandez Ortiz (1952). Ortiz provides a detailed discussion on the etymological origins of the marimba in volume one of his Instrumentos de la Musica Afro-Cubana. His research reveals that the word *marimba* had been derived from the Bantu language, and states that the suffix, *mba* means to sing (Kaptain, pp. 8-9). Kubik elaborates on this theory by demonstrating that the word *rimba* in Bantu can define a single-note xylophone in Malawi or Mozambique and the *ma* is a plural prefix. Hence, *marimba* can mean a complete instrument made up of numerous individual keys (Kaptain, p. 9). Similarities between the African and American marimba/xylophones may be seen in the vibrating membranes attached to the gourd or wood resonators: mirliton or *kazoo* membrane or spider cocoon or cigarette paper used in covering the holes created at the sides of the gourds (although in Latin America, a piece of pig or sheep intestine may be stretched accross an opening in the resonator to create buzzing sound). However, in Latin America, the word *marimba* refers to both xylophone with gourd resonators and types of lamellaphones (Kaptain. p. 10). A modified version of the Latin American *marimba* contains metal tube resonators.

The discussion above has elucidated the definition of drum and the origins of the various drums. Although much of the oral and written accounts discussed above do not provide detailed information about the origin of the African drums, they have explained environmental and historical factors that inspired the origin of the drums, the materials used in constructing some of the drums as well as the interconnection between human beings and other environmental creatures and features. The discussion has also shed light on the borrowing and adaptation of drums that occurred among the Africans and world's peoples. This phenomenon challenges the notion of originality. For a drum borrowed from a given culture may be considered original or new in another culture. Nevertheless, it is important to acknowledge the source(s) of the various musical instruments.

Chapter Two

Drums in African Cultures

In the previous section, we reviewed the origin of drums in African cultures and the intercultural borrowing and adaptation of musical instruments. Groups that have historical ties or live in close proximity to one another tend to have similar musical instruments. In general, instruments found among the various African ethnic groups include stick clappers, bells of varied sizes and shapes, rectangular or squared percussive boxes, percussive gourds which are semi hemispherical in shape, lamellaphones such as *prempensua*, container rattles and bead-netted rattles as well as slit or log drums, pot drums and *gyil*, *bala* or *baan* xylophones. They further include animal tusk trumpets, wooden trumpets, reed pipes, flutes and whistles of varied types; chord or string instruments, such as harps, lutes and lyres; cylindrical, semi cylindrical, curvilinear, conical, rectangular, single-headed, doubled-headed, open-ended and closed-ended drums.

Drums appear to be one of the commonest instruments used in African cultures (especially in West Africa) although some societies tend to use them extensively (in terms of their quantity and frequency of their usage) relative to others. Drums (with a membrane) are reported to have been absent in the music and dance practices of the Zulu, Matabele, Shi, Ngoni, Tukana and some other African groups. These societies usually feature instruments such as xylophones, musical bows and *mbira* in their performance practices

(Hanna, 1987, p. 19). However, it is likely that some of these societies would have adopted some of the drums used by neighboring groups over time, especially in this era of intensified cross cultural interaction. Referring to African musical cultures, one may refer to cultures that make extensive use of drums covered with animals' hides, cultures that make extensive use of xylophones or "wooden drums" and those that make elaborate use of string instruments, etc.

Drums range from very small drums in the form of small bamboo tubes and coconut shells to large or tall drums that are between five to fifteen feet tall. There are tubular drums, bowl shaped drums, kettle-shaped drums and friction drums. Tubular drums include drums that resemble the shape of a barrel, cylinder, goblet, cone and hourglass. Bowl-shaped drums are drums that resemble a bowl. An example of kettle-shaped drum is *gudugudu* of the Yoruba of south-western Nigeria. Friction drums include drums that have special perforation at the center through which a stick is attached, extending through the center of the drum shell, and cylindrical or semi cylindrical drums whose heads are rubbed with special powder or clay, and played with special sticks, to produce desired (glissandi) friction sounds. Examples of double-headed drums are the *iyaalu* (hourglass tension drums and the *bata* (conical) drums of the Yoruba, the *kebero* drums of Ethiopia, *djundjun, sagban* and *kenkeni* drums of the Mande, Mandingo or Manding and Malinke groups. There are also drums made of earthen-ware, or clay, or cement mixed with clay, such as *zevu* or *zenli* pot drum of the Ewe-Fɔn, and slit drums of the Kuba, Igbo, Mangbetu and other African peoples, made from hollowed wood, slit open at the center (forming a pair of lips) (see also Kebede 1982, p. 55).

In some African societies, some drums are referred to as male while some others are referred to as female. For example, among the Ewe of southern Ghana, when two *atimevu* lead drums are used, the one which is tuned relatively higher is regarded as a female while the one tuned in a relatively lower pitch or tonal range is referred to as a male. Also, among the Akan, when a set of two *atumpan* drums are played together (by a single drummer), the drum which is tuned relatively lower in pitch is usually considered the male while the higher sounding *atumpan* is considered the female.

Drums may be played as solo, and in small and large ensembles. They are often combined with bells, clappers, rattles, string instruments such as *kora*; singing, dancing and dramatic enactment in various contexts. Some societies may prefer certain instruments combinations relative to others, due to their environmental influences, contextual requirements and tastes and preferences. The Ewe, for example, usually combine drums of various sizes, rattles, bells and singing in their music/dance performances while some Mande or Mandingo groups often feature *kora*, *bala* (xylophones), voices and drums with a membrane head in their performances. A discussion and examples of African drums are provided under various geographical areas and ethnic groups below:

Drums of Northern Africa

Drums used in Northern Africa include the *naqqara* or double kettle drum (which derived its name from the Arabic word, *naqr*, meaning to strike or beat) found among the Tuaregs of the Sahara; and *darbouka* or *dumbek* or *doumbek*, a goblet-shaped hand drum made with clay, metal, wood or plastic and covered with goat or fish skin (see Eastern Percussion, 2011, http://www.easternp.com/). A similar drum called *daluka* is used by a principal female singer during a spirit possession ceremony called *zur* among the Nubians in Sudan. The drums used in North Africa also include the *tar* (tambourine), a single-headed frame drum which has a hole in the rim for handling with one thumb, which is used to provide the rhythmic component of the Andalusian classical music of Tunisia and Morocco and to accompany the secular songs and dances of the Halfaya of Sudan and Egyptian belly dance (Kebede, p.63; Robinson, 1999, http://www. nscottrobinson.com/framedrums. php). Other instruments are the *riq* (also called, *rik*, *rikk* and *req*), a small tambourine-like single-

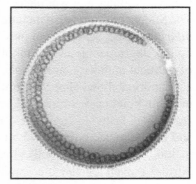

Figure 1. daf.
Source: Pooyan Nassehpoor

headed frame drum (with a hole in the rim for handling), which is between 12 to 16 inches in diameter, and is used in classical, popular and dance music in North Africa, the Mediterranean and the Middle East; Mazhar, a bass version of the riq used mostly in north African popular dance and folk music; *bendir*, a snared frame drum with jingles, used in Morocco, Egypt, Iraq and other countries; *duff*, *daf* or *deff* or *taf*, a large diameter frame drum (without jingles) used to provide bass rhythmic accompaniment to music and dance (Robinson, 1999, internet). Other drums found in Sudan include *bull*, a double-headed conical shape drum, *kola*, an earthen ware pot drum used by the Miri people of the Nubian mountains during rain-making festival; *leleng*, a set of small kettle drums used by the Shilluk people in their ceremonies and war dances. The Sudanese drums also include *nihas*, a copper kettle drum used by the Bagra people as a symbol of political authority and *tumble*, a cylindrical bowl-shaped drum

Figure 2. dumbek or darbuka
Source: asza.com

Figure 3. Moroccan Bendir
Source: Wikimedia.org.

used in kolokua instrumental ensemble during harvest and circumcision festivals (see The Archives of Contemporary music; and Grove music online). Additional drums found in North Africa include, *kidi* double-headed cylindrical drum (also found in Central Africa) played by the blacksmith-musicians among the Tabu of Libya to accompany singing during performances/works (Archive of Contemporary Music; and Grove Music Online).

Drums of West Africa

Drums of the Mande, Susu, Malinke, Bambara and their Sub Groups

A variety of drums are used by the Mande, Mandinka, Malinke, Mandingo and Susu of Senegal, Gambia, Sierra Leone, Guinea, Guinea Bissau, Burkina Faso and Bamana or Bambara of Mali. They include a set of double-headed cylindrical drums called *djundjun*, *sagban* and *kenkeni*, and (goblet size) *djembe* drums of various sizes, ranging between 10 inches to 14 inches in diameter and 24 to 30 inches high; and *tama*, an hourglass drum. The drums found among the Mandinka of Gambia include *tantango* or *saoruba*, a set of three opened-ended drums such as *kutirindingo*, the smallest drum, *kutiriba* the second smallest and *sabaro* the largest. The two (*kutiro*) small drums provide rhythmic background for the ensemble while the *sabaro* leads the ensemble (Knight 1974, p. 32; Tang, p. 33).

A set of *sabar* drums of various sizes are found among the Wolof of Sene-Gambia. They include open-ended drums such as *nder*, the tallest and lead *sabar* drum, which has the narrowest waist of about 17 inches in circumference and 42 inches in height, *m'beng m'beng* or *m'bung, m'bung*, a second *nder* (also called *mbalax nder*) which plays an accompanied part (and has the widest range of sounds)); *m'beng m'beng ball*, the second tallest open-ended *sabar* drum which is about 27 inches in height, 21 inches in waist circumference and 25 inches in base circumference (it has the loudest of the rhythm/bakk part and a very strong bass sound). *m'beng m'beng*, the medium size open-ended drum is between 22-24 inches in height, 21 inches in waist circumference and 25 inches in base circumference. (One of the *m'beng m'beng* is used to provide an accompaniment (*mbalax*); the other plays the rhythms with the rest of the ensemble); *tungune*, the shortest open-ended *sabar* drum, is about 17 inches in height, 20 inches in waist circumference and 25 inches in base circumference. It plays a high pitch accompanying part (*tungune*), and is the most recent addition to the *m'beng m'beng* family (invented during the second half of the 20th century). The *sabar* ensemble also include closed-ended drums

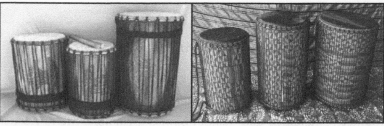

Figure 4. Left to right: Sangban, kenkeni and djundjun: made in Guinea

Source: Dan Rice, motherlandmusic.com

Figure 5. Left to right kenkeni, sangban and djundjun (made in Ghana).

Photo: Modesto Amegago Sept. 2010.

Figure 6. djembe drums made by Christopher Ametefee, Ghana.

Photo by Modesto Amegago. Sept. 2010.

Figure 7. djembe drum from Guinea.

Source: Dan Rice, motherland-music.com

Figure 8. Three kessings attached to a djembe drum

With kind permission of www.djembe~art.de

Figure 9. Kenkeni bells

With kind permission of www.djembe~art.de

Figure 10. Meinl's djembe drum
Source: Meinl USA L. C.

Figure 11. Meinl Headliner djembe
Source: Meinl USA L. C.

Figure 12. nder   **Figure 13. m'beng m'beng**
Both (Sabar) drums are carved from dimbe wood.
Source: Dan Rice, motherlandmusic.com

such as *ndend* or *col* or *thiol,* also called *lamb* (because of its use
in wrestling event), which is about 27 inches in height, 35 inches
in waist circumference and about 26 inches in base circumference
(it produces the lowest sound in the ensemble); *talmbat,* so named
according to its basic accompanying rhythm (also called *gorong
talmbat*), another closed-ended drum (slightly smaller and narrower
than the *lamb* produces a higher tenor sound); it is about 25 inches
tall; *gorong yeguel* or *goron mbabas,* (a new addition to the *sabar*
ensemble, invented by Doudou Ndiaye; also called *goron mbabas*
because of its use as a lead drum for the dance *mbabas* (which is
no longer in vogue). Its head is laced like an opened-bottom drum

Figure 14.
bougarabou drum
Source: Conrad Kubiak

and it produces a unique bright sharp sound. (The *goron yeguel* can also be used as a lead drum in the *sabar* ensemble) (Tang, p. 36; 38).

A variety of xylophones made of wooden slabs mounted on wooden frames with gourd resonators hanging beneath them are found among the Mande groups in Senegal, Guinea, Gambia, Sierra Leone, Mali, Burkina Faso, and Ivory Coast, under different names such as the *bala* (among the Susu and Senufo of Ivory Coast, Mali and Guinea and Burkina Faso), *baan* among the Sambla of the southern Burkina Faso, *balanta* (in Senegal) (see also Strand, pp. 2-5). Xylophones made of wooden slabs/ keys mounted on pits are found in Guinea and Chad while those mounted on banana stems are used in the Kissi country of Guinea and Ivory Coast. A sixteen key xylophone is used by the Bambara of Mali while the fourteen key xylophones are used by the Sara of Chad Republic (see Nketia, pp. 81-83). The gourd resonated xylophones are used by a number of linguistic groups such as Senufo, Bobo and Samago; Gouin, Turka and Karaboro; Bwaba and Bugali; Malinke and Birifor, Dagara, Gan, Jan and Siamou in Burkina Faso (Strand, pp. 3-4; 65-66).

Drums found among the Jola (Buluf, Fogny and Kalunai) of Senegal, Gambia and Guinea include a set of three or four *bugarabu* or *bougarabou* (also called *bugarab* and *bugareb*). These may be accompanied by a hunter's harp, hand clapping, dancing and singing, used to back *djembe* and *tama* in percussion ensembles.

A set of ceremonial drums called *bogolo*, carved standing on three legs and covered with cow hide, and ranging between 11-13 inches in diameter and 22-26 inches in height and drums used in other contexts are found among the Dan and Baule of Ivory Coast respectively. Xylophones with a narrow compass of one to four keys are also found among the Baule (Nketia, p. 81).

Figure 15. Bogolo, Dan ceremonial drums
Source: Dan Rice, motherlandmusic.com

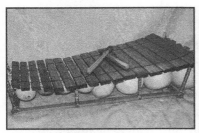

Figure 16. Bamana balafon

Figure 17. Susu Balafon

With kind permission of www.djembe~art.de   With kind permission of www.djembe~art.de

Figure 18. dyi dunni, water drum of the Bambara

With kind permission of www.djembe~art.de

Figure 19. dyi dunni from Guinea, also played by the Ewe youths in Gota and Bamburi

With kind permission of www.djembe~art.de

Figure 20. bara, badas, bendrey, koi or kour Popularly used in Northern Ghana, Burkina Faso and other countries in the Sahel West African Region

Source: Dan Rice, motherlandmusic.com

Figure 21. Gourd percussion played by women of Burkina Faso

Source: Lark In The Morning: http://larkinam.com

Drums of Northern Ghana and the surrounding areas

Among the Dagbamba and related groups of northern Ghana, the *lung, lunka,* or *donno,* double-headed hourglass drum of large, medium and small sizes, ranging about 18-30 inches long and 6-8 inches in diameter are found. The larger *donno* is traditionally used by the Dagbamba for narrating history; the lead part in praise name dances, and the responsorial part in other dances including *damba*; the versatile medium size drums can play the lead (*lundaa*) or answer (*lun kpahira*) part in all musical types (see Locke, pp. 31-32). The Dagbamba drums also include the *gun-gon* or *brekete* a double-headed cylindrical snare drum, ranging between 20-24 inches long and 12-15 inches in diameter. Variants of the *donno* and *brekete* are found in the

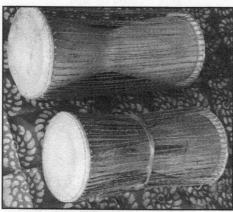

Figure 22. A set of donno drums: Drum maker: Zablong Abdalllah

Photo: Modesto Amegago, Sept. 2010.

Chad Republic, Nigeria, Ivory Coast, Togo, Burkina Faso, Guinea, Mali and Senegal and other parts of West Africa and the world. The *kori* or *kuor* or *koi* gourd vessel drums are used by the Kasena-Nankani, Dagara, Sisala and Lobi of the Upper West region of Ghana. A similar (gourd vessel) drum called *badas or bendrey* is

Figure 23. A set of seyalim rattles
Photo: with kind permission from www.djembe~art.de.

Figure 24. A set of gungun drums: Drum-maker Zablong Abdallah
Photo: Modesto Amegago, Sept. 2010.

Figure 25. nmani gourd vessel drums played by the Dagbamba women and their neighbors.

Photo: Modesto Amegago, Sept. 2010.

Figure 27. gyl xylophone of the Dagara

Figure 26. A pair of gyile xylophone   Lobi and Sisala. Photo: Modesto Amegago, 2010.

used in Burkina Faso and some other Sahel West African regions. The *gyil* xylophone made of wooden slabs/keys ranging between fourteen, seventeen and twenty-two, mounted on rectangular wooden frames with gourd resonators hanging beneath them, is used by the Dagara, Lobi, Dagarti and Sisala of upper West region of Ghana and the southern part of Burkina Faso and north-eastern part of Cote D'Ivoire (see Nketia, p. 82; Wiggins and Kobom, pp. 7-8; Strand, pp. 1-5; 91-114).

Drums of the Hausa

Among the Hausa of northern Ghana and Northern Nigeria, *baba gangan*, a double-headed hourglass drum (similar to the *iyaalu* of the Yoruba), *tambura*, royal kettle drum and *taushi*, a drum which is conical in shape are found (Euba, p. 36). The *sakara* drum which is between 10-12 inches in diameter and one

and half inches in depth (with funnel-like slopping towards the end), made with ceramic clay, covered with goat, cow or antelope skin, is used.

Drums of the Ewe, Fɔn and some neighboring groups

Figure 28. A set of dundun/donno drums of the Hausa
Source: Dan Rice, motherlandmusic.com

Drums used by the Ewe and Fɔn of West Africa include the *atimevu*, an open-ended drum, ranging between four and half feet to six feet tall and 9-10 inches in diameter; the *gboba*, an open-ended barrel-shaped supporting or lead drum which is between 34-36 inches tall and 16 inches in diameter; *sogo*, closed-ended supporting drum which is about 27 inches tall and 9-10-inches in diameter, *kidi, asivui, kpetsi* or *vuvi,* a closed-ended support-ing drum which is between 23 inches high and 8-9 inches in diameter and *kagan* an open-ended slim supporting drum which is between 23 inches tall and 6-7 inches in diameter. The Ewe drums also include the *kloboto* and *totodzi* or *klodzi,* short open-ended supporting drums which are about 16 inches tall and 10-12 inches in diameter; *patenge,* a small double-headed orna-mental (metal) drum, which is between 10-12 inches long and 10 inches in diameter. A set of three or four drums such as *vuvi* and *vuga* or *adzima* of

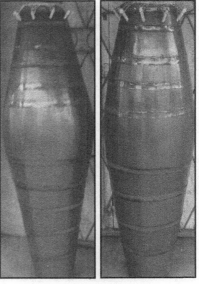

Figures 29 and 30. set of Atimewu drums.
Drum Maker: Freeman Donkor
Photo: Modesto Amegago: August 2010

Figure 31. Gboba drum.
Drum Maker: Freeman Donkor
Photo: Modesto Amegago, August 2010

various sizes, ranging between 16 to 28 inches tall and 8-12 inches in diameter are used by the Ewe in the middle and northern part of the Volta Region of Ghana and southern part of Togoland in *bɔbɔɔbɔ* music/dance.

Agblɔvu, an open-ended (signal or talking) drum is widely used by the Ewe in their political contexts. The *laklevu,* (wolf or sly fox drum) an open-ended friction drum is used by the Like clan of the Aŋlɔ-Ewe in ceremonial contexts. A set of two or three square-framed drums called *tamale* are used by Ewe youths in *konkoma* and *bɔbɔɔbɔ* recreational music and dance, (but they are rarely used nowadays).

The *donno* (double-headed hourglass drum) and *brekete* (double-headed cylindrical drum) which were adopted from northern

Figure 32. kloboto.
Drum Maker: Freeman Donkor
Photo: Modesto Amegago, August 2010

Figure 33. Totodzi.
Drum Maker: Freeman Donkor
Photo: Modesto Amegago, August 2010

Ghana are also used by the Ewe (in traditional and contemporary religious contexts). A set of *asafo* or *vuga* and *atompani* drums (which were adopted from the Akan) of various sizes: the smaller ones ranging between 15 to 24 inches tall and 6-8 inches in diameter, and the larger ones ranging between four and half to six feet tall and 12-14 inches in diameter are used by the Ewe (mostly in ceremonial contexts). In addition, the *adakavuwo* or *adakagovuwo*, (rectangular) box drums or box resonators are used by the Aŋlɔ-Ewe during the period (ranging from a week to about a month) preceding or after a festival celebration, when a ban is imposed on playing drums covered with membranes in the area. This is done in order to maintain tranquility and harmony with the environment and spiri-

Figure 34. kagan,　　　　kidi　　　　　　　sogo
Drum-maker: Christopher Ametefee. Photo: Modesto Amegago, August 2010

Figure 35. A set of wuga and wuviwo, lead and supporting drums of the Have bɔbɔɔbɔ group.
Photo: Modesto Amegago at the second annual *bɔbɔɔbɔ* festival, Ho, Ghana. Nov.4 2011.

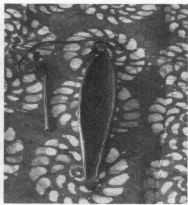

Figure 36. A set of Gangokui bells
Photo: Modesto Amegago, August 2010

Figure 37. Atoke bell
Photo: Modesto Amegago, August 2010

Figure 38. Axatsewo: Rattles
Photo: Modesto Amegago, Sept. 2010.

tual forces before or after the celebration, which usually involves prolong and intense music/dance performances and merry making). Some of these drums are usually combined with bells, rattles, hand clapping, voices and flutes in various performance contexts. One to four slabs xylophones and other drums are found among the Bariba of Dahomey and the Kabere of Togo (Nketia, p. 81).

Drums of the Akan

Drums of the Akan of southern Ghana and Ivory Coast include an ensemble of *adowa* drums such as *petia*, an open-ended (supporting drum) which is between 18 inches tall and 8 inches in diameter, *apentemma*, an open-ended supporting drum (bottle-shaped at the bottom) which ranges between 18-20 inches tall and 7-9 inches in upper diameter, the male and female *atumpan*, open-ended (talking) drums which are between 30 to 36 inches tall and 10-14 inches in

Figure 39. A set of the Akan kete drums of the Ghana Dance Ensemble. Left to right: aburukuwa, kwadum, apentemma and aburukuwa

Drum-maker: Christopher Ametefee. Photo: Modesto Amegago, December 2011.

Figure 40. A set of the Akan fɔntɔmfrɔm drums of the Ghana Dance Ensemble. Left to right: brenko, oprenten, bɔmmaa, male and female atumpan and bɔmmaa drums.

Photo: Modesto Amegago, Sept. 2010.

Figure 42. tamali frame drums
used by the Ga, Akan and Ewe
youths recreational music/dance
Source: Dan Rice, motherlandmusic.com

**Figure 41. gome drum used by the
Ga youths**
Source: Dan Rice, motherlandmusic.com

diameter. They are used to communicate in ceremonial and social
contexts and as lead drums in *adowa* and *fͻntͻmfrͻm* ensembles.
The Akan drums also include an ensemble of *kete* drums such as
two (small close-ended supporting drums) *aburukuwa*, or *akukua*
or *akukuadwo*, which are between 12 inches tall and 6-8 inches in
diameter, *apentemma* (as described earlier) and *kwadum*, an open-
ended lead drum which is between 18-22 inches tall and 12-14
inches in diameter; a set of *fͻntͻmfrͻm* or *bͻmmaa*, open-ended male
and female drums which are about 5 -5 ½ feet tall and 14-16 inches
in diameter, *adukurogya*, an open-ended drum which is between 30
inches tall and 8 inches in diameter, *brenko* an open-ended bottle-
shaped drum which is about the size of *apentemma*; *paso* (*apasoͻ*), a
relatively small high pitched drum, *ͻperenten,* an open-ended bottle-
shaped drum which is a little bigger than *apentemma, adedemma*, a
bottle-shaped drum (which is slimmer and taller than *apentemma*)
which is about three and a half feet tall and eight inches in diameter,
asafotwene, an opened-ended drum which is about 18-24 inches
tall and 8-10 inches in diameter (which may be played alone or
along with *ntahera* elephant tusk trumpet ensemble, to herald the
movement of the Akan leaders). Other drums used by the Akan are
mpintintoa, gourd vessel drums which range between 10-12 inches
in diameter, *donno*, hourglass drums of varied sizes (the large one is
called *monka*; medium one is called *agyesowa* and the smallest one

is called *dawuro*); *gyamadudu* a double-headed cylindrical drum, which is about 28 inches long and 13 inches in diameter; *osekye* (*atenten*) and *sanga*, double-headed cylindrical drums which are between 20-24 inches long and 9-12 inches in diameter. The *tamalin*, square-framed drums (which are also used by the Ewe youths) are used by the Akan youths in some contemporary musical types such as *sikyi* and *asaadua* (see also Nketia, 1963, p. 86; pp. 177-182).

Drums of the Ga-Adangbe

A set of *kpanlogo* drums: *kpa*, *pati* and *twerenshi*, ranging between 20-26 inches tall and 8-10 inches in diameter, *tamalin* square-framed drums (also used by the Ewe and Akan youths (and by the Yoruba who call it Samba)), *donno* and *brekete*, (which had been borrowed from the North as described earlier), *asafo* or *bɔmmaa* or *fɔntɔmfrɔm* drums (which were adopted from the Akan) are used by the Ga of southern Ghana in social, ritual and ceremonial contexts. A set of the Ewe (*sogo, kidi* and *atimevu*) drums are also used by the Ga-Adangme who live in close proximity with the Ewe (by the west).

Figure 43. A set of Ga Kpanlogo drums made by Christopher Ametefee, a master drummer of the Dance Ghana Dance Ensemble.
Photo: Modesto Amegago, Sept. 2010.

Drums of the Yoruba

Drums used by the Yoruba of south-western Nigeria and south-eastern Benin include a set of (double-headed conical) *bata* drums, which include iya, the large drum (the mother), *itotele*, the medium drum (the father), and *okonkolo*, the small drum (the child). The larger part of the drum's head is called *enu* while the smaller part is called *chacha*. These drums are often decorated with small bells and chimes called *saworoide* or *saworo* by the Yoruba at home and *chaworoide* or *chaworo* by the Yoruba descendants in Cuba.

The Yoruba drums also include the *dundun* ensemble, consisting of *iyaalu*, the largest tension drum that leads the ensemble and dictates the pace of the music. It has between 9-10 jingles (*saworo*), attached to the lower part of each head and is between 19-21 inches long and 28-34 inches in circumference; *kerikeri*, also known as *aguda* (and *dabu* in Ondo State) which may be similar to, or bigger than *iyaalu*; *isaaju* (front guard) (also known as *omele ako, ilewa* (in ijebu-Igbo) and *kekeke* (in Ikorodu) provide high pitch sound; it is between 15 and 19 inches long and 22 and 28 inches in circumference; *ikehin* (rear guard) (also called *gbamgbala, omele abo* and *ebele,* or *emele*) is between 18 and 18.5 inches long and 26 and 27 inches in circumference. The *ikehin* and *isaaju* are collectively known as *kanran* (Euba 1990, pp. 113-114). The *dundun* ensemble also includes *gudugudu*, kettle-shaped drum, which is between 24-31 inches in upper circumference, 15-20 inches in bottom circumference and 4-7 inches in height. Another Yoruba drum is the *gangan*; it is similar to the *iyaalu* but has elongated cylindrical trunk or neck separating its heads areas. With the exception of the *kanango*, all drums of the *gangan* sub family have their tension strings coloured brown. The *gangan* (also called *kajukaju* by Ajimo Asimi) is the biggest of the *gangan* type of instruments, followed by *adamo* which is identical to but smaller than the *gangan,* followed by the *kanango*, the smallest of all the tension drums (which has white tension strings similar to *iyaalu*). In addition, *ipese*, special drums used in rituals associated with Ifa; and *apinti*, a set of two or three drums accompanied by iron bell(s), and the *igbin* ensemble played for Obatala, the god of creation, are used by the Yoruba (Euba, 1988, p. 8). The Yoruba drums also include *ashiko*,

Figure 44. iyaalu
Source: Dabi Kanyinsola,
dabi@kanyinsola.com

Figure 45. atele
Source: Dabi Kanyinsola,
dabi@kanyinsola.com

**Figure 46. omele(omele abo), and
Isaju (omele ako)**
Source: Dabi Kanyinsola,
dabi@kanyinsola.com

Figure 47. gudugudu
Source: Dabi Kanyinsola,
dabi@kanyinsola.com

Figure 49. A set of sakara drums
Source: Dan Rice, Motherlandmusic.com

Figure 48. A set of bata drums
Source: Dan Rice, Motherlandmusic.com

straight-sided open-ended drum which is narrower at the bottom
(originally carved out of solid wood and now carved of staves) and
sakara, a round clay stick beaten drum which is between 10-12
inches in diameter and one and half inches deep (slopping inward
funnel-like towards the back (Wikimedia Commons). The Ashiko
was later introduced to Haiti, Cuba and USA. In Eastern Cuba,

Figure 50. ashiko drums
Pam Fleenor: wildwoodinstrument.com

the *ashiko* is known as *boku*.
Most of these drums are usually
combined with human voices,
sekere or rattles, *agogo* or gongs,
hand clapping and flute called
agidigbo in various performance
contexts.

**Figure 51. Ceremonial drum of the
Yoruba**
Source: Hamill Gallery of Tribal Art

Drums of the Igbo and other Eastern Nigerian Groups

Drums used by the Igbo of south-eastern Nigeria include a
set of three or four *udu* or *abang mbre*, (pot for playing) drums,
each with a hole on its side (with the exception of some large ones
which may not have a hole on their side). As noted in the previous chapter, some newer *udu* are now made by Frank Georgini,
Jamey Haddad, and the Latin Percussion Company in The United
States of America. The Igbo drums also include a set of *igba*, open-
ended cylindrical drums carved out of padauk wood and covered
with antelope skin, surrounded by wedges and pegs which serve as
tuning devices. These drums range from about six inches in diameter and 38 inches tall to 7.5-9 inches in diameter and 40-42 inches
tall. The *ekwe*, a two-pitched slit drum of yellow and red colours,
carved of *ube* (white) wood and orji, padauk red wood are also used
by the Igbo and their neighbors (Motherland Music.com, internet).
Xylophone with narrow compass made of up to four slabs, and

Figure 52. udu drum of the Igbo
Source: Dan Rice, motherlandmusic.com

Figure 53. udu drum of the Igbo
By courtesy of asza.com

Figure 55. Frank Georgini's Claytone Udu drums
Frank Georgini: http://www.udu.com

Figure 54. Frank Georgini's hand made udu
Frank Georgini: http://www.udu.com

Figure 56. Short igba drums
Source: Dan Rice, motherlandmusic.com

43

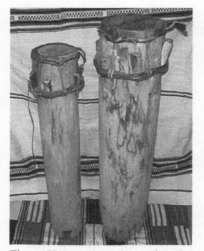

Figure 58. ekwe, Igbo log drum made of orji, Red wood.

Source: Dan Rice, motherlandmusic.com

those with slabs/keys tied over pots are found in Igboland in Nigeria (see Nketia, pp. 81-82).

Figure 57. Long igba drum of the Igbo

Source: Dan Rice, motherlandmusic.com

Drums of Eastern, Central and Southern Africa

The *kebero*, a large double-headed drum made of hollowed out log and animal hide, is common in Ethiopia, Sudan, and Egypt, and is used in religious processions. The interior and exterior of the drum are filled with iron and smoothed with sand-paper. The two open faces: one larger and the other relatively smaller, are covered with pieces of ox hide (Kebede, p. 64). It is used in traditional music of Eritrea and Ethiopia and in their Orthodox Christian liturgical music and secular performances.

Drums used by the Hutu of Burundi include an ensemble of *karyenda*, royal drums which consist of *inkirinya*, lead drum which is usually placed in the middle of the drum circle, *amashako* which provides steady beats, *ibishiko* which follows the rhythms established by *inkiranya*, and *rukinzo*, which is played to herald the movement of the Mwami, the king (Wikimedia Commons, last modified, February, 2011). Drums used in Uganda include the largest royal drums called *mujaguzo* (meaning, jubilation); the 16 *entenga* (drum chime, formally played at the royal court of Kabaka, the traditional ruler of Buganda); and a set of *engalabi*, long single-headed cylindrical high pitch drums, *embutu*, a large kettle drum, *ombala or embula* (the largest bass drum-which derived its name from its purpose of counting aloud the thirty or more Ganda clans to the public during social functions), *empuunyi*, another large and higher bass drum and *nankasa*, a higher pitched small drum (Blades, p. 61). The performer of the royal drum is often equipped with leopard skin apron similar to the bass drummer in the British regimental band (Blades, p. 61; Kebede, p. 67; National Music Museum, 2006-2010). In addition, the (seventeen keys) *akadinda*,

Figure 59. kebero, a double-headed drum used in traditional music of Eritrea and Ethiopia in Orthodox Christians liturgical music and secular celebrations.
Source: Wikimedia.org

embaire and *amadinda* are used by the Ganda of Uganda (in the court of the Kabaka in the past) while a seventeen-key xylophones are found among the Chokwe and Pende of Angola and Zaire respectively.

A set of drums which are generally called *ngoma* (which also means ceremony) are found in the Swaziland and parts of central, eastern and southern Africa. They are used in festivals, funerals, political and religious events and other ceremonies, along with clapping, singing, chanting and dancing. Variants of the *ngoma* are found in the central, eastern and southern parts of Africa. For example, the *kihembe ngoma* is a double-headed drum, with one head bigger than the other. They are found among the Ganda people of Uganda in various sizes (and are laced with zebra skin). The *kihembe ngoma* is much shorter and wider than the Congolese *ngoma*. The Venda and the Zulu *ngoma* is very short and wide, and is covered with ox-hide and played with sticks. Some of the most beautiful double-headed *ngoma* are found in Uganda and the Great lake regions. The skins of both faces are joined together by ropes, laced around the drum from top to bottom, with the skin covering almost the entire wooden body (Kebede, p. 64). In addition, a slit drum idiophone made of single hollowed log which is slit open at the center is common among the Lokele and other ethnic groups in Central Africa. It is used to convey messages in their tonal languages, hence, it is sometimes referred to as a talking drum in many African societies) (Kebede, 1982, p. 55). The *babonda* or *bangoma*, an upright slit drum with two or more pitches and its variants are found among the Kuba, Yaka and other ethnic groups in Congo Brazzaville and Democratic Republic of Congo (http://www. congo~brazaville.org/ art).

Figure 60. A set of engalabi long open-ended
Figure 61. embula bass drum
Figure 62. Drums of the Buganda
Face music: http://www.face~music.ch/instrum/uganda_instrumen.html

Drums used by the Akamba of the Ukamba region of Kenya include the *kyaa*, also known as *muvungu* or *mitilu*.

Figure 63, Figure 64. empuunyi higher bass drums in Buganda ensemble
Face music: http://www.face~music.ch/instrum/uganda_instrumen.html

Kavyu notes that the word, *muvungu* seems to have been derived from the word *ivungulu*, meaning a "hollow object" or wood; and the name *mutilu*, (singular, *mitilu*), might have been derived from the word *kitula*, verb, *tila* and *ku*, the prefix, to hit or stamp with a blunt surface; *muti wa utila* (the act of stamping). The drum is played in the (now extinct) *kyaa* dance. The Akamba drums also include *ngoma*, a set of four to six drums used in spiritual dance (but which are now rare although variants of them are found in Inyamezi country of Tanzania where the Akamba had established a dynasty); *ngutha*, formally played to accompany *ngutha* dance, and to communicate cultural messages; *mbalya*, used to accompany *mbalya* dance; and *kithembe*, a cylindrical honey container or

Figure 65. akadinda

Figure 66. embaire

Figure 67. amadinda

Face music: http://www.face~music.ch/
instrum/uganda_instrumen.html

Figure 68. ngoma and nsakalas

Kenneth Wilson: brazzabeat.com

large open-ended drum used to accompany a religious dance associated with rain ceremony and women connected with it. The Akamba drums further include a set of *mukanda* or *mbeni* used to accompany a dance bearing the same name and musical activities of young people, *kathembe*, a small metal (military) drum used in Christian worship and schools, and *mwase* drum dance played by a woman on the first day of a new moon to appease her spirit (Kavyu, pp. 85-87; 98).

A variety of *timbila or* xylophones that have between ten, twelve, sixteen and nineteen keys are found among the Chopi of Mozambique. They are grouped according to their range, such as treble, *cilanzane* or *malanzane*; alto, *sange* or *sanje*; tenor, *dole* or *mbingwe*, bass: *deblinda*, and double bass, *gulu* or *kulu*. *Timbila* are usually played in large ensembles ranging between fifteen to thirty instruments, although some are played solo to accompany the *ngalanga* children's dances, accompanied by *incinga* and *ngoma* drums (with animal hides), bells and flutes (Tracey, 1970, p. 119).

While the construction of these xylophones is generally uniformed, the keys of the *gulu* are suspended between two wooden bars, as

Figure 69. Ceremonial drum of the Chokwe of Angola.

Tim Hamill: Hamill@hamillgallery.com

opposed to the other xylophones whose keys are tied together, and rest upon a hide-covered frame.

Xylophones with twenty keys are used by the Venda of South Africa while those with one to four slabs are used by the Nsenga and Valley Tonga of Zambia. In addition, xylophones with slabs mounted over a pit, clay pot and box are found in Central African Republic among the Azande and Kala; in Kenya, and among the Kusu, and Zaromo of Tanzania (Nketia, pp. 81-82). The *silimba* or *shinjimba* gourd resonating xylophone is found among the Lozi peoples of Barotseland in Western Zambia. It is used by the Nkoya people of Western Zambia at traditional royal ceremonies like the kazanga

Figure 70. Kuba drums of the Dem. Rep. of Congo

Tim Hamill: Hamill@hamillgallery.com

Figure 71. Slit drums of the Yaka. Democratic Rep. of Congo

Tim Hamill: Hamill@hamillgallery.com

Figure 72. Slit drum of the Mangbetu. Democratic Rep. of Congo

Tim Hamill: Hamill@hamillgallery.com

Nkoya, and is now used in most parts of Zambia (zambiatourism. com).

Drums found among the Venda of Transvaal include large and small *ngoma* drums and the *murumbu*, a single-headed hemispherical drum and the *burumbu*, another single-headed small drum similar to the *murumbu*, carved out of solid wood with cow hide pegged to the shell and ornamented with handles (Blades, pp. 51-52). *Hazolahy*, a double-headed conical drum with the heads lapped by a cord that zigzags between them) and the *antakaran* (lit. drum on a cooking pot), a kettle drum made with shallow clay bowl and covered with animal hide, are found in parts of Madagascar (Blench, internet; Brooklyn Children' Museum, w w w . b r o o k - l y n k i d s . o r g). The *antakaran* is played by women and young men for recreation and entertainment; it is also played during circumcision and funerals. These drums are performed in solo, small and large ensembles to the accompaniment of vocal melodies, chants, bells, rattles, hand clapping, flutes and string instruments.

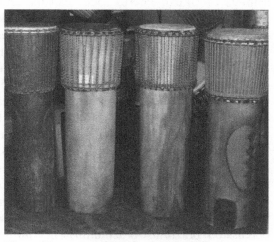

Figure 73. ngoma of the Central, Eastern and Southern Africa, carved in Ghana

Source: Dan Rice, motherlandmusic.com

Drums in the African Diaspora

As a result of the intercultural contacts (noted earlier), certain drums which were originally used by specific African groups may now be seen among a number of ethnic groups across certain geographical areas. For example, variants of the *djembe, lung* or *donno, tama* and *dundun* hourglass drum (popularly known as talking drum) and double-headed cylindrical drums such as *gangan, gyamadudu* and *dundun*) can now be seen in countries such as Senegal, Mali, Guinea, Ghana, Nigeria and South Africa. Some African performing arts institutions have a collection of drums from various African countries and African Diaspora settings. The Ghanaian School of Performing Arts has a collection of *djembe, dundun, sagban, kenkeni, bata*, steel pans, jazz set and conga drums. African derived drums can also be seen in the United States of America, Europe and the Caribbean and other Diaspora settings of Brazil, Puerto Rico, Panama and other parts of the world. They include the *bata*, conga, *iyesa*, double-headed cylindrical drums similar to (*djundjun*) and *cajon*, a box resonator with a hole at its back (made from fish crates and dressers) and a set of *bongo* drums in Cuba, a set of *atabaque* drums (*rum*, a large *bass* drum, *rum-pi* medium pitch drum and *le*, the smaller and higher pitch drum), *cuica*, a friction drum of (Angolan origin) in Brazil; *bomba* large barrel-shaped bass drum used in Puerto Rico (similar to the *gboba* of the Ewe), the *bongo* and other drums in Haiti; the *timpani*, Jazz set and congas in the USA. The African related drums found in the Panama include singled-headed rectilinear, curvilinear and cuneiform drums (*tambors*) and the *caja* (*tambora*) doubled-headed cylindrical drums of various sizes found in the Cuti Province of Daren (George http://www.arcmusic.org/features/archives/percussion_brazil/inst-brazil.html) They further include an ensemble of *repicador, pujador* and the *caja* (redoblante) found in the Los Santos Province; the *sequero* (seco), *claro, pujador* (pujo) and the caja (tambora) and a largest caja called *cumbiero* found in the mulatto areas-La Chorrera in the Province of Panama and its environs; and the *repicadors, pujador, jondo* (hondo and the caja (*tambora*) in the Daren-jungle near the Choco or Columbia region (Jackson, 1985, pp. 173-188). The African derived instruments in

Figure 74. conga drums

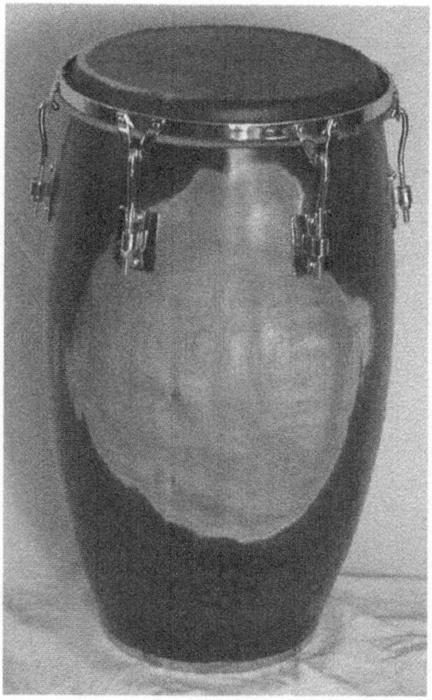

Figure 75. conga drums

Conrad Kubiak: http://www.spiritinthewood.com/conrad.html

Figure 76. Brazilian large atabaque

www.virtualcapoeira.com

Figure 77. Small atabaque ceremony.

www.virtualcapoeira.com

Figure 78. Puerto Rican bomba drum
Source: Conrad Kubiak: http://www.
spiritinthewood.com/conrad.html

the Diaspora further include the *marimba* which is found in Guatemala, Latin America and other Diaspora settings. These instruments are used in performing African derived music/ dance, such as the American Jazz, Blues, Afro-Cuban Salsa, Rumba, Haitian Vodu, Jamaican Reggae, Trinidadian Calypso, Afro-Brazilian Samba and Candomble and other performance styles in both social and ceremonial contexts.

The process of globalization culminates in constant movement of African peoples to and from the Diaspora and other parts of the world. This movement, coupled with the interest generated in African drumming in various Diaspora settings and global settings, culminated in the proliferation of African drums in Europe, United States of America, Canada, Australia and various parts of the world. Thus, one would find drums that traditionally belong to the Akan, Ewe, Hausa, Mande, Yoruba, Lokele and the Hutu, such as *djembe*, *dundun* or *donno* or *tama* or *lunka* hourglass drum, *ashiko*, *sagban* and *kenkeni*, *kpanlogo*, and *udu* in North America, Europe, Asia, Australia and other parts of the world. As noted earlier, some of these drums are now constructed or manufactured by individuals and companies in Germany, the United States of America and other parts of the world in response to the demands of the world peoples. In view of the current processes of globalization, it is obvious that intercultural borrowing and adaptation of musical instruments will intensify in the future. There is usually a concern that in the long run, some of the larger drum manufacturing companies would assume monopoly over the drum making processes thereby making it difficult for the traditional drum makers who are the originators and custodians of the drum to operate. For these reasons, it is imperative to acknowledge the sources of the various drums, and protect the rights of traditional drum makers as well as treasure their products, to enable both the traditional and contemporary drum makers to function.

Chapter Three

Uses and Functions of Drums in African Cultures

The uses and functions of African drums refer to the ways the drums are used and the contributions they make to the lives of the peoples. Drums fulfil significant cultural functions. They are played during social gatherings, marriage/wedding of couples, the birth of some new born babies, circumcision of young boys, and during initiation where the youths are taught their future responsibilities. Drums are also played to accompany, or celebrate occupational activities such as farming, fishing and hunting. They are played during religious, political, festive and funerals events, and to entertain peoples. Drums are also used to communicate through signalling and summoning members of communities to gather for events. They are further employed to communicate on the basis of speech and on symbolic levels. The drums provide a means for documentation of significant cultural values. They also heal people suffering from certain disorders. A discussion of the contexts of African drumming and their contributions to such contexts are provided below:

Drums as Symbolic Representation of Cultural Values

A symbol is an object or concept that stands for something else, or an object or concept whose meaning refers to something else. In addition to being a symbol of humanity, existence and the universe, the drums also serve as symbolic representation of socio-cultural values. For example, due to the strong relationship between Burundi drums and nature, various parts of the drum are named after fertility: *icahi*, the skin symbolizes the skin in which the mother rocks her baby. *amabere*, the pegs, symbolize the mother's breasts, *urugori*, the thong stretching the skin, symbolizes the crown of motherhood; *inda*, the cylinder, represents the stomach while *umukondo*, the foot of the drum represents the umbilical cord (Heavenly planet, 2009: http://www.heavenlyplanet.com). Similarly, the *bata* ensemble is said to represent a family: *iya*, the largest drum represents the mother; *itotele*, the middle drum represents a father while *okonkolo*, the smallest drum represents a baby/child (Wikimedia Commons, last modified, 2011). Also, according to Vivian Parques (as stated by Nketia in Wachsmann, 1971), the *tabale* drum of the Bambara (which is encased in copper) symbolizes royalty: the long stick, which has a bell attached to it represents Koumabana, the giver of speech, the first of the eight ancestors in the Bambara ancestral pantheon (Nketia in Wachsmann, 1971, p.12). Among the Hutu of Burundi, some of the *karyenda* drums symbolize Mwami, the king, his fertility and regeneration (Popovic, internet; see also Euba, 1988, p. 36). Similarly, the *taushi*, a single-headed conical drum of the Hausa, symbolizes royalty; it is played by court musicians. Nketia states that the *fɔntɔmfrɔm* drum orchestra symbolized the heroic ideals of the Asante; the small drums, (such as *apentemma, brenko* and *adukrogya*) which were expected to play together as loudly as possible, provided what was described as "fire" to the music and thus symbolized the intensity of the heroic encounters. The lead *Atumpan* drummer assumed a symbolic role of captain of an army and the two heavy *fɔntɔmfrɔm* drums represented the warriors (Nketia, 1987, p. 202). Also, *naqqara*, a double kettle drums used by the Tuaregs of the Sahara and by other northern African peoples symbolized the power of the king; they were often left standing near the throne and were sometimes used to accompany the imperial proclamations before the advent of technological communication (Kebede, p. 63). The Ethiopian *negarit* drum serves similar (symbolic) purpose (Kebede, p. 63). The name, Negarit is said to have derived from Amharic verb, *negere*, which means, talked or proclaimed (Kebede, p. 63).

Some drums symbolize spirits, divinities and ancestors. For example, *tweneboa,* the cedar wood, which is used for carving most of the Akan drums, is considered an abode of Tweneboa spirit. Hence, the drummer of the *atumpan* came to be identified with the spirit, Tweneboa Kodua (Nketia, p. 6; Kebede. pp. 98-99). Symbolism is also expressed through the sounds of certain drums. For example, the deep sound of the *udu,* pot drum which is molded from the earth, water, fire and air is said to represent the voice of the ancestors, particularly when used in Igbo religious ceremonies in southern and central Nigeria (see also Georgini at www.udu. com). As noted earlier, the *etwie* drum of the Akan symbolizes the snarl of a leopard and the roaring of a king (see also Kebede. p. 66) while the *laklevu* of the Like clan of the Aŋlɔ-Ewe symbolizes the sounds of a sly fox or wolf. Some accompanying instruments such as the Egyptian sistrum is said to symbolize Hathor, goddess of love (Kebede, p. 96). The four jingle metal bars on the sistrum are linked with the elements of nature: fire, water, air and earth. In most Egyptian cults, the sistrum was identified with votive power (Kebede, p. 96).

In addition, the paintings, colours and geometric designs on certain drums may communicate on a symbolic level. For example, the white (calico) cloth, which is used to cover certain drums associated with the Ewe traditional military and political systems, symbolizes the bravery, purity or sanctity that is experienced in the absence of war. Similarly, the red and black cloths which are used to cover the Akan *kete* drums symbolize war and peace. Some drums associated with traditional military organizations are painted with red and white colors: the red symbolizes war and the white stands for peace. Nowadays, some drums are painted with the colors of the national flags of the respective African countries to communicate symbolically. These include some Ghanaian drums which are painted with red, yellow and green colors to symbolize the blood that was shed by their predecessors for gaining independence, and the country's mineral and agricultural resources respectively. Other drums are decorated with carvings of geometric designs, human beings, animals, physical features and cultural symbols such as *Gye Nyame*, an anchor which symbolizes the omnipotent God, *Sankofa*, a bird with the head looking backward (which means go back and retrieve what is left behind), and crossed royal swords which symbolize the strength of a political institution.

Symbolism also relates to the usage of certain instruments. For example, in some parts of Nigeria, a net rattle, *shekere*, may only be made for a particular musician; only a son of the musician may inherit it. The gourd used in making the rattle may symbolize fertility; it usually grows near a body of water and its general shape is reminiscent of a woman' womb. In northern Togoland, the sound of snow chimes is said to symbolize the end of the rainy season, and announce the feast of millet harvest (Kebede, pp.98-99).

Drums as an Instrument for Documentation and validating peoples' Identity and History

Drums also serve as an instrument for documentation of peoples's historical and cultural values: their past, social, religious, economic and political lives. They also serve as a symbol of identifying people, and as an instrument for validating peoples' history and culture. Members of particular cultural groups or groups that have historical ties can be identified with the drums that they use in performances. The drums may serve as a tool for identifying sub groups such as the rulers: kings, chiefs, queens; male and female adults, servants and youths within the social structure. Among the Anlo-Ewe of Ghana, a special *brekete,* double-headed cylindrical drum (of northern Ghana derivative) is played in *Zaga* music which is performed in a procession as a deceased who is partly connected to northern Ghana or slaves from this area is being carried toward the burial ground. Also, among the Mande or Mandinka of south-eastern region of Mali, a special dance called *Wolosodon* was performed by the *Woloso*, slaves who used to serve the royal court. The *Woloso* also performed this music/dance to express the pride of their family.

Drums in the Context of Communication

Some drums are used to convey important cultural messages. For example, among the Lokele of central Africa, slit drums are used to convey messages to the community (Kebede, 1982, p.55). Similarly, the *lung* or *donno, dundun, atumpan* and *atimevu* drums and *gyil, bala* and *baan* xylophones are used to communicate important cultural messages among the Dagbamba, Yoruba, Akan, Ewe and Dagara/Dagarti respectively. These instruments may be played to summon the entire or a cross section of the community to gather for a meeting, communal labour, music/dance performance, festival, etc. They may also be played to announce the arrival of foreigners or important visitors to the community or ceremonies, a state of emergency, death and other cultural messages over relatively short and long distances. Specific signals or texts would be played which members of the community understand on linguistic or textual basis. Nowadays, certain drums are played on national radios and television programs of the respective African countries, to introduce, interject or serve as a finale for news broadcast. For example; the *atumpan* drums may be heard on Ghana's radio and television during news broadcast. The *dundun* or *iyaalu* drum may be heard in prelude, interlude or postlude to the Nigerian radio and television news broadcast. In Ghana, the *atumpan, donno* and other lead drums are played in many elementary and secondary schools to announce the various lessons. African drums are used by some institutions and communities in the African Diaspora settings of North America, Canada and Europe, to signal or announce, or interject certain events, or to educate students about the cultural functions of drumming.

Drums as a Means of Social Integration

Drums are effective means of bringing people together. People who have been informed about the drumming event or those who hear the drums on the spur of the moment may be drawn by the power of the drums to the drumming setting. "A story is told of Afa (Ifa) god of divination and Xevieso, god of thunder and lightning; each of them wanting to know how he could gather people around

Figure 79. Aŋlɔga Dɔnɔgbɔ Gohu group featuring young and older performers, playing drums, rattles, singing, dancing and interacting with one another at Aŋlɔga.

Photo: Modesto Amegago, December 1, 2011.

himself. Xevieso tried to gather his children by word of mouth but they ran away from him. Afa simply went and made a drum and gathered various musical instruments together. On a market day, he gathered the instruments and went with his children to the market area and started playing. All of a sudden, people ran away from the market and came to surround them" (a personal conversation with Dr. Date-Kumordzi on August 25, 2010). The drums also serve as a unifying force, they create a forum for people to interact and express their feelings and thoughts. By coming together to participate in drumming/music/dance regularly, individuals who are not on speaking terms with one another may reconcile. The drumming also serves as a viable means for building communities in the African Diaspora, North America, Europe and other parts of the world, in the ways it brings people together. Drums are played at social gatherings, to enliven the atmosphere. The drummers may play specific melo-rhythms to arouse the feelings of the people and inspire them to move in certain ways.

Drums in the Context of Birth, Circumcision, Initiation and Marriage

Drums are played by the Yoruba, Hausa, Mande, Malinke, Minianka and Hutu, and other African and African Diaspora communities in Canada and the United States to welcome a new born baby and celebrate birth and child-naming. Among the Buganda of Uganda, the *engalabi* drums are played to announce the birth of twins (Wikimedia Commons, last modified, 2011). Also, among the Akamba of Kenya, drums are played during *Nzaico nini*, first circumcision rites to make the pains less bearable and to celebrate successful circumcision (Kavyu, p. 53). In Ungula and Pemba areas and lower mainland of Zanzibar, special *ngoma* are played during *inyago*, girls' initiation ceremony to mark their transition from childhood to adulthood. This ceremony is performed in seclusion by the Bi-Kidude and drummers of the *vum*, bass drum, *msondo* and *kingangan*, open-ended tall drums. The ceremony may last from a day to three months, during which time the young initiates are educated in sexual relations, clothing, hygiene, make-up, cooking, and how to care for husbands, in-laws and neighbours (http://www.zanzibar.net/music_culture_music styles/ ngoma). Special drums are played to accompany the *Klama, Dipo* and *bragorɔ* girls' initiation rites/dances of the Ga-Adangme, Krobo and Brong of Ghana. Also, among the Landoma, Nalo and Baga of Guinea, the *djembe* and *djundjun* drums are played in *sɔsɔne* dance/music to celebrate initiation of the youths and to honor *Kakilambe,* the highest Baga deity. Drums are also played during the *Poro* initiation rites of the Senufo of Ivory Coast and Burkina Faso, to mark the transition of the youths from childhood to adulthood. They are also played to celebrate marriage/ wedding in many African societies. Among the Dagbamba (in northern Ghana), *nmani* percussive gourds semi hemispherical in shape are played by women along with singing and dancing to entertain the gathering and advice couples or people about marriage life. The Yoruba *dundun* drummers may play during wedding to accompany a bride or bride-groom to the place of the wedding and during the wedding, to advise, educate and entertain the attendants. In Mali, drums are also played to honour mothers. African drums serve similar purposes in the Diaspora settings of Canada, United States and Europe where they feature in many social events, such as parties, weddings, child naming, birth day celebrations and festivals.

Drums in the Context of Occupational Activities

A single or set of drums may be played to accompany occupational activities such as farming, sowing, harvesting and fishing, to motivate workers, enliven work, eradicate boredom, and to celebrate successful harvest or catch. Some of the workers or a group of drummers may play to accompany the farmers and fishermen. For example, among the Dagara, Lobi, Sisala and Sambla of northern Ghana and southern part of Burkina Faso, the *gyile* and *baan* xylophones, *donno* or *lunka* and *gangan* or *dennin* may be played to accompany farmers in the field, to motivate them and enliven their work (Strand, p. 132). Hunters' associations (*Ode* in Yoruba, *Adelawo* in Ewe and *Aboafoɔ* in Akan) would drum and chant to celebrate successful hunts, the crowning of a chief hunter, funerals of a deceased hunter, etc. On such occasions, the drums may be played to accompany hunters who re-enact their hunting experiences, such as the training of young hunters; tracking of animals, stalking, halting, stooping, squatting, finding the direction of the wind; aiming, firing, misfiring, getting into difficulties and extricating themselves; boys in training cooking, carrying baskets and pretending to have come a long way, imitating accidents that happened along the bush tracks, dropping things in baskets, flipping, falling down while master hunters pretend to be angry with them or help them, as well as demonstration of fire lighting with flints guns (Nketia. p. 87). In the past, hunters played important roles in leading migrations and founding of states; providing communities with means of livelihood, materials for making musical instruments, and the kings' paraphernalia. In recognition of the significant contributions made by hunters to the welfare and development of African states, the Akan in particular, have created the position of the head hunter (*Bommodu Akonnwa*, Bommodu's stool) in their political system. This position has become hereditary (Nketia, pp. 76-77; Amegago, 2011, p. 58). Nowadays, the hunting profession has declined in many African societies but tribute is still paid to ancestral hunters. There are quite a number of hunters in the African Diaspora settings, who may also re-enact their hunting expeditions or celebrate successful hunts through drumming/music and dance. Some African performing groups in the Diaspora and other global settings would perform the drumming/dancing associated with hunters in these new locations, to commemorate the ancestral hunters, and educate people about the roles and activities of hunters in African societies.

Drums in the Contexts of Recreation, Sports, Beauty Contests, Fashion Shows and Arts Exhibitions

Drums also feature within the contexts of recreational and sporting activities, beauty contests, fashion shows, and arts exhibitions. Among the Wolof of Sene-Gambia, a single or set of *sabar* drums are played during *lamb* or wrestling competitions, to charge the atmosphere, motivate wrestlers, provide background music for the event and entertain spectators. A variety of drums are played during local, national and international sporting events such as soccer matches, athletic competitions in schools, communities, national and international stadia. The drummers may usher the sports men and women, or athletes into the sports arenas/stadia; they may play to highlight the beginning and exciting moments of the events, or throughout the events, to enliven the atmosphere; celebrate victory and herald the movement of the sports men and women and athletes from the stadium.

Beauty contests are some other contexts for drumming in African and African Diaspora communities. The contestants may drum, recite drum poetry or texts and dance to demonstrate their knowledge of part of the cultural heritage. In Ghana, drumming and dancing are some of the requirements for beauty contest. Hence, many contestants would put a lot of time and effort into learning how to drum and dance. The contestants may be judged on how well they utilize the drumming techniques in articulating various tones, pitches and texts, and their ability to interpret the drumming on linguistic basis. They are also adjudicated on how well they dance to the drum beats and in conformity with the criteria set by the organizers. An individual or group of drummers may play during beauty contests, in prelude and interlude to the event, entertain people and as a finale to the event. The drums may be played at the beginning of fashion shows, to accompany the movement of each participant or group of participants and entertain people. In addition, African drummers may play to open arts exhibitions, provide background music, enhance the themes or meanings of the exhibitions and entertain spectators.

Drums in the Context of Fundraising

Drums are played during fundraisings organized by individuals, groups, and organizations such as World Vision International, The Olive Branch for Children, Nutifafa Afrikan Performance Ensemble, African Students Associations to support hospitals, patients, disaster victims, educational institutions, community water projects, Youths' Summer Arts Camps, etc. in Africa, Caribbean, Canada, United States and other parts of the world. In such contexts, the drummers may play to represent specific cultures or nations, enliven the atmosphere, and motivate the people to donate for a good course, and to entertain the people.

Drums in the Context of Mass Cleaning

Some drums are played during mass cleaning, to announce, enliven and mark certain stages of the event. For example, among the Aŋlɔ-Ewe, some drummers would play during dɔdede, mass cleaning, which is organized by the state at certain times of the year; during a period preceding a festival or during a period of an outbreak of a disease. The mass cleaning usually begins from (Atiteti) a town in the western boarder of the state and ends at (Blekusu or Flawu) the eastern boarder of the state. It involves the masses cleaning their homes, collecting waste and harmful materials, parading the streets with them while singing and dancing, and dumping, burning and burying the waste materials at designated locations. The drummers may play to announce the mass cleaning, accompany the crowd to the site of dumping or burning waste materials. However, they are not supposed to drum while returning from the dumping site, for, it is believed the disease (which may manifest in the form of spirit) would be attracted by the music and follow the cleaners back to their homes thereby nullifying all their efforts.

Drums in the Context of Storytelling, Plays and Films

A single or set of drums may be played during story telling to introduce certain characters, accompany their actions and interject their stories. The drumming may provide background music to the story, motivate characters to act, create interest and entertain people. During the 13th century, the *djembe* drums and xylophones were played by storytellers or griots who would travel from place to place to propagate the oral tradition and music of Sunjata, the emperor of the Mali Empire. The king's drummers/musicians were regarded as the guardians of the (sacred) word (http://www. afrodrumming.com/djembe.history.php). African drums are also played during storytelling, poetry recitals and drama productions in some communities, institutions and theaters, in African and African Diaspora settings, to fulfil similar functions. Some drums are used to introduce, interline and highlight certain scenes in films and theatrical productions in Africa and African Diaspora settings.

Drums in the Context of Religion/Rituals

Drums are played within the contexts of rituals and ceremonies. Such rituals/ceremonies are performed by group of people who have common faith and worship a common divinity or God. Membership in these groups may stem from people's desire to communicate with a divinity or God, for protection from environmental hazards or problems such as impotence, sterility, loss of children, ill-health, fear of untimely death, fear of witchcraft and sorcery, and the desires to belong to a religious association, to travel abroad, become rich or successful in business, etc. (Nketia, pp. 90-91). These associations usually have places of worship or ceremonies. However, there are private and public rituals or ceremonies that do not involve drumming. There are also rituals that rarely involve drumming as well as those that involve frequent drumming/dancing. Many religious associations have a suite of music/dance that are performed for specific divinities or a pantheon of divinities that form the focus of their religion. Specific drumming patterns, songs and dances that are associated with particular divinities, may bear the names of such divinities. For example, among the Ewe, *Sohu*, a music and dance form of the Yewe religious sect is identified with the God of thunder and lightning, *afavu* is identified with Afa, God of divination. Similarly, among the Akan, *Atoko twene* is identified with the divinity Atoko; *Mframa twene* refers to the drums of the Mframa divinity while *Ntoa Twene* refers to the drums of the divinity Ntoa (Nketia, pp. 92-93).

Drums are also played to glorify or praise the Supreme Being, divinities and ancestors and to dramatize religious activities. The drumming may provide background music for rituals; or it may be in prelude, interlude and postlude to rituals, or form part of a suite of ritual dances and songs. The *bata* and *iyaalu* drums are used to glorify, worship and communicate with Shango, a god of thunder and lightning. They are also played by the Yoruba descendants in Cuba, Pueto Rico and the United States in worshipping the Santaria or Lucumi. The Afro-Cuban version of the *bata* has a set of liturgical rhythms called Oru del Igbodu, or Oru Seco, consisting of twenty three standard rhythms and vocal call and response, performed for all the Orishas. Special drums called *ipese* are played during ceremonies associated with Ifa (God of divination and wisdom). A set of *agere* (fixed pitch) drums are used by devotees in rituals associated with Ogun (Euba, 1988, p. 8). Nowadays, the Yoruba have included the *dundun* (hourglass or tension) drum in their religious practices because of its wide tonal range, mobility and freedom from contextual restrictions (Euba, 1988, p. 9). The *dundun* drum may accompany a chant as a drummer sings *oriki*, an eulogy comprising of poems which recount the characteristics, personality, ancestry, importance and supernatural powers of the Yoruba divinities. Special drums are played to accompany ceremonies performed by Ajagemo, the chief priest of Obatala on behalf of the state, at the shrines, temples and market places.

Some of these drums may be accompanied by gourd rattles called sekere and/or pair of metallophones (*aro*) (Euba, p.17). In addition, the *udu* (pot) drums of the Ibo are used to communicate with the Supreme Being, divinities and ancestors, and at certain stages of fertility and healing rituals to eradicate poverty and avert wars.

Among the Aŋlɔ-Ewe, a solo drummer would play the *kagan*, supporting drum to provide a steady rhythm for *agoyiyi*, ritual procession of priests and priestesses of the Yewe religious sect, during the graduation ceremony of new initiates and the funeral rites of a deceased member of the sect. An ensemble of the *atimevu, sogo, kidi* and *kagan* drums are used to provide music for a suite of Yewe (God of lightning and thunder) dances such as *afɔvu*, characterized by fast paced drumming, singing and agile contraction and release of the torso while travelling across the dance arena; *husago*, characterized by relatively slow paced drumming, singing and contraction and release of the torso, along with gestures and expressions of sorrow and lamentation; *sohu*, a medium paced drumming, singing along with the basic contraction and release of the torso and hand gestures in honour of the sun God; *sogbadzi*, another medium paced drumming, singing and along with the Ewe contraction and releasing torso movement; *adavu*, another fast paced drumming, singing along with sideways shifting of the pelvis, occasional mouth slaps and upward hand punches; and *avlevu*, characterized by slow paced drumming, singing and sideways shifting of the pelvis, followed by fast paced drumming and the shifting of the pelvis sideways, backward and forward to express humour and repressed desires of the priests and priestesses (Amegago, 2011, p. 183). The *sogo* and *kidi* are also used to provide the music associated with Afa (God of divination and wisdom).

An ensemble of Akan a*pentemma*, ɔ*perenten, akukua, atumpan* and *donno* drums, bells and rattles are also used to provide music/ dance for the Akan divinities. The Akan religious musical suites include, *ntwaaho*, characterized by whirling movement; *adaban* associated with circling movement, *aboafoɔ,* hunters' dance, *ta kese bekɔ tachiman*, The great Ta will go to Tachiman, *akamu*, outburst, *sapa*, dance of enjoyment *dwenini ketekyi*- valiant ram, etc. (see Nketia, pp. 92-95).

Nowadays, many of the drums used in African traditional social and religious contexts are also played by church choirs and other (social) performing groups. Thus, the *dundun, kpanlogo, adowa, agbadza,* and *bɔbɔɔbɔ* drums are used to accompany choristers in some African and African Diaspora churches. African drums are also played by some church Cantata groups to accompany the re-enactment of the birth and crucifixion of Christ and other liturgical plays in Ghana, Nigeria and other African countries as well as the African Diaspora settings of Canada, United States and Europe. An example is the Nutifafa Afrikan Performance Ensemble that utilizes some Ghanaian and West African instruments to accompany dancers and choristers in some churches in Vancouver and Toronto (Abbotsford Missa Luba Choir and Etobicoke Centennial Choir). Drums and their accompanied instruments are played by African church groups that adapt traditional tunes and dances to suite their religious purposes. Ironically, most of the African Christians who continue to adapt and feature traditional African drumming and melodies in their worship constantly refuse to participate in African drumming/dancing outside their own religious contexts. Such an attitude continues to threaten the survival of African traditional music and dance since most of the people who would perpetuate the drumming or music and dance traditions are being discouraged from participating in these performances.

Drums in the Context of Politics

Events, such as the installation and coronation of chiefs, kings and queens, which occur in African societies at certain times of the year, take place within the context of drumming/dance. These events may occur in stool houses, chiefs or kings' palaces, at the beaches, riversides, market places, durbar grounds and specific public spaces. On such occasions, state drums are played to announce the events, recount the genealogy and heroic deeds of the leaders, praise them, and to interject the ceremonies. Drums and other musical instruments usually form part of state regalia. Among the Akan, every important king or chief has drums that symbolize his political status and form part of the state paraphernalia. Senior chiefs would be allowed to own the bigger *fontomfrɔm*

Figure 80: An agblɔʋu (royal drum) player heralding the movement of some Aŋlɔ traditional leaders toward the site of the installation of a chief at Aŋlɔga Ghana.

Photo: Modesto Amegago, July 2011.

or *bɔmmaa* drums while the junior chiefs would be allowed to own smaller drums relative to their ranks (Nketia, 1963; 119). As noted earlier, the Guinean and Malian kings Sumaoro Kante and Sunjata had xylophones and other drums that served as symbols of their offices. Also, among the Tutsi of Rwanda, drums belong to Mwami, the king. With the exception of the drums owned by the queen mother, Tutsi custom prohibits the use of drums in other contexts (cited in Euba, 1988, p. 35). The *(karyenda* and *ingendanyi)* drums of the Mwami are kept in a special sanctuary and are traditionally performed at the coronation ceremonies. For other public occasions when the royal drums must be sounded, copies of these drums are used (Euba, 1988, p. 36). Among the Hausa, court musicians (drummers, trumpeters and *narambad,* female praise singers) are attached to the courts or offices of the Sultan or Emirs, the rulers and district heads. For example, *tambura* (also called *astambora*), the royal kettle drums and *kakaki,* long trumpets are played along with female singing during coronation of leaders and weekly Sara which occurs every Thursday, to symbolize the Emir's authority and express his virtues and achievements. These instruments may also be played when the Emir installs the *Madaki* or the *Galadima* (two of his most senior lieutenants) (Euba, 1988, p. 36). Similarly, the *nyikɔvu, agblɔvu, aflui, kufade, wuga* and *asafo* drums are associated with the Ewe political system.

In addition, group of royal musicians were in the past attached to the court of the Ashanti kings and were responsible for providing the court music. The Kabaka of (Buganda) Uganda had court musicians who were selected from specific villages and clans, and trained (for a certain period) to provide the music associated with the court at regular times (Tracey, 1972 as cited in Euba, p. 37). Blades (1970) notes that a class of "kaffirs", also referred to as Marombe (jesters) were responsible for singing the praises of the king (monomotopa) of South Africa. They would sing (with the accompaniment of bells and gongs) to herald the movement of the king and his retinue (Blades, 1970, p. 51).

Similarly, the Gbedu musicians of the Yoruba were responsible for providing the (Gbedu) music associated with the king. The tension drum was later incorporated into the Gbedu repertoire in the 19th century because of its popularity (in central Yorubaland where the impact of Oyo culture prevailed). A group of drummers were attached to the palace of the Alaafin of Oyo and were responsible for playing the praise poetry of the king at regular intervals (dawns, mornings and during the days), beginning with the praise poetry of Alaafin Atiba, and ending with that of the current king (Euba, 1988, p. 41).

In Dahume (now called the Republic of Benin), groups of female musicians called Ajogen were responsible for providing the music and dance in the royal courts of Agbome and Port Novo. These groups comprised of (approximately) 14 royal wives; ten of them playing drums and iron bells while the remaining four would sing and dance. These musicians/dancers would perform on ceremonial occasions such as feasts for the ancestral cults and for the king's entertainment. Similarly, the Dan and Senufo of Ivory Coast had drummers, singers and trumpeters who were responsible for providing the music associated with the courts. Royal drummers are also attached to the palaces of the kings of Dagbon; who would trace their descent to Bizum, the founder of the Dagbamba drummers' lineage.

These royal drummers/musicians would play to announce the awakening of some leaders, their dinner, need for relaxation and entertainment; to herald their movements, and announce the arrival of visitors and enemies. Also, the king or queen may convey important messages through the medium of drums. For example, the male and female *atumpan* drums are used by the Akan to awaken their chief, announce his meal time and communicate other important information to him). The *mpintin* (gourd vessel) and *fɔntɔmfrɔm* drummers would play to herald the movement of the Asante kings during the celebration of the *Adae* (festival) to commemorate the ancestors. Special pieces of *mpintin* and *atɔpre* are played when the chief is carried in the palanquin, when s/he is delaying in arriving at the ceremonial ground, or when he is approaching the ceremonial setting. A piece of *fɔntɔmfrɔm*, called *akyem* is played for the display of shields usually in procession or in conjunction with the movement of a chief. Special pieces may also be played to usher the chief to his seat, and to announce his drinking in public. *nnawea*, a joyful and triumphant piece may be played when the king sits in state or is returning from the assembly (after celebration) (Nketia, pp. 146-149).

Figure 81. The asafo or bɔmmaa drummers heralding the movement of traditional leaders during the Ngmayem festival at Odumase-Krobo, Ghana.

Photo: Modesto Amegago, October 28, 2011.

Similarly, *agblɔvu*, a single-headed royal drum would be played to herald the movement of the Ewe kings, chiefs and their entourage during the *Hogbetsotso* festival celebrated by the Aŋlɔ-Ewes to commemorate the migration of Ewe from ŋɔtsie (an ancient kingdom in the present day Togoland). The royal drums are also played in prelude, interlude and postlude to speeches and prayers performed by the king, priests and priestesses and other dignitaries.

Figure 82. An agblɔʋu drummer heralding the movement of some Ewe chiefs toward the annual Hogbetsotso featival Durbar, Aŋlɔga, Ghana.

by Photo: Modesto Amegago, November 5 2011.

Among the Akan, drums such as *dua korɔ,* or *kɔ* (imitative of the sound of the drum), *kantamanto* (true to his word) and *susubiribi* (ponder over something) are played to summon state councillors (Nketia, p. 123). In the past, the punishment of civil criminals in some African societies would be announced by certain drums. For example, among the Aŋlɔ-Ewe, sacred male and female *nyikɔvuwo* (large drums) were played to announce the punishment of *nuvɔwɔlawo*, or *dugbalawo*, state criminals (at Aŋlɔga). The sounds of these two drums would be interpreted as:

        Vi ne se tɔ gbe: A child should listen to the
                                  father's voice

Figure 83. Dagbamba royal drummers heralding the movement of leaders during the Ngmayem festival, at Odumase-Krobo.

Photo: Modesto Amegago, Oct. 2011.

vi ne se nɔ gbe: A child should listen to the
                    mother's voice,
Vi masetonu: A child who refuses to listen
Neyi Tɔkɔ Atɔlia: Should go to Tɔkɔ Atɔlia
                    (the site of capital punishment).

Upon returning from the site of the capital punishment, the male drum would sound:

Miede za miegbɔ za: we went at mid-night and
                       returned at mid-night

And the female drum would respond:

Gbe woe nye gbe nye: your voice is my voice (thus reinforcing the male voice) (cited from the Ewe oral tradition).

Similarly, among the Akan, a piece of *fɔntɔmfrɔm* suite called *awɔmu* would be played to symbolize the arrest of a victim of state execution (Nketia, p. 137).

Drums are also used by some contemporary African politicians to promote their political ideologies or agendas. The drums, trumpets and other accompanying instruments and dance serve as an effective means of summoning and addressing party members or crowds during political rallies. They may also be used to praise the party leaders and woo people to the party, celebrate the victory of the parties/leaders, and to herald their movements in jubilation. Some royal drums are played in prelude, interlude and postlude to speeches delivered by heads of states, and parliamentarians on special occasions. In Ghana, drummers and dancers would perform at the airport and specific locations to welcome or bid farewell to presidents, members of the diplomatic corps and foreign dignitaries. The drums may also be played to open parliament, introduce dignitaries, during the receptions and entertainment of the leaders, and the closing of parliament. Some African politicians may criticise their opponents through the medium of drumming/music. In the Canadian cities of Vancouver and Toronto, a group of African drummers would play during the barbecue or parties and special events organized by politicians, to enliven the atmosphere, represent the Africans in the Canadian multicultural society and entertain the people.

Drums in the Context of Military Activities

Drumming forms part of the activities of the African traditional military organizations. In the past, special drums would be played to communicate impending battles, frighten enemies, set a marching pace, motivate militants; command them to advance, attack and retreat in combat situations. The drums would also be played to honour warriors, celebrate victory, funeral of deceased warriors, re-enact past wars, renew loyalty to group members and the state, and to entertain people. Drums used in these contexts include the *etwie* and *laklevu*, leopard and wolf drums of the Akan and Ewe respectively; the *asafo* or *wuga* drums used in some Ghanaian political institutions, and some *ngoma* or *ingoma* and single headed *burumbu* and *murumbu* (Venda) drums of the central, eastern and southern Africa; the *murumbu* and *burumbu* were also used to communicate during wars (Blades, p. 52). In peace time the drumming/music may accompany the activities of African traditional military organizations, such as building bridges, extinguishing fire, clearing paths and felling dangerous trees (Nketia, p. 115, 117-118). Some African and African derived drums such as congas and jazz sets are used by contemporary military, police and prison institutions and units to accompany their marching and drilling. They are also used during the graduation ceremonies of some military, police and prison officers and in their concert performances, to entertain and educate people across towns and countries.

Drums in the Context of Festivals

For commemorating and re-enacting historical events and maintaining solidarity with the Supreme Being, divinities and the peoples, festival(s) are instituted around major agricultural rites, state divinities and episodes in the history and migration of the peoples of a nation. Such festivals are great occasions for music and dance and public re-enactment of the peoples' historical and cultural experiences. They include: the Egungun masquerade festival, celebrated by the Yoruba, to commemorate their ancestors, the Hogbetsotso festival celebrated by the Anlo-Ewes to commemorate the migration of their ancestors from Notsie, the Ngmayem millet sharing festival celebrated by the chiefs and people of Manya Krobo, to commemorate their ancestors and the Supreme Being and offer them gratitude, the Fete des Mask, celebrated by the Dogon of Mali to display new masks, and the Id, el Fitri and Id el Kabir, celebrated by the Muslims of northern Nigeria in October to dramatize their historical, religious and cultural experiences. The festivals further include Essaouira Ghaoua and World music festival, celebrated in Morocco to dramatize aspects of African religious and artistic experiences, Timket, celebrated in lalibela of Ethiopia to re-enact aspects of their religious experiences, Hermanus Whale festival, celebrated in South Africa to mark the return of the southern right whale to the waters of

Figure 84. Figure 85. Drummers heralding the movement of traditional leaders in a procession during Ngmayem festival of the Manya Krobo.

Photo: Modesto Amegago, October 28 2011.

Walker Bay (world news network; Kadmus Arts; About.com, internet).

The musicians and dancers may engage in processions, to herald the movement of leaders, state dignitaries and members of the diplomatic corps to and from the ceremonial grounds. The drummers may play in prelude, interlude and postlude to prayers, speeches and as part of the dramatic enactment of the peoples' culture, and to entertain the peoples. For example, drumming/music and dance performances form a major part of the Aŋlɔ Hogbetsotso festival which is celebrated from the middle of September to first weekend in November. During each day (with the exception of market days), a number of drumming/music and dance groups would perform at Aŋlɔga, the traditional capital of the Aŋlɔ state and its environs, to showcase parts of the cultural expressions, create a festive atmosphere and advertise the festival. Drumming, singing and dramatic enactment also form part of the vigil night (featuring *misego* and *atrikpui* Ewe historical and military music/dances) and the grand durbar. The durbar of chiefs usually features a number of performing groups in processions and at the durbar ground, to entertain, re-enact the Ewe's historical experiences, interject ceremonial prayers, speeches and during merry making.

A solo or group of royal drummers would play to interject, or punctuate prayers during the Aboakyir deer hunting festival, Ngmayem

Figure 86. A royal drummer playing to conclude a prayer at the annual Hogbetsotso festival at Anlɔga, Ghana.

Photo: Modesto Amegago, Nov. 5 2011.

Figure 87. A priest dancing to conclude his prayer and offering to God and ancestors at the annual Ngmayem festival of the people of Manya Krobo

Photo: Modesto Amegago, October 28, 2011.

millet sharing festival, Odwira harvest and commemorative festival of the Awutu and Afutu, and the Akwapim of south-western and south-eastern Ghana respectively. In some Muslim communities of Nigeria, *sakara* drums are played during festivals to call the Muslims to feast, and to celebrate Ramadan (Wikimedia Commons, internet).

Drums are also played in contemporary African schools during Speech and Prize giving days and Hall week celebrations, anniversaries and award ceremonies. They also feature during the Arts and Cultural festivals where student-drummers and groups of musicians/dancers representing schools, feature drum recitals, integrated drumming, singing, dancing and dramatic performances.

The drums are played during the African and African inspired festivals that are celebrated in the Diaspora. These include Odwira of the Akan, Homowo of the Ga, Afro-fest, Carassauga, Caribana celebrated in Canada (Toronto), United States and Europe; Trinidad and Tobago and other Diaspora settings. They are also played during Easter and Christmas in Africa and African Diaspora settings. Drums are played in Winter Solstice processions

Figure 88. The Anlo-Afiadenyigba Misego dancers re-enacting the girding of the loin (as the name of the dance/music implies) prior to the exodus of the Ewe from Notsie at the annual Hogbetsotso festival at Anlɔga

Photo: Modesto Amegago, Nov. 5, 2011.

Figure 89. The Anlo Afiadenyigba Misego group re-enacting the migration of the Ewes from Notsie during the early 17ᵗʰ century at the annual Hogbetsotso festival

Photo: Modesto Amegago, Nov. 5, 2011.

Figure 90. Drummers, singers and dancers performing at the Ngmayem millet sharing festival at the Odumase-Krobo

Photo: Modesto Amegago, Oct. 28 2011.

Figure 91. Have bɔbɔɔbɔ group performing at the second annual Bɔbɔɔbɔ festival organised by the Ho Centre for National Culture

Photo: Modesto Amegago. Nov. 4, 2011.

and during the Black History Month celebrations, International Day for Elimination of Racial Discrimination, Emancipation Day and UNESCO day celebrations as a form of cultural presentation, education and entertainment They are also played at conferences of Ethnomusicology, Dance Ethnology, International Association for Neuroscience, African Studies, Visual and Performing Arts, etc., to re-enact cultural values, to create a forum for dialogue and for education, and to entertain.

The Healing or Therapeutic Functions of African Drums

The drum also serves as a healing device. Some drummers maintain that drumming relieves them of physical and psychological ailments and tensions. In narrating the functions of African drumming, an informant, Emmanuel Agbeli states, "It heals me, when I have headache and I play the drum, that headache is gone". Many drummers would attest to the therapeutic functions of drumming. Drums are used to heal certain psychological and physical disorders in certain patients. Such disorders may stem from death of a family member, social conflict, and treatments meted out against certain individuals and social groups. Diallo and Mitchell (1989) have shed light on the use of drums in healing individuals suffering from mental disorders among the Minianka and Senufo of Guinea and Ivory Coast. They note that the most effective music or drum patterns for healing such an individual or society, is monotony. The drummer/musician/healer has to find the rhythms that suit the patient by experimenting with the tonal qualities of the drum. For example, a patient whose illness is caused by trauma may be enervated by low bass tone (and that should be avoided in this situation). The hysterical patient may be more agitated by high slap tones (Diallo & Mitchell, p. 160). Once the right tone or music is found, the musician has to play repeatedly for about two to three hours; the calming, stabilizing rhythm and powerful sound combination that help to restore the disturbed individual to inner balance. They also note that the healing musician does not necessarily have to use rhythms from any traditional repertoire. He or she would have to engage in creative dialogue with the patient through his experience and try to find the appropriate rhythms and tones that would help restore the mood and inner balance of the patient. According to Diallo and Mitchell, agitated rhythm may be useful for healing a patient that needs more movements; they can provoke the disturbed individual to expend excess energy. When the catharsis is triggered, the musician should continue to stimulate it until the patient is pacified. The musician-healer should always try to understand the patient's inner need in order to provide the appropriate rhythms and tones. He or she knows how to provide therapy, to bring joy and to console a patient during the most difficult moments (Diallo & Mitchell, pp. 160-161). Diallo and Mitchell further suggest the need for the healing musician to protect him or her self and the patient. His knowledge includes understanding the functioning of different systems of human bodies since he is sending sounds that affect those systems/bodies. He has to be ready to use plants which may be needed to restore a balance in the patient. The development of divinatory powers is also part of the musicians calling (Diallo and Mitchell, pp. 160-161).

Asare Newman states that, in Aŋlɔga Fiaxor, Hunua Akakpo's shrine, lunatics suffering from some mental disorders have been healed through specific dance movements (stated in a lecture delivered by Asare Newman at the University of Ghana, 1985). People with fractured or dislocated legs could be healed when taken through specific dance movements, accompanied by specific drum patterns. Drums motivate dancers to move in certain ways, express their inner feelings, release physical tension and restore a sense of equilibrium. The drumming refreshes the mind and body, sharpens the brain, strengthens physique and contributes to a healthy life; as a Latin proverb states, mens sana in corpus sano, "a healthy mind in a healthy body". Ruth Williams notes that drum circles that are organized in Canada and the United States are therapeutic in the ways they create a sense of community and well being. They have also been identified to be useful for stroke, cancer and alzheimer patients; people wanting to break addictions as well as assist the body's defence mechanism (Williams, Djembe Drums for Music Therapy, internet).

Drums in the Context of Dance

There is hardly any African dance which is not accompanied by music. A single or a set of drums may be played to accompany dance within social, educational, occupational, religious, ceremonial or political contexts. A given dance may be accompanied by solo or small or large ensemble of drums and supporting instruments, such as bells, hand and/or stick clappers, rattles, flutes, whistles and trumpets. In Uganda, a set of *engalabe* or *emii diri*, long open-ended cylindrical drums (in Luganda and Lusonga languages respectively), *bakisima, embula, empuunyi* larger drum and *nankasa* small drum (all covered with hides) may be used to accompany the *bakisimba, amanjuugu* dances of the Buganda; *themenhga imbuga, amakondere* of *bunyoro*; and *ekizino* of Ankole royal dances as well as the *ajos* performed by the Teso people of Uganda during installation of chiefs. Also, among the Acholi of Uganda, almost every household has a drum for each *bwola* dancer (whose movements are coordinated with the big drum, *bull*) (http://www.ugandatravel guide.come/musical~instruments. html). A set of *djembe* and *dundun* drums are used to accompany the dances of the Malinke, Susu and Baga people of Guinea, whereas the *aburukuwa, apentemma* and *kwadum* drums are used to provide music for the Akan *kete* dancers.

Special drums are played to accompany mask and masquerade dancers in Liberia, Mali, Guinea, Ivory Coast, Nigeria, Cameroon and some other African societies. A mask, or masquerade may conceal the identity of the wearer, represent an ancestor, a mythological being, divinity, a God or a Goddess. Strand (2009) notes that among the Tusia of Burkina Faso, a special xylophone with an extremely elongated gourd called *tɔn* hanging beneath its bass keys, is played only for a mask called *Dutɔn*, which comes out once in every twenty-five years and dances for a special initiation rite (Strand, p. 113). In ensemble performances, there is usually a player of a bell or a small drum which provides the basic timeline for the performance while the supporting drums provide rhythmic background for the performance. There is also the lead drummer who coordinates the sounds of the various instruments, and engages in dialogue with the supporting instrumentalists, singers

Figure 92. The Dagbe Cultural Centre's Troupe performing Gahu at Kɔfeyia, Volta Region, Ghana

Photo: Modesto Amegago, July 2011.

and dancers. Signals for changing, or intensifying, accelerating and decelerating the drumming patterns, songs and movements would be provided by the master drummer. In performances, such as *agbekɔ, adzogbo* and *atsyia*, the music and dance are closely intertwined. A series of rhythmic patterns would be accompanied by specific movements so that changes in the lead drum patterns would be accompanied by changes in movements. In these performances, the lead drummer may communicate with the dancers on textual or linguistic and melodic basis (this will be elaborated under a discussion of performance processes). It should be noted that in this contemporary era, some individual or group of dancers may dance to a recorded version of the music instead of live drumming/music. A dancer who uses recorded drumming has to rehearse with the drumming and cues it appropriately in order that he or she may be conversant with the music and its relation to the dance routine. This would enable the dancer to avoid making unnecessary errors during the performance.

Drums in Contemporary African Music

Drums are also played in contemporary African musical bands such as the Senegalese *mbalax*, the Ghanaian highlife, Nigerian *juju*, *waka*, *apa*, the Congolese *soukous* and other types of African popular music. Performers of these music and dance genres usually combine Western melodic and harmonic instruments, such as accordions, string guitars or African string instruments (such as *kora*, *ngoni* and *thum Nyatiti*), lyrics, African percussions and trumpets, flutes and synthesizers. They express themes ranging from social, historical, topical, religious, to political, philosophical and individual experiences. They also use electronic equipment such as microphones and loudspeakers to enhance their performances. While some of these performers use African or African derived drums such as twin highlife drums, congas, *djembes*, *kpanlogo*, *iyaalu*, *lung*, *and gyil*, *bala*, *baan* and *balafon* xylophones to provide rhythmic background for the performances, others combine the various percussive instruments to provide a strong percussive section in the performances. For example, the Yoruba *juju* or highlife or *waka* bands often employ the *gangan*, *kanango*, *adamo* and *iyaalu*, and string guitar to provide a strong percussion section for their music/dance. Some Malian, Guinean and Senegalese groups would use *djembe*, *bala*, xylophones, *kora* and rhythm guitars in combination with other instruments to provide the percussion section of their performance.

The Nigerian *waka*, women's singing group may play to accompany a mother of a new born baby when she takes the baby to greet the father's family; or it may accompany a family to dance around the town after celebrating a burial outing at *Jimo*, the weekly Friday mosque service, in return for a fee (see Euba, pp. 437-448). In addition, the Ghanaian, Nigerian, Guinean, Malian, Senegalese, Cameroonian and Zairean contemporary bands may perform at weddings, birthday parties, political rallies and other national and international festivals, to entertain, celebrate important days or events, educate people as well as portray their cultural heritage. Members of these groups may make a decent living (although some may have to supplement their earnings through workshops and production and sale of their CDs and DVDs).

Drums in Contemporary Schools

Drumming now forms part of the curricular and extra – or co-curricular activities in some African and African Diaspora schools and communities. In such institutions and communities, the youths are taught the various drumming techniques, their historical and cultural functions, and the meanings of some drum texts. They are also encouraged to create drumming patterns within the performance structure and perform in small and large groups. The potential drummers are evaluated on their mastery of the drumming skills, their knowledge of the linguistic or textual and cultural basis of drumming, their ability to play selected drumming patterns, dance and sing as individuals and in small and large groups on regular basis, and during the middle and end of the learning period.

Drums in the context of Entertainment

Drums are played by individuals or group of people for their own enjoyment and for the enjoyment of other people. African drums are played in the Diaspora settings such as Canada to provide recreational entertainment for seniors and within the context of a multicultural community. It should be noted that there is an entertaining aspect of every drumming, and drumming which is geared towards entertainment may also communicate significant cultural values.

Drums in the context of Funerals

In African traditional societies, funeral celebrations are great occasions for drumming/music and dance. Among the Dagara/ Dagarti, Lobi and Sisala, and the Sambla of northern Ghana and southern part of Burkina Faso, the *gyil* (or *kogyil*) and *baan,* xylophones are used to announce funeral messages. A Dagara or Lobi or Sisala *kogyil* player may play a song, *gadaa yina, gadaa yina, gadaa yina, gadaa yina nikpe yina gadaa yina,* (meaning, a prominent person is dead), to announce the death of a prominent

Figure 93. The Klikɔ Kpegisu group performing at a funeral at Dzelukɔfe, Ghana

Photo: Modesto Amegago, July 2011.

person in the community (a personal conversation with Aaron Bebe, 2005; 2006). He may play another song, *Namwine Gon Doya*, which means only God knows the sufferers, to reflect on the life experiences of the deceased (Vercelli, musicweb.ucsd. edu~percussionpapers/rs_mvercelli.pdf). Specific songs would also be played during the funerals of men (Daarfo and Daarkpen), women, elders, chiefs and children. Drums are also played during pre-burial, burial and after burial rites. Blades notes that after the death of an African leader, a royal drum may be played at his shrine to release his spirit from the power of the drums. In this context, the sounds of the drum would be interpreted as "I am now free" (Blades, 1970, p. 63).

The duration of funeral rites and their associated performances may vary according to the rank or status of the deceased and the drumming groups to which he or she belonged. A funeral celebration of a king, chief, priest or community leader may be more elaborate than that of an ordinary member of the community. The funeral rites of a deceased who belonged to many performing groups would involve many performances. Among the

Aŋlɔ-Ewe, drumming/performances during funerals may occur on certain days preceding the wake keeping, during the day and night of the wake keeping, and on the day of the burial. Performances may continue on a day after the burial, during the second wake keeping, which may occur between four to seven days after burial (depending upon the deceased's clan), on a day after the second wake keeping (when the deceased's soul would be brought from the cemetery to a family house and fed). A number of performing groups may perform during the final funeral rites of a deceased, which may occur after six months or a year after the burial. The drummers/musicians and dancers may perform during the second, fifth or tenth anniversary of a deceased.

On such occasions, the drumming groups that the deceased or family members belong to would perform to mourn and eulogize the deceased, sympathize with the bereaved family, express group solidarity, reflect on life experiences and social ethics, entertain and heal the community. Thus, among the Aŋlɔ-Ewe, the *nyayito* or *leafelegbe* or *dekɔnyanu* may be performed during the funeral rites of a deceased elder. A corpus of *avihawo* and *konyifahawo* are sung during Ewe funerals, some of which may be accompanied by drumming. The *agbadza, gohu, kinka* and other social music/dance groups may perform to mourn the deceased and express lineage sentiments. Also, among the Akan, the *adowa* and *kete* orchestras may feature lamentation songs along with drumming and dancing during funerals.

Much of the traditional musical/dance performances occur during local rural funerals rather than the urban ones where most people have to work in factories and offices for longer hours during the days in order to earn their living. It is worth noting that there has been a gradual decrease in music and dance performance during local funerals, partly because of the current socioeconomic pressures on individuals and families, increased Christianization, and alienation of African youths from their traditional cultures. Nowadays, live drumming/music and dance performances hardly take place during pre-burial wake keepings in many local Ghanaian communities. Instead, a DJ would be hired to play music and keep the place alive. There has also been a reduction in the number of performances during post-burial rites. In addition, live drumming rarely takes place during funeral rites among the Africans living in the Diaspora settings in Canada, the United States, and Europe, where funeral rites are observed for a few days. On rare occasions, some family members would hire drumming/music groups to perform during pre-burial or post burial rites at funeral homes or in community halls. Some Ghanaian-Canadian and other Africans living in Canada may celebrate funerals of some family members who passed away in their original countries. Some may engage some drumming or music and dance groups in their communities to entertain the mourners for a short period.

Societal Restrictions on Drumming as a form of Checks and Balances

Although drumming forms an integral part of the African's life, it is also socially controlled in time and place. Among the Akan, Ewe and Ga of southern Ghana, a ban is placed on drumming (for about two weeks to over a month) during a period preceding or following state ceremonies or festivals, such as the *Hogbetsotso*, *Homowo* and *Odwira*. The ban is aimed at maintaining tranquillity and harmony with the environment. As noted earlier, drums performed in a given context may not be performed in another context unless a special permission is obtained for doing so. Certain drums/music may only be played at certain times of the day, month or year. The Akamba for example, may allow more drumming/music and dance during the dry season while prohibiting all drumming and dancing (except *kilumi* spirit dance) during rainy season. This may be aimed at keeping young people on the field during the rainy season, and preventing them from performing energetic stamping movements on the wet and soft ground (Kavyu, 199. p. 55). In Cuba, the *bata* are rarely played after sundown; in Matanzas toque ceremony, playing only begins at midnight. Further, ordinary people may not be allowed to play the drums associated with some traditional religious and political groups. For example, in Cuba, only initiates of Santeria divinity could play the *bata* drums. Similarly, only the court musicians may be allowed to play the court's instruments. During the colonial era, the British government considered recreational drumming an offence unless a special pass had been obtained from the police for drumming (Nketia, p. 73). This rule, somehow, prevails in some present African societies. It is worth noting that in this contemporary era, drums that were originally confined to certain traditional religious and political contexts may now be performed by theatrical and semi-professional groups in various contexts, especially in the urban settings. This may be considered a way of sharing the contributions made by the various sectors of the society but it may conflict with the values of certain groups within a broader society.

Chapter Four
Drummers in
African Societies

Figure 94. Modesto Amegago playing the lead drum in Gohu performance at Aŋlɔga, Ghana

Photo: Senyo Amegago. December 1 2011.

A drummer or *Azaguno* as he or she is called among the Ewe; *Akyerema* (as he or she is called among the Akan); *Jembefola* (as he or she is referred to by the Mande or Manding and its sub cultures), and *Nguni ya mukunda* (as he or she is referred to in Kikhamba) occupies a very important position in African societies. His or her role is directly related to the ways the drumming/music/dance functions in African societies. It has been noted that drumming is integrated with socio-cultural events such as child birth, games, socialization, marriage, education, occupation, religion/ceremonies, politics, festivals and funerals. In African traditional societies, drumming is considered a natural talent or a gift from God. Hence, the Akan particularly refer to a drummer as a divine drummer. The Akan believe that drummers are among the first people who were created by God. A drummer is considered an intermediary between God, the ancestors and the living. As I have stated earlier, drumming is the very foundation of the rhythm and motion of the universe, and drummers are the people who mediate the rhythm and motion of the universe, and project humanity's utterances, feelings and thoughts. The act of drumming requires knowledge, skill and perfection which only a few people attain. The fact remains that opportunities for learning to drum are not open to all. Drummers are also regarded as cultural historians, communicators, social critics and commentators and mouth pieces of societies. They are educators, researchers, and philosophers, advisors to leaders as well as musicians and entertainers. Drummers are required to have great command over language, be able to master lyrical, eulogistic verses and detail the heroic deeds of leaders and ancestors (Nketia, p. 155).

Categories of Drummers

There are drummers who specialize in playing a particular type of drum, such as a royal drum used to herald the movement of kings and chiefs, or priests and priestesses. There are also drummers who perform with other drummers in orchestras, such as the *dundun* and *djembe*, *bata*, *agbadza* and *karyenda* ensembles of the Mande, Yoruba, Ewe and Hutu respectively. In addition, there are drummers who specialize in playing the secondary or supporting drums of a particular or various musical styles. There are also master drummers who specialize in playing the lead drums of a particular, a few drumming repertoires or style(s) as well as those that are versatile in playing various repertoires and styles. There are also drummers who are fluent in hand drumming, those who are very good in stick drumming as well as drummers who excel in various drumming techniques.

The master drummer is the leader and conductor of the instrumental and dance ensemble. He or she coordinates the various instruments and gives the performance its unique character. He or she has great command over language and is well versed in the oral literature and history of the society. He or she is able to memorize a vast amount of rhythmic patterns, texts, proverbs and melodies and articulate, ornament and improvise drumming/musical patterns and texts. The master drummer may be a choreographer and/ or a song composer and dancer. He or she is expected to have flexible wrists and be highly skilled in the dynamics of drumming and the techniques of sound production. He or she cues the bell and other instruments to begin their parts at the appropriate times. He or she also provides the complementary and supporting drummers their correct times of entry in case they have difficulty (finding them), and corrects them by tapping the basic rhythms for them if they falter. The master drummer provides the necessary signals for change of patterns or rhythms, style and for heightening certain moments of the performance (see also Nketia, p. 154-155).

Nketia notes that among the Akan, the player of the talking drum is considered the greatest of all drummers because of the breadth and depth of his knowledge, and his skill and leading role in performances (Nketia, p. 154). "He is called the creator's drummer (Odomankoma Kyerema), because he is closest to the spirit of the ancestor chiefs whom he addresses in drumming. He recounts the genealogy and names of the ancestor chiefs, their place of settlement and accomplishments and praises each of them during the celebration of festivals (such as *Akwasidae*, which commemorates and offers gratitude to the ancestors). He is also called the creator's drummer because he is close to nature. He conjures the spirit of creation from whom the components of his drums were obtained, and he calls upon the Supreme Being, lesser gods and ancestor drummers capable of interfering with his work and well being" (Nketia, p. 154). In addition, the drummer of the talking drum calls himself the creator's drummer because, as he says on his talking drum, he is among the first important people to be created, as expressed in the following drum text:

> When the creator created all things,
> When the manifold creator created all things,
> What did he create?
> He created the court crier
> He created the drummer
> He created the principal State Executioner (Nketia, p. 154).

"The drummer of the talking drum also calls himself the creator's drummer because he tells about the origin of kings and states and performs his duties with other beings of creation: with ɔkyerema Nyanɔ, the man in the moon, regarded by the Akan as a drummer; and with the drummer bird kokokyinaka", as expressed in the following drum text:

> Drummer bird, what is your greeting response?
> We answer you with Anyaado
> We answer you with the response: the drummer's child
> The drummer's child sleeps and awakes with the dawn
> The drummer bird Kokokyinaka Asamoa
> Firampon, condolences! Condolences! Condolences!
> (Nketia, p. 154)

Supporting, Secondary and Complementary Drummers

Next to the master drummer are the complementary or supporting drummers who usually engage in dialogue with the master drummer, or provide steady musical background for the performance. Among the Ewe, players of the *sogo*, *kidi* and *gboba* come next to the master drummer: They engage in dialogue with the master drummer by playing rhythmic patterns that complement and ornament the master drum patterns. They are followed by players of the *kagan* supporting drum, bells, rattles and clappers who usually provide steady musical background for performances.

Some Renowned African Drummers and Xylophonists

Among the renowned African drummers are Kwabla Ladzekpo,
Alfred Ladzekpo, C. K. Ladzekpo, Midawo Foli Alowoyie, David
Locke, Godwin Agbeli, C. K. Ganyo, Guy Warren, popularly known
as Kofi Ghanaba, Pascal Younge (specialists in Ghanaian and West
African drumming and based in US). Modesto Amegago, Kwasi
Dunyo and Stephen Gbolonyo (specialists in Ghanaian and West
African drumming and based in Canada), Mustapha Tettey Addy,
Johnson Kemeh, Salomon Amankando, Emmanuel Agbeli (special-
ist in Ghanaian and West African drumming and based in Ghana),
Kuwor Sylvanus (a specialist in Ghanaian and West African drum-
ming and based in UK), Atifose Amegago, Deya Duga, Eda Agorvi,
Detsi-Kwasi Kugblenu, Eyra Kusorgbor, Kwasi Avevor, Robert
Awutey (some renowned Ewe drummers who operate at the local
setting). The renowned African drummers further include Akeem
Ayanniyi, Ayo Adeyemi, Dabi Kanyinsola, Lamidi Ayankunle,
Yusufu Ayankulade, Babatunde Olatunji, Alhaji, Durolu, Olawore
Ayansina, Laisi Ayansola, Salami Ladokun, Ayanleye Popoola and
Sola Akingbola (specialists in Yoruba drumming from Nigeria);
Mamady Keita, Amara Kante, Famoudou, Kouyate, Afaran Toure,
M'Bemba Bangoura (renowned *djembefola* from Guinea), Adama
Drame, Zoumana Dembele (*djembefola* from Burkina Faso),
Abdoul Doumbia, and Soungalo Coulibaly (*djembefola* from Mali)
and Martin Klabundi (in Tucson, USA) (see also http://djembe-
fola.com/artists/index.php). The renowned African xylophonists
include, Kakraba Lobi, Benard Woma, Aaron Sukura Bebe, S.K.
Kakraba, William Diku and Joseph Kobom (all from Ghana),
Famoro Diaoubate (Guinea), Fana Soro (Cote D'Ivoire), Kassoum
Diamoutene (from Mali), Bob Becker and Stephen Wittaker (from
USA). These lists can be greatly expanded.

Relationship among Drummers

Drummers in African traditional societies are supposed to
maintain cordial relationship with one another. Each drummer
recognizes his/her role and contributes his/her best to the performance. Cooperation among the drummers of a group is essential

for the smooth running and success of the group and performances. Occasionally, there may be some misunderstanding or
conflict among some drummers regarding the behaviors or actions
of their colleague but these issues are usually resolved by the
drummers themselves or through the mediation of group members
and leaders. There is usually a feeling of solidarity among drummers within a town or an area although occasionally, there may be
some rivalry and conflicts regarding the behaviors, attitudes and
utterances of certain drummers, or group members towards other
drummers or groups pertaining to their performances or skills.
Usually, drummers belonging to different groups or towns relate
well whenever they come together to observe or participate in the
performances of their neighbors or rival groups in the vicinity or
town. It is worth noting that each drummer is unique and each role
is equally important and contributes to the harmony and success
of the performance. Quarrels among drummers regarding the roles
and treatment of certain drummers, or utterances and attitude
toward one another may break groups.

Women and African Drumming

There are historical references to female drummers in some
African societies. For example in Dahume, the female drummers
were the wives of the king and members of the royal clan, who
would perform the music called *zenli* and *ajogan* at the palaces
of Agbome and Port Novo (as stated earlier). Their performances
involved the playing of *zenli* and *livi*, large vase drums, two membrane drums and an earthen-ware pot, which was played by tapping
the open mouth with leather and basketry fan, accompanied by the
playing of rattles, iron bells (*kpanliga*) and singing (Wachsmann,
p. 37). However, in the present day African traditional societies,
drumming is considered a predominantly male activity - hence
women are usually discouraged from drumming. Some societies
would justify the restriction on women with certain beliefs and
statements. Among the Ewe, there is a saying that a woman who
drums would prepare *akple gbɔgbɔ*, badly cooked food. The Akan
hold the view that a woman who touches the drum (particularly
belonging to the state) in her monthly period would defile it. Some

Figure 95. The female drummers of the Klikɔ Kpegisu group performing at a funeral at Dzelukɔfe, Ghana.

Photo: Modesto Amegago, July, 2010.

other African societies hold the view that a woman who drums would become infertile. Indeed, many Africans societies consider the drums as sacred objects. Hence, women are usually discouraged from touching them in their menstrual period. Although these beliefs and statements may seem sceptical, they may have psychological underpinnings. The problem is, the elders may not readily explain to the youths the rationale for observing such norms, in which case, the youths would have to reason or enquire further in order to understand the rationale behind them. For example, the idea that women who drum would cook badly (partially) cooked food, might have stemmed from the fact that drumming is time demanding and hypnotic and may distract a woman who is in the process of cooking, thus affecting the quality of her food. Also, in many traditional African societies, drumming is a strenuous activity that can go on for hours or days, and the playing of drums such as *sogo* (in sitting position) for longer hours would affect the drummer's blood circulation and cause blood to flow through the urine. Excessive playing of the *sogo* may cause severe stomach problems and affect women especially during their menstrual period. It sometimes contributes to the development of hernia in some male drummers. For these reasons, it may be dangerous especially for women to indulge in rigorous drumming as done in most African traditional settings. Such an act may affect the woman's health. Hence, in most African traditional societies, women usually play light percussions such as hourglass drums, rattles and clappers (which are used in puberty rites of the Akan) and calabash, or gourd vessel (played in the northern parts of Ghana, Togo, Benin, Mali, Guinea and some other West African countries).

Recently, some women have revolted against what they perceived to be male dominance in drumming and formed their own groups, in which they would play the various drums. An example is the Aŋlɔ-Ewe women of Anyako who formed the *takada* drumming/music and dance group (1970s) in which some of them would play the drums and other supporting instruments (Ladzekpo, http://homes.comcastnet/~dzinyaladzekpo/repertoire.html). Another example is the Aŋlɔ-Ewe *kpegisu* women's group of Klikɔ, which features female drummers during performances. Some Guinean and Senegalese groups now feature women playing the *djundjun* drums while dancing at the same time, at home and in the Diaspora. The Ghanaian School of Performing Arts and other contemporary arts institutions teach both male and female students how to drum and feature them in performances, except that most female students usually gravitate towards dancing, singing and playing lighter percussive instruments during public performances.

Becoming a Drummer

Drumming as a natural gift or talent is (traditionally) said to be passed on to sons, or to male descendants through paternal or maternal lineage. Among the Malinke, there exists a caste or class of hereditary professionals called *Nyamalaka* (*nyamalao*) and musical verbal artisans called *Jeli* (*djeli, Jelilu* or *Jali, Jalo* or *Jalolu*) who are believed to have inherited the drumming talent from their lineage. For example, in Guinea, the Kouyate family is regarded as the keepers of the *bala* tradition. They have played a significant role in disseminating the xylophone tradition across generations. Among the Dagbamba, every male born into the drummers' family is a potential drummer. The female born is excluded from becoming a drummer, but at least one of her male children has to become a drummer. If she gives birth to only female, one of her daughters must marry a drummer to ensure the continuity of the drumming tradition (Abdallah, p. 2010, 16). Similarly, among the Akan, the duty of drumming is passed on from one generation to the other, within households, from father to son. There is also a common belief of drum prodigies-people born with the drumming talent. It is stated that soon after birth, such a person would begin to show his inherited trait; when he is being carried, he would be drumming with his fingers on the person carrying him (Nketia, p. 55). The Yoruba believed that Ayan was the first talented ancestor drummer who passed on the drumming talent to posterity (as noted earlier). But they also maintain that drumming could be taught to people who did not receive the talent from any ancestor but from God directly.

Among the Ewe, certain families are known for producing talented drummers. Potential drummers may be seen exhibiting their talent in households and in public from the early childhood. There is a wide held belief in reincarnation among the various African peoples. An Ewe child may be said to have reincarnated an ancestral drummer. In some cases, certain rituals would be performed for the child in order that he may become a drummer in the future. For example, during the funeral rites of a deceased Ewe drummer (prior to the burial), his drumming sticks would be handed over to a potential (young) drummer who may be a son, extended family member so that he would perpetuate the drumming tradition. Some of these children would grow up and become master drummers while others would grow without exhibiting the drumming talent or skill. On the contrary, children of certain parents who are not known to be drummers in communities would exhibit the drumming talent; this may lead to scepticisms about the source of their talent. But, the Ewe would trace their talent to their paternal or maternal lineage, or regard it as their gift from Se, law or law-giver, or Mawu, the Supreme Being. It appears the availability of drums and drumming opportunities in a child's environment coupled with his/her personal motivation, interest and encouragement from parents and community members contribute a great deal to the child's development of the drumming talent and skill (Amegago, pp. 62-63).

Training of Drummers

In African traditional societies, drummers are usually trained through informal and formal modes. The informal training involves children's participation in drumming from pre-natal stage, through infancy and learning from their parents, community drummers and peers from the early childhood to adulthood. The formal training usually takes the form of the older drummers and institutions instructing young and apprenticed drummers in the cultural drumming/music traditions. However, the two modes of training usually overlap.

Informal Training

The informal training of drummers begins from the foetal stage. There is a wide held belief in Ghanaian communities that the condition a pregnant woman undergoes affects the infant. Pregnant women usually participate in music and dance and it is believed a child begins to absorb the drumming at this unconscious stage. From infancy, parents begin to sing lullabies that involve non-meaningful drum syllables to their children while rocking them here and there. Mothers usually carry their babies at their backs to music and dance performances where the children continue to absorb the drumming patterns of their society. A potential child-drummer continues to learn by imitating adults and creating rhythms on toy drums made with tins, bottles, acorn pods and hides, synthetic leathers, and improvised materials such as calabash, and wood branches. A child born or raised in a drummer's family has an added advantage of practising on real drums. Such a child may be encouraged by parents or family members to continue the learning process. A drummer-parent may guide or teach his child how to play some basic or relatively challenging drumming patterns. Other drummers in the communities may teach the child some new rhythms sometimes as a reward for running some errands (Jones, p. 71). A child continues to learn through participation, observation and memorization of adults' performances: the young musician may be asked to play the side of the drum (called *Uukorgo* in Ewe), or supporting drums in adult's performances. The child also learns by observing and participating in initiation and other ceremonies that involve music and dance. By the time the child reaches adolescence, he would have absorbed some drumming repertoires of his culture which he would continue to perform and recreate.

According to Zablong Abdallah, the potential Dagbamba (Dagomba) drummers are trained both informally and formally. The informal training involves a child who is about three years old, taking a broken calabash and playing any rhythms that come to his mind (Abdallah, 2010, p. 17).

In his discussion of the training of Yoruba drummers, Euba states that, a potential *dundun* drummer begins to learn how to drum as early as the age of five: He is given a *kanango*, the smallest hourglass drum. After toying with the *kanango*, he would begin the proper training on the *gudugudu*. From the *gudugudu* the child would proceed to learn how to play the *isaju, ikehin* and *kerikeri* musical patterns. After mastering all the techniques of playing the secondary instruments, the potential drummer begins to learn *iyaalu* at which time he would have started going out to the market to play with the elders (Euba, 1990, p. 104). At this stage, the potential *dundun* drummer would continue to imitate what he hears from the elderly drummers. Some elderly drummers may sit by him and hold his hands to play certain patterns and correct him if he plays wrongly. He is also taught some drum texts, poetry and their interpretations and is encouraged to ask questions about the drumming. The potential drummer may be given the opportunity to play for a short while during adult's performances under the supervision of an elderly drummer as part of his assessment, and if he does well, he may be given the opportunity to represent an *iyaalu* player for longer period until he reaches a stage where he is allowed to lead the ensemble throughout the entire performance. In these ways, the trainee gradually assumes the role of the master drummer (Euba, 1990, pp. 104-106). The informal training could last for many years.

Formal Training

Children are given formal training when the musical type is in fulfilment of certain functions in society. Among the Akan, the male and female *atumpan* drums are used to communicate important cultural messages, and a young musician must be trained to fulfil this role. Also, the Ewe, Dagbamba and some other African societies have to ensure that there are drummers who fulfil the drumming functions in their societies. Therefore, a potential drummer may be entrusted to an elderly or professional drummer (who may be a father, a master drummer in the vicinity or nearby town) for a certain period (ranging from three months to over a year). In addition, potential court musicians among the Dagbamba, Akan and Yoruba would be recruited from certain households or lineages (of commoners and royals) and the vicinities, and be trained for their services. Similarly, the neophytes of the Yewe religious sect of the Ewe would be trained to master a suite of music and dance, a secret language and other ritual practices during initiation.

The training of drummers may take place in a house, compound, farm, beach or secluded location. Among the Akan, some parents may delay the teaching of their offspring for fear that they might be hastening their life on earth. Such a belief implies that a parent who teaches his or her own child how to drum may die earlier than expected. Hence, they may request other drummers in the community to instruct their children. Part of the formal training involves sending an adult drummer to another village and town, to

Figure 96. Young drummers and singers led by a master drummer Reuben Agbeli in a performance at the Dagbe Cultural Institute, Kɔfeyia, V/R. Ghana.

Photo: Modesto Amegago, July 2010.

learn new drumming styles. It further involves sending an invitation to a drummer in another location to come and teach the drummers of a performing group. The formal training also involves attaching drummers to traditional political or religious institutions to learn the drumming associated with such institutions.

The formal training process among the Akan and Ewe further involves the professional/elderly drummer holding the child's hands and playing the rhythms with him on a drum or an improvised object, such as a piece of bamboo, wood, table and branches of trees. The elderly drummer may tap drumming patterns/on the child's shoulder blades to enable him to feel the distribution of sequences of the drum beats, rhythms and drumming techniques. He may express the rhythms in non-meaningful syllables and as meaningful texts, teach the child the cultural contexts of the drumming, drum poetry and proverbs, praise names and genealogies of kings/chiefs where appropriate. The young musician would be led to performances where he would observe, listen and participate by playing the side of the lead drum and supporting instruments, and might sing and dance.

The young musicians would be assessed regularly through questions that would require them to play or recite certain drum patterns, texts and exhibit their playing skills through a series of performances and graduation ceremonies that would involve, drumming, drum recitals, singing and dancing. It is worth noting that most supporting or secondary drummers do not undergo the rigorous training process since they can pick up the art by listening to others play. The period of apprenticeship can last for a very long time. Therefore, a potential or apprenticed drummer needs to be patient and obedient to his masters in order to acquire the requisite knowledge and skills in drumming (See also Jones 1959, pp. 70-71). Some Akan instructors would charge a small fee in return for their services. Similarly, an Ewe, instructor may be provided with *dza* a small fees especially if he has to travel to the place of instruction.

A discussion of the formal training process among the Dagbamba is provided by Abdallah (2010) who states, a male child who is about six years old is given a small *lung* and made to follow the elderly drummers to village or town performances, where he begins to learn how to play supporting drums. In the evenings (after supper), the child would be taught drum poetry, praise singing and oral tradition of the Dagbamba through appropriate drumming techniques (this involves teaching him a few verses at a time). He continues to learn during festivals, funerals, weekly performances in communities and market places. Apart from learning how to drum, he would help the trainer on his farm, and tidy his compound (*sanbani*) every evening (around 5:45 P.M.) before supper and lay the mat or skin (depending on the status of his trainer) (Abdallah, p. 17). Abdallah states further that the potential drummer (child) would also be taught how to play proverbs, poetry, and praises, beginning with tribute to God as follows:

> *Dakol nye bi* ba Nam lana
> Meaning
> The bachelor is the junior but his father is God almighty.

> Pag' lan nye kpem ba Nam lana:
> Meaning
> The married man is the junior, also his father is God almighty.

> Nwum mal lan nwum dim ba Nam lana.
> Meaning
> Whoever has a guardian or a father should eat, again his father is God almighty.

> Nwum kong lan nwum ziya ba Nam lana.
> Meaning
> He who has no guardian or father must sit down or go hungry, yet his father is God.

> Such proverbs appear to be referring to the history and experiences of Bizun, the first lung drummer in Dagbon and some other drummers in the state.

Abdallah also states that the trainee would be introduced to other proverbs that express tribute and praises and omnipotence of God and his creations/deeds as follows:

Nwum yel ni pa Wunni yul Naa nwum mi o tooni
ka yul nyenga Ka bang ni Wunni sagi naa Nam lana,
meaning
Meaning
Whoever disputes the supremacy of God should look
in front of him and turn to look back, it is then that
he would admit the kinship and greatness of almighty.

Nwum yel ni Wunni pa Naa, nwum zang, shigban yini
bang di tooni bang di nyanga ka bang ni Wunni sagi
Naa Nam nala.
Meaning
Whoever disputes the Supremacy of God must take a
piece of bee wax and try to identify the front and back,
then he would realise that, God is actually the king of
kings.

Nwum Wunni nam Sagim lan bia, o tab diri ka odol
vehiri nmana.
Meaning
Who is this God who created the owner of food' child
who licks his colleague's calabash? (Abdallah, 2010,
pp. 20).

After, learning how to play these tributes, the trainee is taught how
to play human actions and deeds: the achievements and praises of
Naa Nyagse (the king) and his children. He is later taught how to
play the names and appellations of his ancestors, and *Nam*, the
kingship or genealogy of the Yendi skin (equiv. throne) beginning
with the name of the king or Naa Zangina to the present king, the
lineages of other kings in neighboring states, their siblings and
birth places, and later, the historical review-achievement of the
leaders (Abdallah, p. 20). The trainee continues to learn during
performances and is corrected whenever he falters. Any proceeds
received by the trainee during performances is given to the trainer
who may take some portion and give him the remaining (Abdallah, p. 17) and pray for God's guidance and protection for the
trainee(Abdallah, p. 18). The training period may range between
ten to fifteen years (Abdallah, p.17). Part of the graduation assessment is referred to as *Zeri tobu*, literally means the pounding of

ingredients); this is a form of drum recital that precedes the historical reviews by the elderly drummers about the history, migrations, achievements, genealogies of chiefs/kings and their enskinment (equiv. enthronement), etc. The performance is presented for the king who passed the night in *Katini Duu* (royal room). The final examination takes place during any Islamic festivals or social occasions, such as *Damba* (celebrated to commemorate the birth of Prophet Mohammed) and *Bugum* (fire festival) where the new drummer would be asked to serve as the lead appellator, lead praise singer, or lead historical reviewer (Abdallah, p. 18). Upon satisfactory performance, the trainee would be recognized as a drummer in the community.

In all these situations, the apprenticed drummers would observe and listen to the elderly drummers and dancers, and be introduced to the various drumming techniques and repertoires, linguistic basis and cultural functions of the drumming.

Limitations Posed by the Traditional Training Process

The limitations posed to traditional training process/method include the lack of opportunities for some trainees to learn the drumming repertoires that belong to certain religious, occupational and political groups. Contextualization of performances is a way of maintaining social harmony, by allowing individuals to participate in the mainstream performances and in specific contexts. It also provides opportunities for potential drummers to learn the repertoires that relate to specific stages of their lives. However, it may not allow them to fully grasp the drumming repertoires of certain religious and political groups unless they become members or reach a certain stage. For example, a potential drummer who does not belong to a hunter's association or Yewe religious sect may not readily learn the drumming associated with these associations (although s/he may absorb or imitate them from a distance). Also, the traditional method does not encourage many women to learn the various drumming repertoires. In addition, the banning of drumming during the period preceding or proceeding certain ceremonies or festivals may affect the training of potential drummers, although such a period may allow the community to rest in preparation for or after certain celebrations. It is worth noting that, among the Aŋlɔ-Ewe, performing groups usually play improvised drums, such as wooden box drum during the period of banning drumming. The decline of traditional structures due mainly to the superimposition of the Western structures and educational system on the African ones continues to hamper the training of potential drummers in the traditional settings. Many potential drummers now lack opportunities for learning through participation and slow absorption from early childhood. Moreso, many parents are now discouraging their children from learning how to drum because of its perceived lack of economic benefits. These phenomena continue to hamper the process of learning drumming in African societies. Hence, there is the need to reconsider the cultural significance of drumming, and create opportunities for children to learn in both traditional and contemporary institutions from the early childhood, to enable them to develop their talent, skills, understanding and appreciation of drumming that would enable them to serve the global communities. Such a move would require the removal of the barriers than hinder the youths' and women's participation in certain contextual drumming.

Training of Drummers in
Contemporary Arts Institutions

The introduction of African drumming in the contemporary African and African Diaspora and world institutions was made possible through the concerted efforts of African leaders such as Dr. Kwame Nkrumah, Leopold Senghor, and Africanist scholars and educators such as Professors Kwabena Nketia, and Akin Euba, who strove to revive African cultures and develop programs in African performing arts and cultures. From the 1960's African drumming was introduced into some African elementary, secondary and tertiary institutions as curricular and extra curricular activities. In Ghana, African drumming was introduced into the elementary and secondary schools, as curricular and extra curricular activities. It also forms part of the programs of the School of Performing Arts, University of Ghana, Legon, the National Academy of Music, Wineba (in the Western Region), University of Cape Coast (Central Region), Ghana Dance Ensemble and Centres for National Culture. It further constitutes part of the programs of the University of Ile Ife and some other African Universities. In addition, African drumming is now taught and performed in some European and American communities and institutions such as University of Surrey, Roehampton University, University of California, Arizona State University, the University of Arizona, University of North Texas, Denton, York University and University of Toronto, and some elementary and secondary schools. These institutions continue to employ drum instructors who have received traditional and Western education. They have developed drumming courses in relation to the various educational levels and learning periods, and try to provide equal opportunities for both male and female students to learn the various contextual drumming/music.

Contemporary Drumming Teaching/Learning Methods

The teaching of African drumming in these new institutions takes the form of group and individualized instruction. Potential drummers are introduced to the historical and cultural contexts of African drumming; timbre, orchestration, tuning processes, drumming techniques and linguistic or textual basis of African drumming. Students are encouraged to observe, listen and take note of their drumming activities in class. Instructors usually go round to help or correct students who are in difficulty. They also assess students on daily, weekly and periodic basis (in large and small groups) by asking them verbal questions on specific aspects of the drumming, and through quiz and essay questions, and by leading students to drum, sing and dance in small and large groups and as individuals, thereby testing their understanding of the cultural contexts, concepts and acquisition of the drumming skills. Students are awarded grades according to their performances in the various areas (ranging from A to D and below). The instructors emphasize both group and individual performances in the evaluation process.

A review of both the traditional and contemporary teaching methods has elucidated the fact that although the new institutions have tried to create equal opportunities for various students to learn the drumming repertoires of diverse cultures, most of these students lack the opportunity to participate in drumming from infancy. This prevents them from absorbing the drumming/musical traditions of their own cultures from the early childhood, which would have served as a solid foundation for their future education, creativity and performance. While in the contemporary settings, African drumming is usually taught for a relatively shorter period: about one and a half to three hours per session, once or twice in a week, potential drummers in the African traditional settings learn through repetition of the various drumming patterns and styles and participation in performances for several hours, days and nights. This enables them to acquire in-depth knowledge and skills in the various drumming repertoires. Another problem is that many elementary and secondary schools (in Africa) that would have provided opportunities for the youths to develop their drumming skills/knowledge from childhood do not appear to have taken the drumming/cultural lessons seriously, in part because of its perceived lack of economic or career opportunities and prestige in societies. Unfortunately, the higher institutions alone may not be able to train all the societies' potential drummers/musicians. The African children in the Diaspora are more vulnerable to this situation although some elementary and secondary schools in these new locations are trying to provide opportunities for the youths to engage in drumming.

Should the current situation prevail, African societies may no longer be able to produce many talented drummers in the long run. In this situation, there is the need for a reconsideration of the traditional learning methods. Communities and families should encourage their youths to continue to participate in their cultural music and dance forms in order to develop their drumming skills and knowledge from the early childhood. This would provide avenues for recruiting and training potential drummers for the contemporary arts institutions and would facilitate the work of these new institutions.

Status of Drummers in African Societies

The status of drummers in a particular society depends upon how the society values drumming. Societies that consider drumming as a significant part of their lives may regard drummers highly while societies that do not value drumming may not regard them as such. Some people may value the drummers when they are in the act of drumming, and may undermine them outside the contexts of drumming/performance. Societal perceptions or attitudes towards drummers also depend on the drummers' personality, behaviours or actions in the community. For example, if a drummer is in the habit of drinking, or is known to be lazy, he or she may not be highly regarded in the community. Among the Ewe and the Akan for example, drummers are usually admired for their talent, skill and ability to play and communicate historical and cultural experiences; arouse the feelings, thoughts and actions of peoples, educate them as well as express aesthetically pleasing sounds. They are often praised for their performances and offered token of financial remuneration and gifts in kind. Some people who are very impressed by a drummer's talent and performance may befriend or fall in love with him/her.

Euba states that, the Yoruba, *dundun* drummers enjoy popularity because of their personality and skilful use of language in narrating cultural stories, teaching wisdom and building images of individual clients and community as well as creating a sense of humour and entertaining the people. The rhetorical gift of the *dundun* artist includes a disposition toward witticisms even in the process of making philosophical statements. By virtue of all these, the *iyaalu* drummer is a well regarded and favoured member of the community (Euba, 1990, p. 93).

Among the Dagbamba, the *lunsi*, hourglass drummers think of themselves as aristocrats because their great ancestor Bizun was in line to become the king of Dagbon. They serve as philosophers and advisers to the politicians through the witty proverbs that they play on the drums (Locke, p. 1990, p. 13). However, they also compare themselves to slaves and women because of their traditional obligations to provide a unique social service. They further compare themselves to beggars since some of them earn money as receivers of alms as sanctioned by Islamic custom (by drumming in the market and vantage locations (see also Locke, p. 13). Societies give the drummers the freedom to criticise or comment on the behaviours of all its members regardless of their statuses. The drummers can address the leaders without using their appropriate titles through drumming. In performance contexts, the *iyaalu* drummer may critique or comment on the behaviours of all kinds of people in the community: ordinary, rich and poor, kings and queens. The drum gives the drummer a kind of freedom to the Oba's palace which only the royal wives enjoy (Euba, 1990, pp 93-94).

Drumming Titles

Some societies may confer honorific titles on particular drummers, based on the recognition of their services to humanity. For example, the Ewe would refer to an experienced and knowledgeable drummer as *Azagunɔga* (lit. great or senior drummer). They would also refer to a junior or up and coming drummer as *Azagunɔkpe*. According to Euba, the Yoruba drummers have their own chieftaincy titles which are similar to the titles borne by traditional chiefs of an Oba. The most important drumming title is that of the *aareelu*, known in Ile Ife as *Bale Ilu*, which is given to the person appointed as the traditional head of all the (*dundun* and other) drummers in a town. In Osogbo, such titles include: *Aareelu, Otun, Giwa* and *Aare Ago* (*Aare Agoro*). In Ede, seven principal titles are usually conferred on drummers such as *Aarelu, Otun, Balogun, Seriki, Aare Gangan* (leader of the gangan players), *Jagun* and *Babaasale*. The *Aarelu* is usually an elderly drummer and a man of integrity (Euba, 1990, p. 100). Also, some contemporary African performing art institutions and communities may confer the title "master drummer" on highly skillful, experienced, efficient and versatile drummers.

Chief of Drummers

Some drumming groups or communities may appoint a member of the group as their chief. Among the Yoruba, such a chief would be automatically accorded recognition by Oba and his chiefs. Drumming titles, such as those given by Oba are held for life (See Euba, 1990, p.100). Similarly, the *Lunsi* of the Dagbamba constitute an association of drummers who reside (with their sons and grand sons) in the *Lunsi* quarter of the towns, or state and who have their own chieftaincy and council of hierarchy (*lung nannima*) of drummers, such as the *lung Naa* (chief drummer), *Sampahi Naa* (deputy chief drummer), *lunga* (practicing drummer), *lunga paga* (female drummer or drummer's wife) and *lungbih* (young and up and coming drummer) (Locke, 1990, p. 13; Abdallah, 2010, pp. 66-67).

There is an office of a drummer chief in the Akan court, which is usually apportioned to household of commoners or households of king's or chiefs who are responsible for providing artists and servants. These *akyeremafoa*, drummers' group reside in a quarter of *Akyeremade*, drummers' town or quarter. Some drummers, however, live in other sectors of the town. A drummer chief is not necessarily an expert drummer but a leader who maintains a link between the chief/king and state drummers.

In an ordinary life, a drummer may be treated like an ordinary person; even though he may be well known in his immediate neighbourhood, s/he may pass unnoticed in other neighbourhoods. The drummers enjoy equal rights to be heard despite their differential roles. However, as societies continue to shift their emphasis from social values to economic values, the status of drummers begins to fall on the socio-economic ladder (with the exception of a few that are holding other social titles or have been financially successful through drumming). Some people came to look down on drummers especially out of the performance contexts. Thus, an Ewe drummer may be alluded to such as *Azaguno mahadua*? (a drummer for me to eat?). Abdallah also notes that among the Dagbamba, the very mention of the *lunsi* invokes lazy begging intruders, and comments such as *Kaa Lunga mei*, what worth is a drummer may be made in reference to drummers. However, such negative perceptions of drummers may change as societies continue to critically reflect on the drummers' roles in relation to their history and cultural formation and contemporary problems or issues.

Drummer Remuneration

As noted earlier, court drummers/musicians and their families in the past depended on traditional leaders for their living. For example, the *Lunsi* of Dagbon and the *dundun* drummers of the

Yoruba and *Jembefola* of the Mande operated as professional or craft guilds, and earned money by performing for chiefs/kings and sub groups at market places, praising people and collecting gifts of money from spectators. Benevolent spectators may offer individuals or group of drummers some tokens (of money) in appreciation for their services. As noted earlier, some traditional drummers may derive some income by charging small fees for teaching potential drummers. Money derived from such performances may be distributed equally or on the basis of seniority and one's role in the performance. A very talented and skillful lead drummer or singer may earn a comparatively large share but every drummer would receive his fair share (see Locke, 1990, p. 13). In group performances, the greater proportion of gift (in cash or kind) is given to drummers. However, many traditional drummers are not adequately remunerated for their services. Hence, they have to engage in other activities such as farming, fishing and carving for their living. Needless to say, in this contemporary era, some popular or highlife bands that continue to tour their respective countries, regions or overseas usually employ some drummers and pay them decent wages. Some African performing arts institutions are employing talented, skillful and knowledgeable drummers on full or part time basis to teach African drumming courses, or play to accompany dance classes, or in school drama and opera productions. The same applies to national music/dance companies, such as the Senegalese Ballet, Guinea Ballet, Ghana Dance Ensemble and Centres for the Arts and Culture. Although, such groups employ both traditional and contemporary drummers, the drummers residing in the urban areas have easy access to such opportunities. In addition, some institutions and communities in the United States of America, Canada, Europe and other parts of the world have been hiring some African drummers, drum/music instructors to teach or play in productions or performances on part time or full time basis. Some drummers in African and the Diaspora may also derive additional income from recording their music and playing in music and dance video and film productions. It is imperative for drummers to take advantage of the emerging markets for performances and teaching in order to raise their socioeconomic status.

However, the art of drumming should not be driven mainly by financial gains but by the love and passion that one has for it. It should be considered a call to duty and service to humanity, which requires dedication, sacrifice and perseverance that would enable potential drummers to develop the requisite talent, skills and knowledge. The drummers have to broaden their knowledge to enable them to effectively serve the global community. Societies need to recognize the role of drummers and find possible ways of supporting them in order to perpetuate the drumming tradition.

This chapter has shed lights on the role of drummers in African and African Diaspora societies; societal perceptions of women and drumming, women's reactions through the formation of their own drumming/dance groups, and the subsequent inclusion of more women in drumming; the traditional and contemporary training processes and the socioeconomic status and remuneration of drummers. It is obvious that changes in the socioeconomic conditions have imparted on the training and status of the African drummers. Hence, a new awareness should be created about the significance of drumming in African and global societies. The various communities should continue to train potential drummers from the early childhood and provide them with the needed supports that would enable them to develop their skills and knowledge. The drummers have to dedicate themselves to the profession, endeavour to excel in their practices and refrain from certain behaviours, attitudes and practices that may tarnish their reputation. They also need to form their own unions in order to educate members about their social obligations, rights and needs and work towards achieving such ends. Finally, the drummers need to remind themselves of the health issues that might result from excessive drumming despite the healing functions of the drums. They will have to act in moderation in the process of rendering their services to humanity.

Chapter Five

Organization of African Drumming and Performing Groups

Drum(s) may be played by an individual or group of people who do not belong to any association, but come together to perform on the spur of the moment, or for specific cultural events. But usually, a group of people who share common interest or values come together to form their own drumming group(s). The drumming or music/dance groups may be formed for the purpose of performing particular or various music and dance styles to the public or state, religious institutions; for offering financial assistance to members and securing the patronage and clients of members. For example, the youths, students, male and/or male adults, hunters, farmers, fisher-folks, drummers, members of religious and political associations and other occupational groups may come together to form their own drumming/performing groups, for the purpose of socializing or expressing or sharing their collective experiences. Among the Ewe, performing groups are formed by the mainstream community, youths, students, male and/or female adults, drummers, hunters and members of some religious and political groups. Examples of these groups are the mainstream *agbadza*, the youths' *gota, gahu, bɔbɔɔbɔ* and *kinka* music/dance groups; the adults' *gohu* and *adzida* and *nyayito* groups, the female *takada* and *kpegisu* groups, *yevevu* and *afavu* (religious groups), *adevu*, hunters' groups), *vuga*, *asafo* and *adabatram* (which are associated with the traditional political and military organizations). Also, among the Akan, there are popular bands such as, *asonko*, *awaa*, *sanga*, *osekye*, and *asaadua* (formed by youths and adult male and female). There are also *aboafoa* and *asafo*, hunters and warriors groups, formed by common people and the rulers. Some Akan *asafo* and *fɔntɔmfrɔm* groups are formed by the traditional political institutions, and their members are drawn from particular lineages, households or localities (Nketia, pp. 67-74; 75-89; 105-151). Similarly, each Yoruba town or division may have drummers' association that may be sub-divided into branches based on age groups. For example, there are senior and junior branches of drummers association in *Osogbo*(a town in south-western Nigeria) As reported by Kavyu, among the Akamba of Kenya dance groups are organized in every (*utui*) village by male youths (*anake*) and female youths (*eitu*) between 14-24 years old, and several elders *nthele* (Kavyu, p. 53). Drumming/music and dance organizations may be observed in other Africa communities.

Some of the drummers' associations may not primarily be geared towards performances. For example, the *Osun* drummers association has representatives from various Yoruba drumming groups, whose aims among other things; include addressing issues affecting the drummers and settling any disagreements among them (Euba, pp. 100-101). On the contrary, many of the drumming groups formed among the Ewe, Ga and Akan of Ghana are geared towards performances, and in addition, making financial contributions to needy members. According to Euba, the *Osun* drummers Association of the Yoruba may meet once every month, each time in a different town and each member of the association would contribute ten thousand naira every two weeks in the association's treasury to cover the running expenses and helping the members of the association. Euba also notes that during some of the meetings of the Association, the patron expressed concerns about the need to have special places for the sale of drums; he also condemned the practice whereby too many non drummers were making and selling drums, and suggested the need for cultivating the trees for making the drum shells and for establishing a school for the study of drumming. In addition, the leaders expressed concerns about fewer engagements due to the influx of popular music and advised members to supplement their income by engaging in other professions (Euba 1990, pp. 100-101). Similarly, the Aŋlɔga *Azagunɔwo fe habɔbɔ*, Drummers Association (in the Volta Region of Ghana) may meet once in a month, or once every three months to discuss issues of common concern, contribute towards the up keeping of the group, assist members in financial need and perform for the deceased members of the association as well as contribute to their funeral expenses.

Group Membership

Members of some African ethnic groups who migrate to some urban areas would come together to form their own performing groups. The same applies to some other Africans who migrate to African Diaspora settings of London, United States of America and Canada. Examples of these groups are the Nɔvisi group of the Ewe community of London, Ogedengbe drumming group in Vancouver, led by Kwasi Oruogye (of Nigeria), Afrikania group in Denton, North Texas, led by Professor Gideon Foli Alɔwoyi (from Ghana), Martey and the Akwaaba Ensemble, led by Peace Elewonu (from Ghana), Nutifafa Afrikan Performance Ensemble, led by Modesto Amegago (from Ghana). The groups further include Lebagatae African Drum and Dance Ensemble, led by (a Guinean) Mustapha Bangoura. Sankofa African Drum and Dance Ensemble in Brockport, led by (an American) Clyde Alafiju Morgan, the Shona Sarif African Drum and Dance Ensemble founded by Willie Anku (of Ghana in 1982) at the University of Pittsburgh. Some of these groups are formed by schools, churches and professional artists.

Membership in the mainstream performing groups is open to all on the basis of one's enthusiasm, availability and ability to attend the groups' meetings and rehearsals, and participate in its performances. Groups formed within the local areas are usually made up of people from fairly homogeneous ethnic groups, who reside in the vicinity. Some local Aŋlɔ-Ewe groups attract the Ewe who reside in various towns and villages within the entire state, region and country. Similarly, membership of the Yoruba drummers associations is opened to *dundun* and other drummers in the community, town or area. In the urban areas, many traditional drumming/performing groups are formed by members of a homogeneous ethnic group who live within certain areas of the city or spread across the city. The same applies to groups that are formed in cosmopolitan cities of Canada, US and Europe whose members are drawn from fairly homogeneous ethnic groups, who migrated from specific or a number of African countries. Some of these groups attract people from multiethnic or multiracial communities.

Group Repertoires

Groups formed in the indigenous African communities usually specialize in a particular type or a suite of drumming/music and dance that form part of their cultural heritage. Nowadays, a number of local groups may feature more than one drumming/music and dance style in their repertoires. Groups formed by people from the same ethnic group who migrated to urban areas may specialize in one or more than one drumming/music and dance style. On the contrary, drumming/ performing groups that are organized by arts institutions and professional artists may feature a number of pieces belonging to various ethnic groups that form part of the nation-state. Some of these groups may feature drumming or music/dance styles of neighboring African countries and their own compositions during productions or performance processes. Depending on the style, the repertoire of the *dundun* and *lung* or *donno* may be predominantly drumming, interwoven with chants, singing and dancing.

Rules and Regulations Governing Group Membership

There are rules and regulations governing the conducts of group members. These generally include respect for one another, elders and audiences; punctuality and regularity at rehearsals and performances, and dedication to the group's activities. Violators of such rules and regulations would be advised, reprimanded or punished, depending on the gravity of the offence. For example, late comers and arrogant members of the group may be advised to avoid lateness and put up good behaviour. Habitual late comers may be fined to pay a certain amount of money or to provide some drinks to the membership. An individual who is in the habit of quarrelling with other members of the group may be dismissed.

Organizational Processes

Variations exist in the processes of forming drumming/ performing groups across contexts, but similarities may also be observed in the various processes. The formation of an African drumming/performing group usually revolves around a lead, drummer, song composer singer, instructor or artistic director. In the absence of a lead drummer, cantor/singer and instructor, the groups would request the services of such leaders from other associations or localities to help train its members. A group of people who express the desire to form a drumming/performing group would inform the leaders in the community or institution, and solicit their support and guidance. Based upon the consent of the leaders or authorities, the pioneering members of the group may raise funds and purchase some drums, or look for some instruments for use in the group formation process. They would also hold preliminary meetings at anywhere deemed appropriate to discuss the purpose, type and name of performance or performing group, rehearsal and performance venues, schedule and process.

Selection of Leaders

Community drumming/performing groups usually select male (*Uumega* in Ewe and *agorɔhene* in Akan) and female (*Uudada* in Ewe and *agorɔhemma* in Akan) leaders who would serve as the group's mentors, guardians and supporters. Groups formed by only male or female may have one or two male or female leaders respectively. As noted earlier, the Akan, Yoruba and Dagbamba societies have drummer chiefs who usually serve as mentors for the groups and maintain a link between community elders, chiefs/ kings and state drummers. Kavyu notes that, the Akamba drumming/music and dance groups consist of a dance council, made up of several elders (*nthele*) who advice the group on certain musical and social matters. They are followed by *ngui* a composer and solo singer, *nguni* or *mukuni* an instrumentalist, or *nguni ya mukunda*, a drummer and *asungi* beautiful and skilful dancers who play their respective roles (Kavyu, pp. 53-54.) Some drumming/performance groups have chairpersons, vice chairpersons, secretaries, assistant secretaries, treasurers, auditors, financial secretaries and legal advisors (Euba, 1990, p. 101).

Drumming groups formed by students in the African elementary and secondary schools usually have male and female peer leaders and one or two teachers (preferably, male and female) who would serve as over all leaders. Groups that are formed by students or professional drummers/musicians/dancers in institutions and communities may be led by master drummers or dancers who may also be referred to as artistic directors. In some cases, the initiators of the group, who have the requisite artistic skills would become the group's artistic directors or over all leaders. In other cases, a performing group may have an artistic director, board of directors, advisors, public relations officers, stage managers, secretaries, treasurers and costume mistresses, etc. who would be responsible for the day-to-day management of the group, artistic direction, advertising the group's events, liaising with the public and designing or purchasing costumes.

Rehearsal Schedule

At the initial stages, the master drummer/xylophonist or musician or choreographer may begin to review the prevailing repertoires and/or compose new drumming patterns/melodies through reflecting on cultural experiences or relevant themes, and through selection, elimination, modification of the initial compositions at anywhere deemed convenient. Upon receiving the consent of the leaders or authorities, the founding members of the group may begin to rehearse the initial compositions and/or prevailing drumming repertoires. Among the Ewe, the pioneering members of the group would begin preliminary rehearsals in a lead drummer/

composer's house. These rehearsals usually take place in the evenings after dinner (8:00-10:00 PM).

After reviewing the initial or existing compositions, the pioneering members of the group would schedule major rehearsals that would involve all members of the group. These rehearsals are usually organized around work schedules of the members. Some African traditional societies would schedule their rehearsals around lean farming or fishing seasons, market days, in the evenings (with the exception of the market days). These are usually held in or outside the composer or patron's compound or communal space reserved for public events. Groups formed by elementary and secondary school students may schedule their rehearsals around music/dance period, or during the last two periods of classes, or after school, in a classroom, studio or school compound. In addition, groups formed by students in some African Performing Arts institutions would rehearse during class periods, and in the evenings after classes. Drumming/performing groups formed by workers in the urban African areas may rehearse in the evenings and during weekends at the master drummer or patron's house, or communal space.

Similarly, drumming groups formed by African communities in the Diaspora settings may rehearse in the afternoons of Saturdays or Sundays when members are relatively free. These groups may rehearse at their own community centers or the city's community centers and churches, in a patron's house or at any convenient location. Drumming groups formed by students or schools in the Diaspora may schedule their rehearsals around school hours, after classes and may rehearse in the school's studio. Professional or semi professional groups formed in the Diaspora may rehearse in the evenings, or weekends, two to four times a week, depending on the drumming type, repertoire or production. These groups may rehearse at community centers, private studios, or school buildings or studios. The rehearsals may last for over a month to over a year, depending upon the drumming/performance type/style and circumstances.

Group Rehearsals

Drumming/music and dance groups whose performances emphasize singing usually focus on rehearsing the song component of the repertoire during the rehearsals, in which case the drummers would gather in their leader's house or at anywhere deemed convenient to rehearse or re-create the drumming aspect. Groups whose music and dance are closely intertwined would rehearse both the drumming/music and dance elements during the main rehearsals. Such groups are usually led by versatile composers-choreographers, and their rehearsals require greater collaboration between the drummers, singers and dancers.

The composition, learning and rehearsal processes are interwoven. In the process, a master drummer/xylophonist/composer or instructor may inform the group members about the rationale for composing the pieces, and the meanings of the compositions. He or she would introduce specific drumming patterns (beginning with the call or supporting patterns), involving the use of appropriate technique such as hands, hand and stick, and sticks; and encourage a drummer or group of drummers to repeat after him/her (this may be done a number of times). He or she would express the drumming patterns in speech and non meaningful syllables and emphasize the proper articulation of the patterns and texts. He or she would comment on the group and individual's performances and correct those who have difficulty playing the drumming patterns. The lead drummer would introduce new rhythmic patterns after the group/drummers have learnt the previous patterns. He or she would play in unison and speak with the supporting drummers and relate the drumming to the songs and movements, and encourage the group to memorize the various performance components. In addition, the leader would encourage those who know how to read and write to write down the drumming patterns, to serve as a source of reference, and to facilitate the rehearsal process. Nowadays, some institutions, communities and leaders encourage some group members or a videographer to video or audio tape some of their rehearsals, enabling them to reflect on the process and make the necessary adjustments or corrections.

As the rehearsals progress, other leading drummers, cantors, dancers, rehearsal overseers would be selected to assist the leaders in the process. New drumming/musical patterns would be created during rehearsals through inspirations received from fellow drummers/participants. In the process, an experienced composer/

drummer or instructor would be invited to observe the rehearsals and offer feedback or advice to the group on possible ways of improving upon their drumming/music/dance or performance.

Ritual Performances in the Rehearsal Process

Some groups may perform certain rituals during the rehearsal process. Such rituals are aimed at paying tribute to the Supreme Being, divinities and ancestors who are the originators and custodians of performances, protecting group members from any uncertainties and regulating their conducts. These rituals may include traditional, Islamic, or Christian prayer which may be performed at the beginning of rehearsals, or during the rehearsal process by some leaders on behalf of the groups. Among the Aŋlɔ-Ewe, a ritual referred to as *Blatso*, (tie and untie or bind and unbind), is performed for the ring leaders (master drummers and cantors) of the group (upon divine recommendation). It is aimed at protecting group members from uncertainties stemming from unfavourable environmental conditions and any malevolent human thoughts and feelings that are likely to affect their performance). In the process, a priest would gather certain medicinal herbs, and knot them into fourteen long ropes, and ask the leading drummers to sit by the sides of their drums and drum sticks while stretching their legs forward. The priest would acknowledge the presence of the Supreme Being, divinities and ancestors and proceed to tie each drummer together with his/her drum and drum sticks at seven parts of his/her body (head, neck, torso, legs, knees, ankles and feet). He would leave and then return to the ritual setting momentarily and begin to call the name of the drummer/client, to which the drummer would respond, *agoo!!* The priest would ask, "why is everybody interacting freely here but you have been tied in these ropes?". The client would again respond (as directed by the priest), eku, edɔ, enya, ahe kple nuvɔwo dzeasimedzenuiwoe blam de ka sia me, meaning, "death, sickness, words, curses and evils, fall-in-hand and into mouths/poverty have tied me in these ropes". The priest would again ask, ne bokɔ tso ka siawo kata na wo eye nekpoe gbe deka de nukae nawɔ ne?, "If the diviner/priest unties (or cut) all these ropes for you and you see him one day, what will you do to him? The drummer performer/client would again respond, *Mabliba nae*, (I will revere him). The priest would then cut the ropes with a knife while saying. "Today, I have cut the ropes of death, sickness, gossip, curses, evils and fall-in hand and into the mouths/poverty for you". After the initial round of the ritual, the client would untie all the knots in the ritual materials, gather them and exit to throw them at a place invisible from public eye. The process is repeated, after which the client would gather the remaining ritual materials and take them home for use as medicinal antidotes against the phenomena mentioned above. In the end, the clients/leading musicians/performers and the priest may share drink and/or food before dispersing to their various homes. The significance of this ritual lies in its provision of avenues for performers to experience the phenomena mentioned above at real and symbolic/imaginary levels. It is also aimed at liberating the performers from such phenomena (Amegago, 2000, p. 285; 2011, pp. 204-205).

Further preparations towards the unveiling of the group would include designing or purchasing of new costumes, organizing dressed rehearsals on specific dates at a public or communal or private space; a house or school compound, studio and theater. These rehearsals would be attended by groups' patrons, who would later provide feedback on the performance and advice the group to put finishing touches to it before the public performance.

Group Inauguration or Outdooring

When the group is ready to perform, it would schedule public performances and send invitations to members of neighbouring performing groups and friends by word of mouth or letters and on the radio. Groups formed by students and contemporary institutions may advertise their performances in local and national news papers, on the radio and television and on line. On the performance date, the group would clean the performance setting and surroundings (open spaces), raise tents and decorate the settings with flags and big umbrellas; arrange furniture for the performers and invited guests. Groups organized by students, institutions and other professionals whose performances take place in theaters or studios may also design the setting according to the themes of the performance (although they may not raise flags and bigger umbrellas).

On the inaugural or performance date, the traditional groups would engage in drumming procession towards the performance settings. In particular, members of groups formed among the Aŋlɔ-Ewe would wake up at dawn and walk to *Gbedzi*, an outskirt of the town, where they would begin the procession, making sporadic stopovers in neighbouring wards and exhibiting short versions of the performance (this is referred to as *hadzadzra*, song or group selling). From about two or three kilometres away from the main performance setting, the group would form two to four lines and engage in procession towards the main performance setting. On arrival at the setting, the group would feature short versions of its repertoire for about an hour, and break for an afternoon performance. The afternoon session would begin from about 2:30-3:00 PM. and end around 6:30-7: 00 PM. About three or four rounds of integrated drumming, singing and dancing would be featured in the afternoons. The entire inauguration performance may last between three to seven days, after which the group would be recognized in the community as a performing group, and would be invited to perform on certain occasions such as wedding, child naming, festivals, political rallies and funerals (Amegago, 2000, p.119-134; 2011, pp. 69-70; Ladzekpo, 1971, pp. 6-22).

A similar organizational procedure may be observed by African drumming/performing groups formed in other African and African Diaspora settings (albeit with some local variations). These groups would seek informed consents from the elders or authorities, review some of the prevailing pieces and new compositions, rehearse, solicit feedback from leaders or experts in the field, purchase musical instruments and costumes; advertise their performances by words of mouth, posters, text messages, emails and radio and TV. They may also invite critics and media houses to report or cover their performances, and may perform for a day, or during a weekend, or for a season, which may last between three to six months. However, most of the groups formed in the urban African and African Diaspora settings may not engage in elaborate processions during inaugural or public performances (although some may do so during major festivals such as Caribana) because of the challenges of living in bigger cities and due to the cold whether conditions in some Diaspora settings

The discussion above is based on the participation and observation of the processes of forming or reviving African drumming/ performing groups among the Ewe, Ghanaians and multi-ethnic groups in Canada and United States of America. It should be noted that drummers who do not belong to any established groups but come together to perform on the spur of the moment or within the contexts of economic, recreational and other social activities also create or rehearse their drumming/musical patterns (in their minds or at any convenient locations) in preparation for their performances. Their compositions, rehearsals and performances are interwoven into their contextual activities, which in turn inspire the creation of new artistic elements. For example, during a recent visit to the Tetekorfe-Keta beach, the fishermen composed a song on the spur of the moment in reference to the data the writer was collecting while they were dragging a net, singing and moving rhythmically backward while some members of the group swam (Amegago, 2011, p. 72).

Further, some contemporary African performing groups (such as *adzido*, *waka* and Highlife bands and some renowned singers) in London, Nigeria and Ghana may now commission a gifted composer/drummer to compose or teach the group his/her composition in return for a fee. In this case, the performer or group may brief the song/drumming composer on specific themes on which the drumming/song should be composed. Upon completion, the composer would teach the newly composed drumming patterns or songs to the performers through practice, by rote and other modes of learning; and his/her contract ends as soon as the performers have mastered the drumming/song. Euba notes that as far back as 1990s, such a composer in Nigeria would be paid about 10.50 Naira for a six minute song. A song/drumming which has been paid for by a performer may not be sold by the composer to any other performer (Euba p. 437).

This chapter has elucidated the processes of organizing African drumming/performing groups, the aims and objectives of forming such groups, membership, rules and regulation, leadership and the rehearsal/compositional and inaugural processes. By coming together to form drumming/performing groups, group members acquire social and leadership skills necessary for communal living, social harmony, problem solving and future careers. It is obvious that changes in socio economic and political conditions are affecting the rate of forming drumming/performing groups in African traditional societies, and the duration and activities of their creative and performance processes. In this situation, societies have to reevaluate the benefits derived from such groups in order to find ways of perpetuating the African drumming traditions. In the following chapter, I will discuss the African drum making process.

Chapter Six
Drum Making

Makers of African Drums

In chapter one, we have learned about the origins of African drums: their attribution to hunters, blacksmiths, leaders, neighboring creatures, mythological beings, divinities and the Supreme Being. With time, certain individuals and families came to be recognized as drum-carvers or drum-makers. Among the Wolof, a carver is referred to as *lawbe*. The *lawbe* are members of the wood worker's caste (Tang, pp. 38-40). Also, among the Ewe a drum-carver or drum-maker is referred to as *Ʋukpala* or *Ʋublala*. The *vukpalawo* or *vublalawo* are individuals who specialize in the carving or construction of the drums used by their society, and who have learned the trade from their parents or family members. Among the Ewe drum makers are, Kwasi Avevɔ of Aŋlɔga, Gilbert Dɔnkɔ of Akatsi and Christopher Ametefee of Anyako and based in Accra. Among the Chopi of Mozambique, the *wavati watimbila* are the people who make the *timbila* xylophones. Their craft/art is passed to the succeeding generations. Traditionally, drum-makers are usually males, who combine drum making with other activities such as farming and fishing for their livelihood. However, as the demand for drums continues to rise, some drum-makers in both local and urban settings may now derive more income from their craft. In the traditional settings, drums are usually carved or made to order, however, some drums may be made for display and with the hope that they would be sold in the future.

Most traditional drum-makers perform multiple tasks of felling and cutting the tree, carving the drum shell and pegs, designing and painting the wood, preparing twines or ropes, finding or purchasing hides and fixing them on the drum-shell. Some drum-makers engage in limited division of labour whereby a carver would carve the wood and another carver would design it with cultural images or symbols while the carver himself or another person would attach the skin to the drum-shell. For example, among the Ewe, the *vukpala* (wood carver), or *vublala* (wood constructor) would prepare the pegs, rings/rims, skin and fix them to the drum-shell. Most southern Ewe drums are now carved at Akatsi or Mɔnenu in the southern part of the Volta Region; some are carved at Aŋlɔga, Abɔ and other Aŋlɔ towns. In the present days Wolof and Yoruba societies, specialist wood carvers carve the drum-shells and sell them to the drummers or other specialists who fix the skin and some of the accessories, such as stripes and jingles to them. Akin Euba (1990) informs us that Yoruba drum shells are carved in Abeokuta, Ibadan, Oyo, Illa, Saki, Osogbo and Ife and Odan, but the best shells are carved in Abeokuta (in the past there were carvers in other Yoruba towns such as Ede). Also, according to Euba (as narrated to him by Adenji), the best carver anywhere in Yorubland is the Abeokuta craftsman, Lawani Omoolugbon. The sole carver in Osogbo was Shittu Adenji who learnt the craft from Lawani Omoolugbon (Euba, 1990, p. 132). Some Yoruba carvers belong to the Carpenters Association (Euba, p.132). Most carvers are not drummers but it is an advantage for a carver to be a drummer.

There are similarities and differences in the various modes of making African drums. Societies that live close to one another and use similar drums tend to employ similar drum making methods. Thus, one would see similarities between the drum making methods of the Akan, Ga and Ewe who live in close proximity along the southern part of Ghana and use similar drums. One would also observe similarities in the methods of making *lung* or *donno*, *lunka*, *tama*, *iyaalu* hourglass type of drums; and the *gungon* or *brekete*, *dundun* and *gyamadudu* double-headed cylin-

Figure 97. Drum-maker Christopher Ametefee in the process of measuring a log at the University of Ghana, Accra.

Photo: Modesto Amegago. December 2011.

drical type of drums among the Dagbamba, Mande or Mandinka sub groups and, Senufo, Hausa and Yoruba of West Africa.

Materials used in making African Drums

The materials used in making African drums depend to a large extent on the geographic location of the people and materials available in their environments. The drum-making materials are carefully chosen with due consideration of the desired timbre or sound quality, contextual functions, size and shape of the drum. Some drums may be designed to produce low, intermediate and high pitch sounds; others may be designed to produce heavy, light or medium weight sounds while some other drums may be designed to produce clear, bright, crispy, dull or blurring, soft, or dumpy sounds. Most of the Yoruba, Ewe, Akan and Hutu drums are usually designed on the basis of the social structure and tonal languages, to represent the voices of youths, adults, male and female leaders in societies. Some drums are also designed to imitate the sounds of certain animals and environmental features (as noted earlier) (Nketia, 1963, p. 7). The timbre of the drum also depends upon the type, quality and size of wood and the skin used in making them. For example, mahogany lowers the frequency of low pitches and keeps higher pitches at about the same pitch level. Drums with longer diameter or bigger volume produce lower pitches. Depending on the size of the drum shell, thicker drum skins may produce lower pitches and deep loud sounds. Among the Ewe, antelope skins are considered more elastic and capable of producing wide range of pleasing sounds, while goat skin is viewed as lighter and is usually used for covering a drum which is not sounding well due to the nature of its wood (a personal conversation with Donkor, an Ewe drum-maker at Akatsi, August, 2010). Any coating or stripe on the drum skin affects its timbre.

In general, African drums are made from hard log-wood, and template or stave wood, bamboo tubes, tortoise shells (in the past), earthen ware or clay, calabash or gourd vessels, nut shells, tins, metals and skins of animals such as antelope, deer, goat, cow, elephant, zebra, ox, leopard, lizard and bat as well as twines or ropes from local trees and other materials. In particular, cultural groups that live within the tropical forest zones tend to use relatively larger or bulky wood and hides of forest animals such as antelope, deer, elephant and other domestic animals such as goat, in making their drums. For example, the Akan who live in the tropical area of Ghana usually use hard wood from Tweneboa or Tweneduro (cedar) tree (in carving the heavy drums) and some light wood from Seprewa, Nyamedua and Akyeampong trees (in carving the light drums such as gyamadudu and donno) as well as hides from the elephant's ear, duiker, deer and cow in making most of their drums. Similarly, the Ewe who live in the tropical and coastal areas of West Africa utilize the wood of Logo-azagu, silk cotton tree, Odum and Mahogany (hard wood) in carving most of their drums. Some newly invented, or adopted Ewe drums such as *patenge* which is used to provide ornamental rhythm in *kinka hatsyiatsyia* (main singing section) is constructed with iron metal and antelope or deer hides. The Ewe use thin but tough hides of (avegboe) antelope, (*adzɔki*) red-flanked duiker and (Sade) deer, in covering most of their drums. They also use skins of duiker and ram for making *nyayito* drums that are designed to produce low timbre.

The shells of the Yoruba *dundun*, tension drums are made from *Apa* (ajezelia Africana) (Mahogany bean), *goji* or *ayunre* (albizzia of any species) (Mimosaceae). "The species of *ayunre* known as albizzia Gummifera appears to be the favourite of Yoruba carvers, for, according to Abraham, it is soft and easily carved into spoons, images," etc.(Euba, 1990, p. 118). The Yoruba drum makers use the skin of *obuko* (billy goat or *ewure* (goat) for making the drum-head (Euba, 1990, p. 125). Traditionally, only non castrated male deer or goat skin is used in making the *bata* drum, but nowadays, other types of skins and synthetic leather are also used in making the *bata*, especially in some African Diaspora settings.

Groups that live in semi deciduous and Savannah areas of West Africa, such as Senufo, Mande, Malinke, Mandinka, Minianka, Baga, Susu and Bambara of Senegal, Guinea and Mali, Burkina Faso and Ivory Cost; the Dagbamba of Ghana, and Hausa of northern Nigeria, usually use logs from local hard wood such as shea-nut trees, (dimba) bush mango, (Lenge) bois rouge, acajou, iroko, hare, khand and dugura trees, and gourd vessels as well as the hides of cow, alligator, lizard and goat in making their drums. In rare cases, some of these groups may use hides of antelope, zebra, deer and calf in making their drums. In particular, the Dagbamba drum makers usually use cedar wood in carving their *lung* and *brekete* drums, and goat skin for the drum-head (see also Locke, p. 26). The Wolof drum makers utilize dimbe or mahogany (hard wood) found in the forest of Casamance and Saloum for carving the *sabar* drums as well as thicker skins of goat or gazelle or sheep (which does not have any defect or much fat) capable of resisting rupture, for covering the drums (see also Tag, p 38).

Among the Hutu of Burundi, the trunk of the local D'umuvigangoma (cord Africana), (meaning the tree that makes the drum speak) is usually used for carving royal drums while dried and stretched ox and cow-hides are used for covering the wood. Nowadays, the Akamba of Kenya carve some of their drums from the local wood such as *Tsavi* (Newtonia pencijuga, Mimosaesae), *Itula Mukau* and *Muvuti* "Arythrina Abyssinica" (*Tsavi* and *Itula* are used for carving the light *mukanda* drums while *mukau* and *muuku* ("Terminalia brawnei frensen") are used for carving the heavy *kithembe* drums. The Akamba also use cylindrical metal containers of different sizes for constructing some of their new drums (Kavyu, 1986, p. 93) and skins of goat, monitor lizard (which is said to have clearer tone), or python to cover the *mukanda* drums; and cow hides (which are said to be more durable) for covering their large *kithembe* drums (Kavyu, pp. 94-95). Variants of the *ngoma* drums used in the Eastern, Central and Southern parts of Africa are covered with hides of cow and ox and some other environmental animals. Children, especially in many West African societies usually use tins, bottles, acorn pods, animals' hides, synthetic leathers or papers in making their (toy) drums.

In general, African xylophones are made from wood, banana stems, bundles of grasses, boxes, pots and pits; strings from animal hides, barks of trees and nylon; gourds, spider egg cases or cocoons and intestine of animals (Nketia, pp. 81-84; Kebede, p.52). In particular, the Chopi xylophones makers (of Mozambique) would utilize local materials such as *mukusu* wood for the wooden frame, *mwenje* wood for the wooden slabs/slats, *matamba* gourds, *upula*, bees-wax of the ground bee, *ingoti* bark strings or thongs of animal hides; *mbungo* rubber for the rubber-headed beaters, and *ivondo* (*ya kwewa*) the diaphragm of the jerboa, or the peritoneum of cattle for the reverberating membrane (Tracey, 1970 pp.129-130). Similarly, the Dagara *gyil*, xylophone makers usually use *liga* or *nirra*, rosewood (Dalbergia melanoxylon) and a particular type of mahogany (which they consider spiritually dangerous) for making the slabs; some local light wood (which grows along the rivers/lakes) for making the frame; cow, goat and antelope hides for making the strings; hollowed out gourds, spider egg cases/cocoon, and cigarette papers for making the resonators (Wiggins and Kobom, p. 9; Harper: http://contexts.org/articles/winter-/2008/harper/). Similarly, makers of the *baan,* xylophones among the Sambla of Burkina Faso utilize local hard wood, stripes of animals, synthetic cords, oblong-shaped gourds, chalky red rock and water (Strand, pp. 104-113).

Many of the African drum-makers in the Diaspora use some of the original materials imported from Africa and the local materials as well as wood, animals' hides, synthetic leathers and metals. Some of the new materials may affect the timbre of the instruments. For example, the quality or texture of the wood, animal hides and synthetic materials used in Canada, the Americas and Europe differ from those found in the African environments.

Figure 98. Drum Maker Christopher Ametefee in the process of designing the drum shell.

Photo: Modesto Amegago, December 2011.

Drum Making Process

The process of making African drums involves a carver or specialist going into the forest to inspect the wood and assess its resonance by tapping its trunk or branches, choosing the appropriate tree and cutting it. The process also involves a carver who utilizes staves of wood going to the market or shop to buy the wood (such as Odum or Mahogany).

Some carvers perform certain rituals before felling the tree or carving the drum. Such rituals are aimed at paying tribute to the source of material, seeking protection from spiritual forces and maintaining harmony with the environment. Euba states that, a Yoruba carver may sometimes perform a ritual for the *ako* (masculine wood), which is believed to be inhabited by a spirit and is recognized (a) by the existence of a hole within the tree, (b) by the tree shedding of water which is some times visible on the ground as if there had been rain, or (c) by the tree lighting up at night. This ritual may involve sacrificing a goat and food made of cow pea and cola nut at the foot of the tree while addressing it with the following words: "we wish to cut you, if there is a spirit inside you, let it depart. May it not harm us or our children; this is your offering of pacification that we bring" (Euba, 1990, pp. 118-119). A Yoruba carver may wait for two or three days after the ritual before felling the tree.

The Akan associate *Tweneboa* trees with powerful spirits, hence, an Akan carver may sacrifice an egg and pray to seek protection against harmful spirits before felling the tree. Kebede notes that the Akan drum making process also involves the carver carving the wood while drawing an eye on the frame of the drum that always stares in his direction. The watchful eye of the carver is intended to prevent misuse or any foul play on the drum as well as enable the carver to commune with the patron deity of music (Kebede, p. 64). Similarly, an Ewe drum carver may pour libation to Egu, the divinity responsible for metal, iron or technological works, and Mawu, the supreme and omnipresent God, to seek their guidance and protection in the carving process. The Hutu, drummers would surround the tree used in carving the drum and beat the drums carried on their heads while their leader would spray the tree with herbs in order to chase away the python which is said to inhabit the foliage of the tree before felling it (Kebede, p. 64).

The Dagara, Lobi and Sisala *gyil*, xylophone makers may sacrifice a black hen to the mahogany tree which they consider very dangerous (and capable of interfering in the construction process), before felling or cutting it. Similarly, the Sambla of Burkina Faso may sacrifice chicken to the very long oblong gourd believed to represent the ancestral xylophonists or spirit before beginning the construction process (Strand, pp. 104-113). Following the sacrifice, the tree may be felled with (*fia* in Ewe, and *aake, ikegilule* in Yoruba) a sharp axe with a wooden handle on the same day or after some days. A Dagara xylophone maker may cut the roots of the tree and leave the tree until it falls.

After felling the tree, the carver may roll/move the log/wood to a good location, peel and chop it into desired pieces. Some carvers (among the Yoruba, for example) may begin carving immediately after felling the tree. According to Euba (as stated to him by a Yoruba carver, Adenji), a shell is best carved while the wood is still wet for it is more difficult to carve the wood when it is dry (Euba, p.121). Other carvers (among the Ewe, for example) may allow the wood to dry for some days or weeks before they begin to carve it. Some carvers may begin to carve the drum-shell at the site of felling the tree, especially when the log/wood is bulky to convey to their workshops. Kavyu states that, the Akamba carvers (of Kenya) would roll the log to a good site, and erect it upside down to rest on a good standing stone or a planted Y shape pole, with the wood leaning towards the carver (to keep the log in stable position) and begin carving (Kavyu. p. 94). In other cases, the log or staves of wood would be conveyed to the carver's workshop, which may be a shade, under a tree, or a temporary structure of wood and palm, or coconut branches, or a block building. After the wood has dried up, the carver would shape it with a sharp machete or an axe into the desired shape, and use a chisel or suitable tool to hollow its interior. In carving a slit drum, the carver would slit the log opened at the center and hollow the inside, to form a pair of lips (each of which would be shaped to produce a definite pitch when struck with a beater). The interior part of some drums is carved appropriately. For example, the interior part of *djembe* may be carved or decorated with spiral design.

The carver usually uses his own judgement to get the exact thickness of the drum. He inspects the shell and its extremities by striking the various parts of the wood with his hands, or a heavy stick and listening to the resulting sound. The pitch of the sound determines whether or not more carving is required at a particular point (Nketia, p. 7). The drum may be carved to a thickness of two or three centimeters. The carver would shape the head and bottom of the wood in the desired (round) shapes. In the case of the Akan *atumpan* and *apentemma* drums, both ends would be narrowed, with the bottom narrower that the head in the shape of a bottle (like most semi cylindrical drums such as *bɔmmaa, mpebi, nkwawiri, adedemma* and *akukuadwo* (*aburukuwa*). The opening at the base of certain drums, such as *sogo, kidi, akukuadwo* or *aburukuwa* would be closed by inserting a flat circular board one or two inches from the bottom. A small (round) hole or opening would be bored at the center of the Akan *aburukuwa*, or at the side of the Ewe *sogo* and *kidi* drums a few inches from the bottom. Such openings allow easy passage of air and water into the drums for proper resonance and tuning. In carving some Akan, Ewe and Yoruba ritual drums (such as *adedemma* and *afluivu*) and some central and southern African drums, a number of three or four little wedges or feet would be carved a few inches from the base, to serve as a seat for the drum.

A drum-maker who utilizes staves of wood would saw the wood into pieces; plane them and continue to make the drum. An Ewe drum-maker, Gilbert Dɔnkɔ who uses staves of *Odum* and Mahogany wood in making some Ewe and conga-like drums narrates the process as follows, "You buy the wood, put button on it (or measure it), cut the width into two to make it half an inch, plane it and put it into a vice, shape it and cut it into pieces. After cutting the wood, you arrange them into about 19 or 20 pieces, depending on the size of the drum. In the past, we used rope to tighten them into the desired shape. But now, our system is changing, so we use another metal rims or loops to tighten them and make the ends narrower. When you notice that the wood wants to break you set fire inside the drum-wood with saw dust, to enable it to

Figure 99 - Figure 104. Gilbert Dɔnkɔ and son demonstrating the drum making process.

Photo: Modesto Amegago, August 2010.

Figure 105, Figure 106. Gilbert Dɔnkɔ exhibiting his newly made drums at Akatsi, Volta Region, Ghana.

Photo: Modesto Amegago, Aug. 2010. All Rights Reserved

expand and bend easily (then it does not break at the stomach/ middle). After some days, you remove the old metal strips or rims and re-tighten the wood by putting new metal rims one after the other around the drum-wood, and hitting them downward with a chisel and hammer, to push them to the appropriate positions of the drum until the process is completed" (a personal conversation with Gilbert Dɔnkɔ, an Ewe drum maker at Akatsi, in the Volta Region of Ghana on August 29 2010). He would then paint the drum afterwards with certain colours of his choice or as requested by the customers, to make it look appealing to buyers. Asked if he drums, he responded, "I tried to learn it but I am not a drummer".

For most Ewe-Fon, Akan, Ga and Wolof drums, a number of (equidistant) small round holes (ranging from six to twelve or more) are bored or drilled around the drum-wood by means of a hot round metal, or chisel about 4 or 4 ½ inches away from the top (according to Dɔnkɔ), to serve as sockets for suspending the drum pegs that would hold the skin in required positions and tension. There are 9-10 peg holes around the Ewe *atimevu,* 14-15 peg holes around the *gboba,* 9-11 around the *sogo* and *kidi* and 6-8 holes around the *kagan* drum. The peg holes or sockets on the Akan drums are usually seven in number except the ones on drums with narrow surface, which may be five in number (Nketia, p. 8).

The process of carving the Yoruba hourglass, tension drums (as described by Euba) involves the carver cutting the tree or tree trunk, chopping it into the right length for a shell with *aake ikegilule,* an axe with a wooden handle, marking the lines which will be the middle of the narrow cylindrical trunk of the hourglass structure and using *aake,* flare-blade axe to define the rough shape and size of the narrow cylindrical trunk by chopping of the wood in defined areas. The process further involves the carver marking the line of the circumference of the "bell" (outer side/edge) of the shell on one of the two flat surfaces of the portion of the trunk and chopping the wood in this surface away to make contact with the empty space created near the middle and to reveal the rough side and shape of one of the two bells of the shell. This process is repeated on the other flat surface of the portion of the wood, to create the other "bell" of the shell. After removing the thick outer skin, the carver uses the *iso* (an axe with a long narrow blade) to bore a hole in the rough hourglass structure, to create the sound chamber of the shell. He then uses the *ifanu* (a sickle-shaped implement) to plane the inside of the shell and uses *aake boro* (an axe with a short narrow blade) to refine the outer surface of the shell (Euba, pp.119-121). The carver divides the sound chamber of the drum shell in three sections: *keke, kurun* and *agogo*. The *agogo* is the narrow trunk of the drum shell; the *keke* begins at the edge where the shell makes contact with a drum head while the *kurun* begins with the line separating the narrow trunk from the bell on either side; the *keke* and *kurun* meet around the line where the bell on either side is at its widest. The length of each half of the drum shell, excluding the trunk is known as *oru*. Euba notes further that, a Yoruba carver Adenji conceived of the *keke, kurun* and *agogo* in terms of volume while Ayansola described them in terms of pitch. According to Ayansola (as stated by Euba), the *keke* is the low tone of the drum; the *kurun* the middle tone and the *agogo* is the high tone. The carvers, have definite idea of what the outer dimensions of the drum shell should be and Adenji uses a combination of tape rule and the span of the hand to gauge these dimensions (Euba, pp.121-122). Euba further informs us that in carving, a carver would put the shell to the ear to see how much it hums, however, a carver can tell if a shell is likely to sound well. The shell which has not been properly planed inside will not sound well. The curves inside the shell must be smooth and without irregular bulges or depressions (Euba. p. 124).

Some Ewe *sogo* and *kidi* drums are molded with special clay or cement. The same applies to the *udu* drums of the Igbo (of south-eastern Nigeria) which are molded by women from clay collected from sacred locations. The process of molding these drums involves finding the right type of clay or cement, mixing the clay or cement with the right quantity of water, mixing or pounding it with one's feet, hands, suitable rocks or objects, envisioning the shape of the drum and coiling up the form little by little, shaping or molding it with hands, or hand-made wooden paddle into the desired shape, smoothing its interior and exterior with hands, wooden paddle or special object and some water, creating a hole to the side of the *udu* and burning the drum for a number of hours, removing it from fire and dipping it into water for some time and letting it out (Georgini http://www.udu.html/

aboutudus.html). Also, the process of making gourd vessel drums, such as *kori*, *mpintintoa* of the Kasena-Nankani and Akan respectively involves finding or purchasing the right type of gourd from the farm or market, removing the seeds from the gourd, cleaning and polishing its exterior part. Metal drums such as *patenge* are

Figure 107. Decoration on Kpanlogo shell

Drum Maker: Christopher Ametefee
Photo: Modesto Amegago, September 2010

Figure 108. The interior part of a Kpanlogo shell

Drum Maker: Christopher Ametefee
Photo: Modesto Amegago, September 2010

usually constructed by blacksmiths or welders, who would mold the iron metal into drum shapes, attach the skins to the heads by tightening them with metal screws and bolts instead of pegs.

Drum Decoration

After carving or constructing the drum shell, its exterior and the mouth are smoothed with sandpaper or other local materials. The interior and exterior parts of the Ethiopian *kebero* are filled with iron and smoothed with sandpaper (Kebede, p. 64). Similarly, the exterior of the Ewe drums are usually smoothed with sandpaper and polished and/or painted with a combination of blue and green; blue, yellow and red, or red, yellow and green colours. The names or initials of the master drummers may be printed on some lead drums (or this may be done later by the drummers themselves who usually keep such drums under their care for convenience sake). Some Akan drums are decorated with two or three rows of saw edge designs (series of recurrent alternate triangle) starting below the socket and with the rows varying from ½ to ¾ of an inch in width; one or two rows of short vertical lines in fish bone formation (a little way below the sockets), followed by plain ring, ½ to ¾ of an inch width and vertical line decorations covering the whole or nearly the remaining length of the drum, leaving a band or plain surface at the foot (Nketia, pp. 8-10). Most of the bottle-shaped Akan drums are decorated by hatching, which involves shading the whole exterior part of the drum with straight lines. For some other Akan drums, the surface may be divided into vertical bands of plain surface, by one, two, three or four line grooves and band of horizontal line surface 3-3 3/4 in width. The line decoration on Akan drums further include alternating square patches of lines and plain surface, arranged in bands so that a plain surface is bounded on all sides by a patch of lines, and a patch of lines by patches of plain surface. This decoration may be seen on *aburukuwa* and *brento* drums. Additional decorations on the *atumpan* drum include a rectangular patch marked below a portion below the sockets and rings of vertical saw-edged design, to serve as an eye of the drum; this part of the drum is intended to face the drummer. The signal drum and the male and female *atumpan* drums which are used in the Akan political contexts are usually decorated with brass in a similar way the *tabale* drum of the Bambara is encased in copper. The *etwie* drum is covered with leopard skin while the *nkrawiri* are dressed in camel blanket (Nketia, pp. 8-14). Other decorations on the Akan drums include carved symbols such as royal swords, anchor (Gye Nyame), symbolizing except God, crossed swords (symbolizing the strength of the political institution). A set of the Akan *kete* drums, are decorated with red and black cloths to symbolize war and peace.

Additional decorations such as carved human figures, breasts of a woman, a human being or divinity carrying a ritual bowl and other objects may be seen on some Yoruba drums and those of some other African ethnic groups. Some *dundun* drums of the Yoruba are decorated or labelled with the names and symbols of the carvers. According to Thieme, the carver's symbol represents the house of Ayan (Euba 1990, p. 125). There are also images of human beings, kings, queens, priests and priestesses, animals, birds, reptiles; animal tusk trumpets, cowry, raffia and intricate abstract designs on certain ceremonial drums of the Yoruba, Baule, Senufo; Kuba, Mangbetu, Chokwe and Yaka; and Makonde of Nigeria, Ivory Coast, Democratic Republic of Congo, Angola and Tanzania respectively (Hamill (Gallery of Tribal Art), 2001). Some of these drums are carved in the form of anthropomorphic figures; human beings and human beings with animals and birds sitting on their heads.

Some Uganda drums are decorated with the skin of a zebra and a small pebble-sized knot of hide referred to as the heart of the drum is placed inside some of the drums before covering them completely with hides. Similarly, some southern African drum shells are decorated with the skin of a leopard, and *mwedi*, stones believed to have come from the stomach of a crocodile which is the clan totem, are placed in the shells of the drums of the Venda of northern Transvaal. In the past, bone remains of vanquished enemies would be attached to drums of certain military organizations to symbolize utter degradation but these practices are no longer in vogue (Blades, p. 58).

Nowadays, some Ghanaian carvers would decorate certain drums with the colors of their national flag, images of environ-

Figure 109   Figure 110

Figure 111
Kpanlogo drum shells decorated
with images of Africa, giraffe and
Sankofa bird

Drum maker: Christopher Ametefee Photo: Modesto Amegago, Sept. 2010.

mental animals, such as giraffe, elephants; houses, trees, etc. Similarly, the *sabar* drums of the Wolof are decorated with bands carved around the base and middle of the drums, carvings of palm trees, map of Africa, traditional mask-style faces and other geometric figures. Some *sabar* drums are named after important people (having a *sabar* named after someone is an honour) (Tang, p. 40). Some other drums are covered with white or red, or indigo clothes, raffia skirts and special animal skins on festive or ceremonial occasions. Also, some *lung* or *lunga* and *gun-gon*, or *dundun*, *sangban* and *kenkeni* may now be covered with special African fabrics to make them look aesthetically appealing to people. In addition, one may see some Ghanaian *Adinkra* and other African symbols on some drums of Suriname and other Diaspora Africans.

Carving Drum Pegs

The *tsotsiwo* (in Ewe) or *obua* (in Akan), drum pegs are carved from durable sticks that are capable of resisting the tension of the skin and the ropes suspending them. They are carved in round shape in relation to the size of the holes, and in such a way that they can be inserted and removed from the holes fairly easily. The carving of the drum pegs reflects cultural particularities or styles. For example, the Ewe drum pegs are carved from *Xetsi* (a relatively short thorny tree), *Setsi* (destiny or God's tree; another short tree), *guwati*, guava tree and other durable trees found in the immediate environment. The pegs range between 6-7 inches long. They are cut deeper around the (front of the neck) portion intended to hold the twines or rope-loops), and face the drummer or observer, and straight around the part facing the drum-wood. The Akan drum pegs are usually carved from *ɔfema* tree; the portion of the peg inside the drum may be half of the total length (Nketia, pp. 11-12). The head of the Akan drum peg is usually cut round in the form of a cap (about 2-5 inches in circumference), at the area which is designed to hold the twine, or rope-loops connecting the skin to the drum-wood. Drums with the largest skin surface, such as *atumpan* and *bɔmmaa* tend to have bigger size pegs. The *sabar* drum pegs are carved from apple tree, kel (tiliacee), a hard wood similar to oak, or nim (meliacee) (Tang, p. 38). The drums

Figure 112. Samples of the Akan (round-necked) drum pegs inserted in the holes of the kete drum set

Drum maker: Christopher Ametefee. Photo: Modesto Amegago, at the School of Performing Arts, University of Ghana, December 2011.

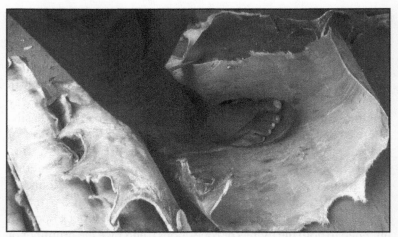

Figure 113. Drum Maker Christopher Ametefee in the process of shaving the skin that would be attached to the drum head

Photo: Modesto Amegago, September 2010.

pegs for the *mukanda, kithembe* and *ngoma* drums of the Akamba of Kenya are carved from the local *mutulua* tree and are about six centimeters in length (Kavyu, p. 96). In carving, the pegs are usually inserted into their holes regularly to ensure that they fit properly into them. The pegs may be left to dry after carving for a number of hours or days before being used. Nowadays, some drum-makers in the African Diaspora settings such as Canada would prepare or buy metal hooks which are screwed around the drum-wood instead of the wooden pegs.

Attaching the Skin to the Drum Shell

The next stage of the drum making process involves attaching the hide to the drum shell. The *awo* (in Yoruba) or *lagbale* (in Ewe), animal hide is usually purchased from the dealers in the market. The Ewe *agbadza* drum-maker would purchase relatively thin and tough antelope skin that would enable the drum to produce a wide range of clear and pleasing sounds. The maker of the Akan *bɔmmaa* or *fɔntɔmfrɔm* and *atumpan* drums would look for the skins of an elephant's ear or duiker (*ɔtwe*) that would enable the drums to produce the desired sounds. Some Akan believe the skin of (the ear of) the female elephant produces a very rich sound. In the case of the *Etwie* (snarl drum), the skin of a leopard would be found and shaped to paper thickness, to enable the drum to produce the desired roaring sound (see blades, p. 53). A Yoruba *dundun* maker would find the skin (*awo*) of *obuko* (billy goat or ewure (goat).

The hair may be removed from the skin before it is attached to the drum. For example, an Ewe *vusila*, (a term that refers to an individual who attaches the skin to the drum-head) would remove the hair from the skin by pouring ashes on it and letting it stay for a while, and using a rough stone, brick, or a knife to scrap it loose, or by shaving it with a razor or knife (this process is referred to in Ewe as *agbaletekpe*) and then soak it in a bucket or bowl of water (*agbalededetsi* in Ewe) six to twelve hours or over night, to make it pliable. A Yoruba drum-maker would first scrub the skin with tagari (fruit of adenopus brevifloris) and soak it in a mixture of water, ashes and cut-up bits of tagiri for about a day before removing it from the water and scrapping the hair from it. Similarly, the *sabar* drum skin is soaked in water before being shaved. The skins used in covering Akamba drums are cut in relation to the size of the drum before being soaked (Kavyu, p. 96). The cutting of the skin before soaking it is due to the fact that such cow and ox skins are usually thick and large and only a smaller portion of them may be needed for making specific drums. The skin for making the Ethiopian *kebero* is first treated with animal fat, to prevent it

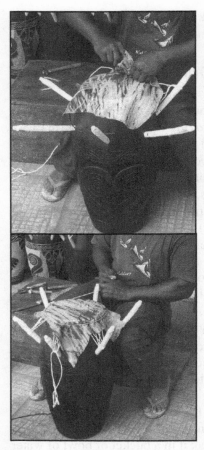

Figure 114 and 115. Christopher Ametefee in the process of assessing the string, lacing the skin to the shell via the pegs and readjusting the strings.

Photo: Modesto Amegago, Sept. 2010.

from cracking (Kebede, p. 64). The duration of the soaking period varies in relation to the type and thickness of skin and the required timbre. Thicker antelope skins may be soaked for longer period while thinner skins may be soaked for a relatively shorter period of time. In some cases, the thicker skins may be buried for several days to enable it become soft and loose its fat.

In the process, a circular ring or hoop is prepared with flexible wood, rope, or wire a little larger than the diameter of the drum-head. The softened skin is washed (and any fat remains removed from it) and is stretched proportionately over the drum-shell (extending about one and half inches downward) and the circular ring or hoop (called *agbakɔ* in Ewe) is placed on top of it. An assistant or apprenticed-drum-maker, or a young boy usually helps in holding the edges of the skin and stretching it proportionately downward over the top of the drum. In the absence of an assistant, the skin may be stretched and held proportionately by the drum maker or nailed around the drum shell. Following this, a string (*ka* in Ewe and *obofunu* in Akan) which is long enough to lace the entire skin to the pegs is found. For example, three yards of string may be long enough to complete the lacing of a skin on an Ewe drum. The drum-maker would begin to roll or fold the skin over the hoop and use a sharp knife, or a long needle to perforate it and sow, or lace the string or twine through it with pointed twine, or wire, or bicycle spoke (bent together in the form of a long needle), to form double or triple loops of strings around the pegs that sit in the peg holes. In sowing the membrane, the drum-maker always has to ensure that the skin is properly stretched across the shell to avoid making a loose and poor quality drum (Jones, 1959, p. 59).

After sewing the hide around the drum pegs, the double or triple twines or rope-loops are removed from each peg, and re-adjusted by pulling them proportionately downward, and stretching or shortening their lengths. The string or rope-loops are then twisted together and placed around the pegs that are inserted slightly inside the peg holes. The drum pegs are hit slightly inside the peg holes again, to enable them to hold or stretch the membrane proportionately across the drum. The excess skin at the edges of the drum is trimmed or cut about a quarter of an inch from the sowing area. For some Akan and Ewe drums, a little bit of the skin

would be left and pierced at the center, to form a loop, which could serve as a handle or buckle through which a sling or belt could be passed. The heavy *atumpan* and *bɔmmaa,* and *atimevu* drums do not have this handle. After completing the process, the drum is left to dry under the sun or at an airy place for about six to twelve hours or a day, after which it may be tuned properly to the desired pitch or sounds.

The process of making the royal drums of the Hutu of Burundi and some *ngoma* drums of Eastern, Central and Southern Africa involves the drum-maker stretching the dried ox or cow-hide across

Figure 116. Christopher Ametefee in the process of trimming the skin and displaying the drums.

Photo: Modesto Amegago, Sept. 2010.

Figure 117. A display of drums made by Christopher Ametefee.

Photo: Modesto Amegago, September 2011.

the drum-head to its maximum, and pegging it around the drum-shell. For some other drums (of eastern, central and southern Africa), the hide may be pegged to the drum shell with the use of a hammer, or glued, or nailed across the drum-head and left to dry under the sun for a whole day.

The wooden or clay shell of some friction drums may be covered with thin membrane and laced or lapped with twine or string. For some other friction drums, small perforations are made at their center, through which a straw or cord is passed to the underside, holding the membrane tight. Special powder may be applied to the heads of *laklevu,* the Ewe (wolf or sly fox) friction drum, to enable it to produce the desired (glissandi) gliding sounds.

In addition, the process of making the *djembe* involves placing the wet skin with the ring system on the drum and pulling the ring down gently with the rope verticals, around the whole drum. After completing the process, the drum is left to dry completely under

Figure 118 and 119. Ghanaian drum-maker in the process of attaching the goat skin to djembe drum shell and shaving the remaining hair after drying the drum.

Photos: Modesto Amegago, University of Ghana, Sept. 2010.

the sun and is then tuned by rigorously pulling and twisting the rope around it. The drum skin is shaved once again after tuning to get rid of any remaining hair.

In attaching the skin to the m'bung m'bung (*sabar* drum), (as has been noted by Patricia Tang) three slits are made in the edge of the skin through which the drum pegs are inserted into the peg holes. On the *col* (supporting drums), five slits are made through which the pegs are inserted into the holes. The wet skin is stretched tightly over the drum head with the help of an apprentice until all pegs alternating from opposite sides of the drum have been inserted. Following this, *xir,* a long piece of string is wound around the skin, starting about midway between the top of the drum and the pegs. A small slit may be made in the skin of the *col* to thread the initial ring of the string and hold it down. This string is tightly wound around the top of the drum; when it reaches the pegs and it is wound beneath the pegs for at least four times and knotted at the end. The excess skin is then trimmed off by pulling on the skin and cutting it with a knife just below the bottom ring of the string, leaving a small tab of string between each peg to tuck back up into the bottom rings holding the strings in place (Tang, p. 40).

For some other *sabar* drums (other than the *col*), a series of small slits approximately one centimeter interval are cut half way between the top of the drum head and pegs and a thick string called *fer* is threaded through the holes by twisting one side of the thread over the other, using a v shaped metal or wooden threader. The *fer* is wound around and secured in the starting knot. Next, strips of *mees* wide nylon ribbon or cow skin are threaded through the slits in the skin above the string. These are threaded between each peg and looped around the bottom of each peg. The drum is then left in the sun to dry for a number of hours after which it is tuned by tightening the mees/strings loops, and knotting it securely to enable it to produce the desired bright and sharp sound. The drum head is shaved once again to get rid of the finest hair (Tang, p. 40).

The process of attaching the skin to *zevu* or *zenli*, earthenware or clay pot drums of the Ewe and the Fɔn, and *kori or kuor* and *mpintintoa* gourd-vessel drums of the Kasena-Nankani and Akan involves stretching the skin over the drum-head to about two or three inches down, sowing strings of animal's hide or cotton-singer through the hide and tying the strings to the circular iron ring (which is about five inches in diameter and a quarter of an inch in thickness), attached to the bottom of the drum(s). The process further involves tying two or three strings around the body of the drum and to the vertical strings, to keep the vertical ones in position. The *mpintintoa,* gourd vessel drums of the Akan has a pair of braces (attached to some of the vertical strings, forming a pair of loop-handle (about 18-22 inches from the edge of the drum) for carrying the drum around each shoulder, leaving it to rest in front just below the chest-line (Nketia, 1963, p. 14).

The fixing of the *awo*, skin to the *egi* drum shell of the *gugudugu* (as reported by Euba) involves putting the soft skin on the drum shell and stiffening the edge of the head to which the *osan*, strings are sewn with extra layer of *egi* or *asele*, leather, sowing the skin with *osan*, twisted leather strings to the strings which are arranged in groups of four to six, around the body of the drum and attached to (*egi* or *asele*) the edge of the head which is looped around *kusanri* or *kusanni*, a circular iron frame at the base of the drum shell. As each line of the *osan*, string is put in place, it is pulled tight and the drum is then put in the sun to dry. The strings (*osan*) are pulled tight once more on the next day to make the drum-head taut, after which the tuning pegs are inserted between *kunsanrin*, the circular iron frame and the base of the shell. The head is tied again, and if the drum-maker is satisfied with the sound, he affixes *ida* the tuning paste on the center of the head, and attach the *oja* neck strap made of cloth, by means of *ifina* or *mojawere oja*, twisted leather strings. The *ilagba* or *bilala*, drum sticks are also attached to the *ifina* by means of *ogan* leather strings (Euba, 1990, pp. 116-117).

In addition, the construction of hourglass and double-headed cylindrical snared drums, such as the *lung* or *donno, tama, dundun,* and *brekete* involves stretching the soaked goat skin about one or two inches over both edges of the drum-wood, attaching a small loop of about a quarter of an inch in width to each edge, and sowing the skins with *lun dihi* (in Dagbani) or *osan* (in Yoruba) vertical antelope strings or cords made from *igala* or *ewure*, goat skin or bush buck (in the case of the Dagbamba and Yoruba hourglass drums); or strings of other hides and cotton through (the loops) one edge of the drum to the other (back and forth) to keep the head in position until the process is completed. Leather straps are wrapped between the lacing of the *brekete* to serve as tuning devices.

The process of fixing the skin on the Yoruba tension drums such as *iyaalu* also involves inserting *kekere*, thin bamboo sticks between the *osan* strings (in divisions of one stick per six lines of *osan*) to twist the *osan*, thereby exerting pressure on the drum heads. The strings of the drum are then bound loosely, and the drum is left in the sun for about a day to dry, after which it is removed and the strings unbound. The *osan*, strings of the drums that belong to *iyaalu* family are rubbed with hard stone, to make them look whitish. The strings are then adjusted or pulled to one end proportionately and tightened together. The *dundun* drum may be placed in the sun for another day and be removed from the sun and tuned to make it ready for playing.

Attaching Snares and Tuning Pastes and other Accessories to the Drums

Chahira, a piece of twirled or twisted goat skin is tied across the upper portion of the *brekete* drum-head to enable it to produce snared and buzzing sounds. Also, *ida*, tuning pastes are attached to the center of the *gudugudu* and *bata* drums to serve as supplementary tuning devices. This paste is obtained from *ogbagba* or *aba* tree and is made by extracting the sap of either tree by beating it together with charcoal and palm oil. The *dundun* drummer may make this paste by himself or buy it from *bata* players (Euba, p. 130). Some tuning pastes or patches that may be found on other African drums are made from a mixture of bees wax and roasted peanut powder (Blades, p. 60). A scarf is tied to the central part of the *lung* or *donno* shell for use in suspending the drum on a shoulder while carrying or playing it. Similarly, the *apa*, shoulder strap made from a piece of *kujipa* cloth is tied to the Yoruba tension drum and *igbaju*, a piece of decorated cloth lined underneath with leather and *saworo* jingle bells made from brass are fixed to the shell of *iyaalu*, the mother tension drum (Euba, 1990. pp. 126-127). Also, a cloth-strap is attached to the lacings at each head of the *gungon* or *brekete* for use in carrying it on a shoulder while playing (Locke, 1990, p. 26; 29). A pair of *sese* or *nyanjama* (in one of the Mande languages) kessings, steel or metal rattles may be attached to a *djembe* drum to provide additional percussive sounds to the music/dance.

Children Making Drums

Mention should also be made of children who make toy drums with improvised and real materials such as tins, bottles, acorn pods, synthetic leathers, papers and animal skins. For example, an Ewe child may use *ganugui*, tin, or *atukpa*, bottle, remove its bottom by rubbing it on cemented floor persistently or by chipping it with a chisel, and smoothing the rough edges. He would make a ring slightly smaller than the diameter of the tin or bottle with a creeper, and stretch a piece of synthetic leather or wet hide over the opened part of the tin or bottle and force the ring over it. Toy drums made with wet hides would be left to dry under the sun for about six hours. Jones observes that, an Ewe child may use *alagbago*, an acorn pod (which may be about a foot long and 4-6 inches in diameter) and make a large hole at its larger end (that would be the drum-head) and a smaller hole at the smaller end and remove the acorn from the pod. He would bore additional equidistant holes around the large side of the pod at short distance from the top, to hold the drum pegs in position, and fix a skin to the top of the pod in a manner the skins are fixed to some adult's drums (see Jones, pp.70-71). It should be noted that in this contemporary era, there has been a decrease in children's drum making (especially among the Ewe) due to the gradual disappearance of the contexts of children's musical activities (games and socialization) which was caused by the transformation of African societies and the introduction of new modes of socialization and education.

Constructing African Xylophones

The process of constructing African xylophone may vary slightly from one society to another. The process (as described by Wiggins and Kobom; and Strand) generally involves felling a tree and leaving it to dry for a numbers of days or weeks (some say about six to seven years), selecting the right type of wood, cutting it into slabs or bars, and seasoning them by smoking them on a regulated (low flame) fire for a period of time ranging from a week, several weeks, months to over a year (Wiggins and Kobom pp. 5-8; Strand, pp. 104-113). In constructing the Dagara *gyil* xylophone, the slabs are tuned (from oral memory) to the desired scale or in relation to an existing xylophone. The tuning involves removal of part of the wood at the underside-center of the slabs. The process further involves the construction of a wooden frame by cutting a suitable type of wood into four short thick vertical poles and six to eight horizontal wood (and some flexible sticks), and additional four to six pieces of side-wood, and fastening them together with strips of softened goat, antelope or cow hide, and thongs. The frame is usually taller and wider at the side where the lower keys would be mounted, and lower and narrower at the part where the higher keys would be mounted. According to Wiggins and Kobom, the frame for the fourteen key *gyil* (xylophone) of the Dagara and Lobi is about 96 cm long and varies from 34 cm to 24cm in width. The slabs or keys are then woven with the string of cow, goat or antelope hide or nylon and are mounted on the frame sloping downward in a curve, from the lowest bar to the highest, being about forty cm. high at the lowest bar and 18cm at the highest (Wiggins and Kobom, pp. 7-8). A number of large and small hollowed out, dried gourds resonators, ranging from 7cm.-15 cm. in diameter are tested in relation to the slabs/keys they best resonate with. Two or three holes are cut into each gourd approximately 15mm. in diameter and are covered with spider eggs cases (or cigarette paper, or intestines of certain animals) by means of saliva (slightly slack), to enable the instrument produce a unique buzzing sound. These gourds are suspended beneath the slabs by means of vertical and flexible sticks and strings/ropes made from bark of trees, in two rows, resonating alternate notes, in order to accommodate their sizes within the frame (Wiggins and Kobom. p. 8). However, the gourds beneath some *timbila*, xylophones of the Chopi are arranged in one row.

Similarly, the process of constructing the *baan* (xylophone) of the Sambla (as reported by Julie Strand) involves finding the appropriate (hard) wood, cutting it into slabs, smoking or curing the wood over fire for several weeks, re-shaping and tuning the wood. It further involves constructing a frame with four short thick vertical poles and eight horizontal strips of light weight, flexible wood, held together with strips of softened goat skin, or synthetic cord, wrapping another leather strip around the portion of the frames upon which the keys would rest, to serve as insulation material for each key, hanging hollowed out gourd around which two small holes are cut and covered with thin vibrating membrane below each corresponding key to resonate and amplify the sound (Strand, p.104-108). Some distinctive features of the Sambla xylophone are the oblong-shaped gourds which are painted with earthy reddish colour, obtained by mixing soft chalky red rock with water, and mounted under most of the slabs, and the *nemɔgɔfirin* and *bienkote* (meaning swollen testicle), extremely elongated gourd mounted under the largest/lowest key. Strand notes that, the *bienkote* is made by affixing a small, round cala-bash to the end of a long thin gourd, which is cut and tuned to the pitch of its corresponding key. This gourd is regarded as a spiritual guardian of the instrument and a portal to the ancestors of Sambla xylophonists. It also serves as an altar upon which regular sacrifices (in the form of slaughter chicken) are made to the *baan,* to herald the beginning and ending of the rainy season, express gratitude to the predecessors for creating and sustaining the xylophone tradition as well as providing musicians with means of livelihood (Strand, pp.104-113). Similar and differing methods of constructing xylophones had been observed by Hugh Tracey (1970) among the Chopi of Mozambique.

For the pit, pot and box xylophones, the slabs or keys would be mounted on a pit, box and pot that have been specially designed for this purpose. For the *akadinda,* xylophone of Uganda, a number of *amakundi* navel hernia, (pieces of pointed sticks) are fixed to the banana stems between each slabs/keys and projecting upward, to hold the slabs/keys in place or prevent them from moving off the banana stem in which they are mounted (Kubik, 1994, p. 63). In addition, the slabs may be placed on a human's legs and played, as in the case of some xylophones which are used for occasional purposes (Kebede, p. 52).

Rituals in Completion of the drum making Process

Some drum makers may perform additional rituals during the completion of the carving process. Euba notes that the Yoruba carvers may perform a ritual in connection with the building of the drum from an entirely new shell. One of such rituals as described by Ladokun involves the drummer buying about six to twelve yards of cloth and a pigeon, and providing some food (ekunu) and drinks; placing the drum shell on the cloth when it is given its first heads. The drummer's wife would cover the drum with one of her cloths until such a time that the drum would be played for the first time, where a family member would say a prayer over it before it is played. The prayer goes:

> *The drum will not break in your hands. Your performance on it will be rewarded with gifts of clothings. Your performance on it will be rewarded with gifts of*

*horses. Your performance on it will make you materi-
ally successful. Your performance on it will be rewarded
with marrying of wives. You will not run into debt as a
result of your use of this drum* (Euba, 1990, p. 127-128).

An Islamic prayer may also be said since most *Iyaalu* drummers
are Muslims.

Some drum-makers in African diaspora settings would use
original materials imported from various parts of Africa while
others may use local wood, some of which are similar to the wood
found on the African continent. The drum-makers would also use
singer or nylon strings, screws, hooks, wedges and technological
devices in their immediate environment in making drums. For
example, some drum makers in the Brazil utilize *jacaranda* and
macaiba wood and metals; nylon or singer strings, wood screws,
calf and goat skins in making *atabaque* and *macaida* drums (http://
www.celebratebrazil.com/brazilian.musical~musical~instruments.
html;Wikimedia Commons). Also, the making of African derived
drums in the Afro-Panamanian communities involves the felling
and cutting of the local cedar wood, *el indio, el corotun, balsa,*
coconut palm or *elvolador* (the cedar and corotu are always used
for the *caja*), carving or shaping the wood with chisel and machete,
drying it again (to avoid cracks in the drum) smoothing the edges,
finding the skin of deer, goat, wild pig or cat, removing its hair with
ash, rough stone and knife; putting the skin on rattan vine (*bejuco*)
and mounting it on the drum, making holes in the skin closed to the
ring of the *bejuco* vine and lacing a string or cord through them,
and connecting the cord to the waist band that circles the drum's
body. The waist ban may be located at the bottom of the curvilinear
drums or near the retaining rings of vines of the rectilinear and
cuneiform drums. Wedges are placed on the drum and the waist
band and heads are pulled downward by using a hammer and other
heavy objects to hit the ring or edges. The drum is tightened and
placed in the sun for about six hours to dry, and is tuned to the
desired pitch and tones (Jackson, pp. 177-178). The method of
constructing double-headed cylindrical *caja* (*tambora*) is similar
to that of the *brekete* and *gyamadudu* discussed above. It is worth
noting that the used of new materials and devices may affect the
sound quality of the drums. However, these new materials and

devices enable the Diaspora African to satisfy their musical needs or desires within the new environments.

Mention should also be made of African drum instructors and drum makers such as David Amu, Muthadi, and Dido Morris who would teach the art of drum making to some youths and adults in school and communities in Accra, Ghana, Toronto and Vancouver, Canada. These drum-makers use real and improvised materials, wooden shells, tins, real and synthetic leathers, nylon or cotton strings, wooden and metal pegs and rings in making drums. Their works have exposed many of the youths to the African drum making process. As noted earlier, Meneil and Frank Georgini and other Western drum makers and manufacturing companies are now constructing the *djembe*, *udu* and other African and African derived drums on a larger scale through the use of traditional and newly invented techniques. Such manufacturers use both local and imported wood, clays, fibre glasses, raw hides, synthetic leathers, ropes, screws and bolts and appropriate technologies to construct newer versions of African drums. For example, Frank Georgini's slip-casting of the *udu* drums involves pouring a liquid clay slip into a plaster mold, which enables him to produce consistent quality drums in large quantities within a shorter period of time (Meneil: 2011x 8 drums and Percussion Inc.). These drum makers have added new dimensions to the traditional drum making processes and are serving the global market.

Naming the Drum

A new or existing drum is named in a language spoken by the drum-maker or buyer, to serve as a way of identifying it. A given drum may have more than one name. For example, an African drum may be named after the material used in constructing it. Among the Ewe, the name *atigo*, literally meaning a tree-log, generally refers to drum constructed of log wood (Amegago, p. 77). Among the Akamba of Kenya, the name *kyaa* was derived from a type of wood used in making the *kyaa*, drum. Also, the Akamba word, *muvungu*, (another name for *kyaa*) seems to have derived from the word, *ivungulu*, a hollow object or wood (Kavyu, p. 89). A drum may also be named after the sound it produces. For example, the Ewe drums *kidi, totodzi* and *kagan* derived some of their names from their rhythmic patterns. The creature or feature that the drum is designed to imitate or resemble may lend its name to the drum. For example, the *aburukuwa* of the Akan was named after the singing bird that the drum was designed to imitate, so also the Congolese *ngoma* derived its name from the leopard that it was designed to imitate. A drum may also derive its name from its positioning or handling before being played. Thus, the name *atimevu*, literally meaning, tree-inside-drum, refers to the manner of leaning the drum against a wooden stand before being played. Similarly, the name *asivui,* literally meaning, hand drum, seems to

Figure 120. An Ewe Sogo drum
Photo: Modesto Amegago, Aug. 2010.

have derived its name from the practice of carrying it in the hand while being played (especially in processions) (Amegago, p. 79).

The playing technique may lend its name to the drum. For example, the Ewe name *agblɔvu*, meaning curved-stick-drum, derived its name from the hooked sticks used in playing it. The music and dance in which the drum features may lend a generic name to the drum; for example, *agbekɔvu*, *agbekɔ* drum, *adzidavu*, *adzida* drum.

A drum may also be named after the divinity with which it is associated, for example, *mframa twene*, the divinity *mframa*'s drum; *ntoa' twene*, the divinity *ntoa*'s drum (Nketia, p. 92). It may also be named after a family member or an important person in the community (as is the custom of the Wolof). Nowadays, a drum may also be named after an individual buyer or owner or a performing arts company who owns it, such as the Center for National Culture Dance Company, Ho). The function of the drum or music/dance may lend a name to the drum; for example, the generic name, talking drum given to the West African tension drums and the Akan male and female *atumpan* drums were derived from their predominant use in communication on textual basis. Drum sticks may be named according to their function. For example, among the Ewe, the drum stick is called *vufoti*, meaning drum-beating-stick. Similarly, the Ewe name *vudetsi* or *vuglatsi*, meaning drum-holding/supporting-stick, is given to the drum-stand because of its function in holding or supporting the drums in place.

The keys of some African xylophone may be named according to their relative position on the instrument, socio-cultural and musical functions. Hugh Tracey notes that all the keys of the *timbila* xylophone are named in relation to the tonic called *hombe*, and their relative position on the instrument. Thus, the outside note of the instrument may be called *magumo kanyamboswe*, "end right", i.e. the top note in the treble, or *magumo manyadye*, "end left", the bottom note in the bass (Tracey, 1970, pp.119-121). Also, according to Strand (2009), each note of the *baan* xylophone has a name in relation to the central pitch of the scale, which is referred to as *baana*, the xylophone-mother, and which may be equivalent to tonic or tonal center in Western music. The lowest key of the *baan* is called *tɔrɔntɔrɔn*; the second key is called *baan cɔtenɔ*, the third, *diobaanden,* fourth called *tɔrɔntɔrɔn-cɔtenɔ* and followed by the names of the ensuing keys (Strand, pp.165-166). Similar modes of identifying the instruments and their components and accessories may be observed in other African societies. Some Dagara, Lobi and Sisala xylophonists operating in the Ghanaian School of performing arts would now label their xylophone keys with numbers 1, 2, 3, 4 ,5, or C D E G A, beginning from the lowest to the highest key in an octave according to pentatonic scale. They also identify them by specific sounds.

Tuning the Drum

A newly made or an existing drum is usually tuned to the desired pitch or sound. The tuning method varies in relation to the drum type, socio-cultural functions, tastes and preferences. It should be noted that the *udu* pot drums, slit drums as well as other supporting instruments such as bells and clappers are not usually tuned although they may be remolded, or readjusted (in the case of some rattles).

Tuning Devices

Drums with notched pegs may be tuned with round and hard batons (some of which have special handles), smooth stones, a head of a hammer, a handle of an axe, hands and water. Double-headed cylindrical drums may be tuned with hands while the *djembe* may be tuned with a piece of hard wood, a lever or stick with the help of the hands and feet. Drums to which metals hooks are attached as tuning devices may be tuned with pliers or screw drivers.

The Tuning Process

The drums are tuned according to the desired timbres and their contextual functions. An orchestra or a set of drums are relatively tuned to produce the desired contrasting tones and pitches, and to create interest and harmony. Drummers usually tune the drums with their ears, although some scholars or performers may now use pitch measuring devices and specific intervals in tuning some of the drums. Some drums are tuned on the basis of the social structure (to represent the voices of youths, male and female adults and leaders, as noted earlier). The Akan *fɔntɔmfrɔm* and *Adowa* drums are relatively tuned: the bigger *frɔm* or *fɔntɔmfrɔm* drums are tuned low with one sounding higher than the other, followed by the male and female *atumpan* drums which are tuned relatively higher with the female sounding higher than the male), and followed by the smaller supporting instruments which are tuned relatively higher (to represent the voices of male and female youths, adults, warriors and leaders within the socio-political structure). Similarly, the Ewe *agbadza* or *adzida* ensembles may be tuned to represent the voices of youths, male and female adults in the Ewe society: one *atimevu* would be tuned lower than the other *atimevu*, followed by *sogo*, which would be tuned higher than the two *atimevuwo,* and *kidi* which would be tuned relatively higher than *sogo*, and followed by the *kagan*, which would be tuned to the highest pitch (Jones, 1959, pp. 58-59). However, the *atimevu* in *agbekɔ* ensemble may be tuned relatively higher to enable it to produce high taunting sounds to fulfil its contextual functions. The *gboba*, an ornamental and bass drum in *kinka* music/ dance ensemble would be tuned to the lowest pitch. In tuning the Mande or Mandingo drum ensemble, the *dundun* would be tuned relatively lower than *sagban* while *kenkeni* would be tuned to the highest pitch.

The *atimevu,* (an open-ended lead drum) may also be tuned by standing it upside down and pouring a few cups of water in it and leaving it for about two minutes, to enable the water to soak the underside of it; the drum would be put on its side and rolled around, to enable the water to wet its pegs and wood joints. This may be followed by standing the drum upright and using a handful of water to rub or wet the membrane and leaving it for another three or four minutes. Also, a cup of water may be poured through the hole at the bottom side of the *sogo* and *kidi* and the drums would be turned upside down for about a minute or two and put on their sides and rolled momentarily as done to the *atimevu*. This mode of tuning softens the skin and enables it to regain its elasticity. It also enables the wood to expand and fill any spaces in between the staves of wood and regain its sounds. It should be noted that the wetting of the skin is only done before the performance; if further tuning is required, the wetting is omitted.

Most cylindrical, rectangular, open-ended or closed-ended drums used by the Ewe, Ga and Akan and some other African peoples are tuned by hitting the drum pegs with round and hard baton, stone, or hammer, and hitting the rim or edges of the membrane carefully so that the skin is stretched proportionately and firmly downward. This is followed by tapping the heads of the pegs while testing the pitch of the drum head and its ability to produce the desired tones/sounds. The skin may be pressed with fist hand, or the palm, or the lower part of the hand in order to lower its pitch.

The *djembe* is usually tuned by pulling the vertical ropes evenly and tightly so that a system of metal rings brings the skin down over the drum shell, and tightening the ropes all the way round, taking multiple passes through the ropes (with a lever) and twisting more ropes horizontally through the vertical ropes. This mode of tuning also involves passing the horizontal rope under two verticals and back over one, and under one, making a z or s shape, and pulling the rope hard and downward.

Variants of hourglass drums (such as the *lung* or *donno, tama* and *dundun* sets are relatively tuned, with the largest drums producing the lower sounds, followed by the medium drums which would produce medium sounds and the smallest ones, which produce the higher and highest sounds. These drums may be tuned by adjusting or pulling the loose string toward one end and removing the excess string (which has been caused by over stretching) and re-tightening the string, to enable them to produce higher sounds. In particular, the fixed pitch tension drums of the Yoruba are tuned by having their tensioning strings tightly bound in the middle; they are left unbound when they are not being played (to maintain the looseness of the strings), and, therefore, need to be tuned before every performance. If the heads of the tension drums are found to be too tight, the tensioning strings are bound and the drum is placed in the sun for some hours (Euba 1990, p.137). *Iyaalu*, the principal drum, may be tied and left in the sun for about two hours, after which its tensioning strings would be rubbed with stone, and the drum would be placed under the sun again (with heads exposed in turns to the sun). When the heads of a tension drum are too tight, the tension strings (*osan*) may be loosened one by one (there is always an extra length of strings tucked away underneath the tensioning strings). The strings may be re-pulled one by one, to make them tighter; or the drum may be left untied in the sun for some time when the heads are too loosed. The secondary tension drums are usually tuned to fixed pitch; their required pitch may be reached after the tensioning strings have been properly bound so that they touch one another and the drum heads are tout (expressed as *kan*, sour or sharp taste) (Euba, pp. 137-138). The *brekete* double-headed cylindrical drum may be tuned by tying each pair of laces with the tuning strings. The laces are usually untied in order to detune the drum when it is not in use.

Further, the *mukanda*, *kithembe* and *ngoma* drums of the Akamba of Kenya may be tuned by heating them by fire or sun before the performance. The drums may be placed on the ground or on an object about a meter away, with the playing surface facing the fire, to enable it to heat up gradually. When the drum is ready and the performance is yet to begin, it is placed a few meters away from the fire to reduce the intensity of the heat reaching the head. A drummer may use his palm to rub the surface of an overheated drum in a circular manner to enable him to absorb or distribute the heat across the drum surface. Alternatively, the drum may be placed horizontally under the sun on a sunny day. After tuning/heating the pitch of the drum may be assessed by playing some rhythmic phrases on it (Kavyu, p. 96-100). Under extreme weather conditions in places such as North America and Europe (where drum heads are usually dampened), drums such as *dundun*, *djembe* and *brekete* may be heated for about five to ten minutes, to enable them to regain their desired sounds. It is worth noting that the heating is only a temporary solution and the drummer may continue to heat the drum over and over again during a performance to prevent it from getting detuned. While some detuned drums may create contrast and interest in a performance, a drum which is too detuned may create discord in a performance.

Players of the African drums in America, Europe, Australia and other Diaspora settings are often influenced by the sounds they hear in their immediate environments and the tastes and preferences of the audiences. Hence, they may tune particular drums relatively higher than the ways they would normally be tuned in Africa.

Xylophones are tuned progressively from low to high notes. Some Cameroonian xylophones are tuned in octave pairs; that is a key and the next higher octave are put together with a little gap left between this pair and the next. In north-western Ghana, small and large xylophones are sometimes kept separate because their keys begin on different pitches and are, therefore, not played together. In some other African societies, this differentiation is conceived of in relation to musical roles in ensembles. Thus, among the Chopi, there are treble xylophones with sixteen keys, alto xylophones with nineteen keys, (with three additional lower keys), tenor xylophones with twelve keys (with two keys lower than the alto xylophone), bass xylophone with ten keys (with two keys lower than those of the tenor xylophone), and a contrabass or double bass xylophone with four keys (beginning two steps below the bass). A similar distribution exists in other xylophone cultures having three or four types of instruments, except that the compass of those instruments that play accompanying notes or ostinati may be reduced to the basic notes that they are generally required to play. This scheme is utilized where xylophones of the narrow compass of two or three keys are played in ensembles: the instruments are tuned in such a way that when they are played together, they can share the notes of the melody, as well as those of the accompanying figures (Nketia, p. 82). Xylophones may be tuned in pentatonic, hexatonic and heptatonic scales. For example, xylophones used by the Dagara, Birifor, Lobi and Sisala or northern Ghana and southern Burkina Faso are tuned in pentatonic scale, while those used by some Mende groups are tuned in heptatonic scale (Kebede, p. 54). Both equidistant and non-equidistant tuning systems are utilized although some kind of equidistant tuning appears to be widespread. An equidistant tuning in the African context is a system of tuning which is based not on a concept of small and large intervals but on recognition of steps that resemble one another. For example, the *timbila* xylophones of the Chopi are tuned to equiheptatonic scale, which is based on the concept and tonic, *hombe*, which represents a central unifying key in the Chopi musical system (Tracey, 1970, p. 119). When a key does not conform to this system but is retained on the instrument as something tolerable, it is referred to as a "bad" key (Nketia, p. 83). Among the Lobi, there is another sense of a bad key; it occurs in one particular xylophone tuned to a tetratonic scale, and is placed after each set of four keys, counting from the bottom. If the bad keys are played, they change the scale from a tetratonic scale to pentatonic one, but because they are not supposed to be played, they are described as keys to be avoided. As noted by Nketia, bad keys are built into the designed to give the standard number of keys and facilitate the motor movement that controls the formation of melodic phrases (Nketia, p. 83). Nketia further notes that the use of equidistant tuning facilitates transposition (shifting the normal starting point of the melody up or down to agree with the voices of the singers or to counteract the effects of changes in temperature on the instrument). It also facilitates the use of polyphony; the practice of playing a number of melodic fragments against each other. There are noticeable differences in the quality of sounds of the various types of xylophones such as log xylophones, pit xylophones, box xylophones, frame xylophones, etc. (Nketia, p. 84).

Limits of Tuning

The tuning of a drum may reach its limit when the drum pegs are hit completely inside the drum-wood, leaving only the notched heads or head-caps outside the drums, and when the drum's cords or strings have over-stretched or deteriorated. In these situations, the drum pegs may be removed from the holes and the cords or string-loops be re-twisted and re-placed around the pegs, and hit proportionally inward the drum, to enable the drum to regain its sounds. Similarly, the slabs of a xylophone may be cut beyond the desired range, or they may deteriorate over time, which would make it impossible for the instrument to produce the desired sound. In this case, the slabs would have to be replaced with different ones.

Drum Maintenance and Repair

Drums need proper maintenance to enable them to produce the desired sounds, to prevent them from damaging and to ensure their durability. Drum maintenance also relates to its storage, tuning and handling. Among the Ewe, the art of lubricating the drum-head and softening the wood with water are ways of tuning and maintaining the drum. Tang notes that the Wolof drum makers (*gewel*) would oil the inside of *sabar* drums with palm oil every few months in order to prevent cracking (Tang, p. 40). Drums may deteriorate or damage through improper handling, unfavorable environmental conditions, ageing, or long period of usage. Peg holes may expand or widen over time due to persistent tuning, which may cause the wood to weaken), thereby making it difficult for the holes to hold the pegs properly; the wood may crack; drum skins and strings, or twines may over stretch, wear out or lose their elasticity, and peel off, or become thinner over time, due to the above mentioned factors. Worn out skin and strings may affect the timbre of the drum and may require the player of a tension drum to pull more lines on the strings than s/he would normally do in order to apply pressure on the drum head. It can also irritate the drummer's hand (Euba, 1990, pp. 128-129).

Wax or wood dust mixed with glue may be used to fill the damaged part of the peg hole or the cracked portion of the drum shell. Also, a piece of paper may be inserted in the peg hole to fill the expanded portion and serve as a temporary solution. When the problem recurs, the drum wood may eventually have to undergo a major repair. In addition, the cracked portion of the wood may be parched or replaced with a new piece; or staves of wood may be readjusted and re-tightened with metal rim-loops. The drum-wood which is damaged beyond repair may be abandoned. Worn-out skins or strings would be replaced with new ones in the ways the original ones were fixed to the drum-heads. Among the Ewe, Akan and the Yoruba, the skin that is not too worn out may be converted into drums strings, or twines, or used for making children's drums. Also, the bars and strings of xylophones must be treated with shea butter from time to time to prevent them from drying out or cracking (Wiggins and Kobom, p. 7). The longevity of the skin or strings differs from one environment to another and depends on the frequency of drum's usage and maintenance. Lead drums' skins may wear out more quickly than the skins of secondary instruments. On average, a new skin or string may last two to four years.

During my recent interaction with some drummers in Ghana (July-August 2010), some complained about the ways some people mishandle the drums by putting their feet and food on them and by abandoning them after performance. They stressed the importance of taking good care of drums and stated that drums are like human beings or spirits; if you do not handle them well, the spirit may desert them, which may result in their malfunctioning. Indeed, the practice of some professional drummers carrying drums in special cases and bags to performances is a way of keeping the drums safe and tidy.

Drum Storage/Preservation

Some drumming or performing groups would store their drums in the houses of their patrons. For example, some lead Ewe drums are kept in the houses of the master drummers (who usually use them to signal group members on days of performances). Some Ewe performing groups have special drum houses (*vuxɔ*) or storage rooms in which they store their drums. Drums belonging to some religious associations are kept in religious temples or sanctuaries, or near a place of worship, such as in a house of a head priest or priestess and other leaders of the associations. Similarly, drums belonging to the state or form part of the state's paraphernalia are kept in a stool house, or chief or king's palace. Special drums are kept at sacred locations. Some royal drums of East Africa were in the past stored in sanctuaries and guided by persons of the highest integrity. Such sanctuaries were considered holy and animals entering them would become taboo, so also fugitives and fleeing slaves entering them would be given temporary immunity. If a condemned person succeeded in escaping to such drums, she or he would be safe and become their perpetual servant (Blades, p. 63). Many contemporary music/dance companies and institutions have special storage rooms and studios where they keep their drums. Individuals may keep their drums in their own rooms, storage or at any convenient locations.

It is important to store the drums at places or rooms with moderate temperature. Over exposure to heat may cause the wood and skin to dry and crack, or break suddenly (especially when played in this condition with hands or sticks). To avoid sudden damage of drums kept (in this condition), it would be necessary to lubricate the skins with water before playing them. In addition, storing the drums under extreme cold weather conditions may dampen the skins and cause the drum-shell to develop moulds over time. Under such conditions, drums constructed with staves of wood could develop cracks in between the staves, and the metal rim loops could loose from the wood.

Drum Ownership

Most of the drums used in African traditional societies are collectively owned. But, as noted earlier, certain kings or chiefs are allowed to own certain drums relative to their ranks. Among the Tutsi of Rwanda, drums belong to the king and are played only for him (and the queen) (Euba, 1988, p. 36). Also, among the Akan, only the Asantehene could own the bigger *fɔntɔmfrɔm* and *kete* drums. Some drums are owned by religious associations and performing groups. Due to the emergence of professional drummers/artists and commercialization of certain drums in this contemporary era, many individual drummers, artists, drum enthusiasts; performing groups and arts institutions within and outside Africa may now purchase African drums for use in their instructions, performances and for aesthetic purposes. Regardless of the ownership of African drums, it would be important to regard the drums as cultural products and symbols, and instruments that deserve proper treatment, maintenance and respect.

The discussion above has elucidated African drum-makers, drum making materials and processes as well as the naming, tuning, maintenance, storage and ownership of African drums. It has also shed light on the materials and technologies that are used in the drum making processes, and their impacts on the quality of the drums. It is obvious that changes in environmental conditions would lead to constant emergence of new materials and technologies in the drum making processes. However, a balance should be created between the older and newer materials and technologies. It is imperative to protect the environment to ensure regular supply of the drum making materials, or avoid rapid depletion of the resources.

Chapter Seven

Techniques of African Drumming

Drumming/Playing Techniques

The techniques of African drumming are determined by the purpose of the drum, its desired timbre or sound quality; the type and size of the instrument and aesthetics values of the performers and societies. The techniques require the handling or positioning of the drums in a certain way. A variety of techniques such as hands, hand and fingers, hand and stick, hand and fan, hand and rubber strap, damp fingers and damp rag, and two sticks techniques are employed in African drumming. The two hand technique is used by the Egyptian, Moroccans and Sudanese, etc in playing the *doumbek*; by the Mande, Malinke, Susu, Minianka, Bamana, Baga and Jola in playing the *djembe* and *bugarabu* drums; by the Ewe in playing the lead *sogo, gboba, bɔbɔɔbɔ* and *akpese* drums, and by the Ga in playing a set of *kpanlogo* drums. The *bougarabou* drummers would wear jingling bracelets that add another percussion sound to the music. The two hands technique is also used by the Akan in playing the *agyegyewa, apentemma* and *mpintin* drums in *sikyi, adowa, kete* and *mpintin* ensembles. This technique requires relaxation of the wrists and hands, and positioning them in appropriate manner. The drum may be hit with a slightly scooped hand in order to produce clear bouncing sounds, or it may be hit or slapped near the edge or center of the drum-head with slanted (first three or four) fingers, to produce high pitch sound. The hand technique also involves the pressing of the fingers or finger tips on the drum-head, sliding the middle finger pressed against a thumb on the drum-head (as done by some Ga *kpanlogo* and Ewe *bɔbɔɔbɔ* drummers), to produce clear and sustained sound. The technique further involves the pressing of fist hand or an elbow on the drum (as done by some Ga and Ewe drummers) to produce some muting effects.

Figure 121. A group of *kpanlogo* drummers playing with hand techniques during Ngmayem festival at Odumase-Krobo. Ghana.

Photo: Modesto Amegago, Oct.28, 2011.

A combination of hands and feet are used in playing the Ga *gome* (open-ended square or rectangular) drum. The drummer would sit on the drum wood and press the feet against the center or edge of the membrane, and release them while beating the area near the center and the edge with relaxed or scooped hands, at various tempi and dynamic ranges, to produce varied tones and pitches. The techniques used by the Ewe youths in playing the lead *bɔbɔɔbɔ* drum include the holding of the drum between the knees and lifting it up and down while playing the various zones of the drum-head with relaxed or scooped hands to produce low, mid

Figure 122. A group of *bɔbɔɔbɔ* drummers exhibiting the lifting and hand drumming technique at the second annual *Bɔbɔɔbɔ* Festival at Ho, Ghana.

Photo: Modesto Amegago, Nov. 4, 2011.

and high tones. A similar technique may be observed among some Afro-Panamanian *Tambor* drummers, who would sit and press the drum between the lower legs and play it with hands while raising and lowering it with the knees, for varied tonal effects (Smith, in Jackson, p. 187).

A hand and leather strap are used in beating the mouths or openings of the *livi* and *ajogan* drums of the Fɔn; the *bata* drums of the Yoruba and the *udu* drums of the Igbo, to produce some puffing, deep, rounded and reverberating sounds. Two leather beaters are used in playing the *gudugudu* (bowl-shaped) drum of the Yoruba. The drum may be struck at or near the center to produce the desired sounds.

A combination of hand and stick are used in playing some drums, to produce specific tonal effects. Drum sticks (*lung-doli* in Dagbani; *vufotsi* in Ewe, *nkonta* in Akan) vary in size, thickness, weight and length in relation to the size of the drum and the thickness of the membrane. The right type and size of stick is needed for producing the desired timbre. Drum sticks are usually carved from hard and durable trees within the drummers' environment (although some may be carved from sticks brought from different locations). *ʋufotsi*, drum sticks used by the Aŋlɔ-Ewe are usually carved from *klitsi* or *xetsi*, a local thorny tree, *setsi*, destiny or God's tree, (a short tree found along the coastal Ewe areas), *guwatsi*, guava tree and other durable trees in the environment. The *sabar* drum sticks are made from the local *sideem* (jujube) or *daqar* (tamarind) trees. Drum sticks are usually carved in round shape; some are straight while others are curved, or have knobs at one or both ends. The sticks may range between ten to twenty four inches long, and a quarter of an inch to one inch in thickness (diameter).

Straight sticks are used in playing some Mande/Malinke, Susu, Ewe and Hutu drums for producing clear, bouncing, tonal and rapid sounds. Two straight sticks are used in playing the various supporting instruments such as *sogo, kidi* and *kagan,* for producing clear tones, pitches and rapid rhythms (although the hands may also be used in playing the supporting *sogo* in Aŋlɔga *adzɔkli* performance of the elderly people) and slit drums of the Igbo, Dan and Kuba. For example, two straight sticks between 12 to 20 inches long and ¼ inch in diameter are used by Ewe drummers in playing the *kagan* (smallest supporting drum). The sticks

Figure 123. A group of drummers exhibiting stick drumming techniques

Photo: Modesto Amegago at Dalive-Agave V/R. Ghana, July 2011.

used in playing the *kidi, sogo* and *atimevu* drums are between 10-12 inches long and 3/8 inch to 3/4 inch in thickness. Also, the sticks used in playing the lead *gboba* (large barrel-shaped) drum in *gahu* and *olenke* are relatively thicker and weightier than those used in playing the lead *atimevu* drum (Jones, pp. 59-60).

Sticks with rubber tipped short beaters similar to xylophone or *alo* (long gong bell) mallets are used in playing the Ekwe slit drum. The mallets made with wood of about 30 cm. long and 2-3 cm. in diameter with thin strips of latex wound around one end and, held together with glue to a diameter of four to 5 cm. are used in playing the xylophones. Nowadays, pieces of car tyre are cut round in five cm. diameter and affixed or glued to the sticks; this is more durable since the glue on the traditional beaters tends to soften and become sticky when the temperature rises (Wiggins and Kobom, pp. 7-8). Players of the Dagara, Lobi and Sisala and some other African xylophones would hold the stick or shaft of mallets between the fore and middle fingers; some would hold it between the thumb and fore finger. The South African *mbila* players may hold two (*dibinda*) beaters on the left hand to enable them to play the wide slabs that produce the deeper notes at the required time. The left hand beaters are used alternatively, never together (Blades, p. 80). A player of the xylophone is supposed to maintain flexible wrists and utilize mainly the wrists in the process of playing.

Generally, a player's right hand is employed with the melody (in the case of right-handed players), whilst the left hand assists in octave or playing a counter melody (Blades, p. 80).

One or two straight sticks are used in playing the *dundun, sangban* and *kenkeni* of the Mande/Susu, Malinke, Bamana and Baga, and the *karyenda* and *ngoma* drums of the Hutu. Generally, the sticks used in playing the *djundjun* ensemble and the *karyenda* or *ngoma* drums are relatively heavier than those used in playing the Ewe *agbadza* and the Akan *adowa* and *fɔntɔmfrɔm* drums.

Curved sticks are employed in playing the Dagbamba, Hausa, and some Yoruba (*lung* and *iyaalu*, hourglass drums), the Akan *frɔm* or *bɔmma* and *atumpan* (in both *fɔntɔmfrɔm* and *adowa*, and in speech mode); and in playing *kwadum* and *akukuadwo* for producing deep, and clear tonal sounds. Curved sticks used

Figure 124. William Diku, a master xylophonist exhibiting some playing techniques in a performance with the Ghana Dance Ensemble at the University of Ghana, Accra.

Photo: retaken by Modesto Amegago, December 2011, by courtesy of artistic Director Benjamin Aryetey.

for playing the *lung* or *donno* have a round and flat edge or tip. The curved parts of the *lung* and *dundun* sticks are round at the neck while the curved parts of the *adowa* drum sticks are shaped to about 45 degrees. The curved part of the Akan *adowa* and *fɔntɔmfrɔm* sticks (*kɔtɔkɔrɔ*) may be between 2-4 inches long while the bent part of the *lung iyaalu* and *tama* may be up to 1-2 inches long. *Agblɔ*, curved sticks are also used in playing *agblɔvu* and *laklevu,* royal and friction drums of the Ewe, and the *brekete* and *donno* (northern derivatives). They are sometimes used in playing *kloboto* and *totodzi,* supporting drums in *agbekɔ,* and the ornamental *kloboto,* and *atimevu,* lead drum in *nyayito* or *leafelegbe* or *atigo* or *dekɔnyanu* ensemble, for specific tonal and melo-rhythmic sounds.

Figure 125. The Dagbamba lung drummers exhibiting the arm control, squeezing and curved stick technique at the Ngmayem festival, Odumase Krobo, Ghana

Photo: Modesto Amegago. October 28 2011.

Figure 126. Some hourglass drummers exhibiting some playing techniques at the Ngmayem festival, Odumase-Krobo Ghana.

Photo: Modesto Amegago, Oct. 28 2011.

Figure 127. A group of brekete drummers demonstrating curved stick and hand drumming techniques.

Photo: Fiatikorpe Brekete group.

The sticks may be grasped with or between the thumbs and fore fingers with the remaining fingers bending slightly towards the palm. The wrists are supple and the drummer relaxes the hands when playing bouncing strokes. He or she may press the sticks with the fore fingers slightly downward or grasp the sticks a bit firmer when playing some muting beats. The drum-head may be struck or hit with a stick while pressing it at the center or near the edge of the drum with the other hand (or vice versa), or while pressing the membrane and releasing the hand; or the skin may be hit by hand and stick simultaneously. The drum may also be hit by hand and stick in rapid succession, or the membrane may be pressed with one hand while sliding a stick held in the other hand forward on it.

Some friction drums are played by rubbing the sticks or straws (that run through the center of the drum-wood) with damp or moistened fingers and/or wet rags, at different tempi and dynamic ranges, to produce varied (glissandi) sounds. Some are played by twirling the stick between the palm and hand to produce the desired sounds. In addition, the *etwie* and *laklevu,* friction drums of the Akan and Ewes respectively may be played by rubbing the tip of the *kɔtɔkɔrɔ* or *agblɔ,* curved or bent stick on the vellum backward and forward, or in a circular manner, to enable the drums to produce the desired roaring sounds. It should be noted that most stick drumming usually concentrates on the center of the drum head (although the drummer may play some muted strokes near the edge or snare of the drums for specific tonal effects).

A hand and (straight) stick are employed by the Ewe in playing the lead (*atimevu*) drums in *adzida, gohu, agbekɔ, adzohu, gahu, kinka* and *dunekpoe* for producing clear and loud sounds. They are also used by the Wolof in playing *sabar* drums, and by the Akan in playing some supporting drums of *adowa, fɔntɔmfrɔm* and *kundum,* for producing clear tonal sounds.

A stick and arm control or squeezing technique is used for playing the *lung* or *donno* of the Dagbamba. A combination of curved stick, arm control, hand and squeezing techniques are used in playing the *dundun* and *tama,* hourglass drums of the Yoruba and Mande, Susu, Baga, Minianka and Senufo sub groups, for producing specific tonal and melo-rhythmic sounds. The drums are strapped across a shoulder to rest near the rib cage around the waist area, or below an arm (depending upon its size), to balance horizontally. A thumb of the holding hand may be looped through some of the tension cords to steady the drum. The playing hand and wrist are suppled and the drum is squeezed with an arm against the body while being played with curved stick (*lungdoli*) held in the other hand (in the case of the *lung* or *donno*), or it may be squeezed with an arm against the body and played with a stick held in the other arm, while at the same time muffling or brushing the drumhead with the other hand upward or toward oneself (as may be observed in the playing of *tama* and *dundun*). The Yoruba *iyaalu* drummer would manipulate the tensioning strings with a combination of fingers, wrist and hip bone. When using the smaller drums with shorter shoulder straps, such as the *kanango* and *gangan* for talking, the tensioning strings may be manipulated with the upper arm. The stick may be held at clenched fist with free or supple wrist, and applied squarely to the drum head (at right angle) as near the center of the drum as possible, to produce a bouncing stroke (hitting near the edge of the drum may break the drum-head). The drummer may use the side of the stick some inches above the

Figure 128. An *iyaalu* drummer playing a Medium-pitched sound.

Source: Dabi Kanyinsola, dabi@ kanyinsola.com

Figure 129. An *atele* drummer producing high pitched sound.

Source: Dabi Kanyinsola, dabi@ kanyinsola.com

stick-head to hit the drum lightly for special effect (Euba, 1990, p. 142). The *iyaalu* drummer who is providing music for dance may employ the hand and stick technique to play some punctuation known as *ijalu* (lit. meaning, breaking the drumming). The typical *ijalu* strokes consist of a hand stroke, followed by a stick stroke almost simultaneously (in rapid successions) (Euba, 1990, p. 143). The hitting of an area of the skin near the tuning paste enables the drum to produce a deeper tone (Blades, p. 60). The *dundun/iyaalu* drummer may produce some muted strokes by stiffening his wrist before hitting the drum with a stick or hand. In general, most hand strokes (whether executed with a lose wrist or not) tend to have a slightly muted effect. A high tone is often muted to make it clearer. The drum may be lightly muted by touching its skin with a hand in between stick strokes; or hitting the drum less forcefully, or with less rigid wrist, to create different muting effects. Also, a *gangan* drummer (in *dundun* music) may use the nails of his/her free hand to scratch the drum-head or he or she may touch the drum-head with some of the drum's jingles, to produce some nasal or snaring effects (Euba, pp. 145-146).

Structure of African Drumming

The structure of African drumming is shaped by the sounds of the instruments and related activities that constitute the entire performance. The structure is also shaped by the style or nature of the drumming composition, duration and context of drumming/performance. African drumming structure may be shaped by the sounds of a single, a set, or an ensemble of instruments, songs, dance and dramatic elements. Hence, the structure may be perceived on multi levels. For example, the African drumming structure may be composed of two, three, four, five or six repetitive beats, such as tege dege dege dege... or tegede tegede tegede tegede..., kidikitsi kidikitsi, degedegede degedegede..., kidigidikitsi kidigidikitsi...played by a solo or group of drummers (playing the same patterns in unison). It may also be composed of two or three repetitive drum patterns played by different instrumentalists in an interlocking or dialogic manner. In addition, the structure may be composed of varied and additive patterns (played in linear or multilinear progression). A more complex African drumming structure would be composed of short and lengthy repetitive, additive, varied, dialogic, interlocking and circular patterns provided by the supporting and complementary instrumentalists, lead instrumentalists, singers and dancers. Viewed from an orchestral and integrated perspective, the structure and sounds of most of the African drumming may be described as polyrhythmic and polyphonic. These structural components may be conceptualized as rhythmic patterns, melo-rhythmic patterns or texts or phrases, drum beats and drum syllables.

In ensemble performances, there is usually a bell or a small supporting drum that provides the basic regulative beats or tempo for the orchestra. Some African drum ensembles such as the *lung* and *gun-gon* of the Dagbamba do not feature the bell as a time keeper, but the drummers usually sense or feel the steady beats or timing of the performance. Many of the basic regulative patterns that are played in African traditional performances highlight uneven number of visible beats, for example, the three beat *adavu*, tin-ko-ko-...; and the seven beat *agbadza* bell pattern: tin-ko- koko ko- ko- ko(ti), or tin-go- gogo go-go-go(ti) in Ewe performances; and the seven beat Akan *kete* and *adowa* bell patterns, ken ki ken ken ki ken ken, or ken- ki-ke-keren-ken-ki. In drum ensembles, the hand or stick clapping and rattles complement the bell patterns by providing three to twelve beats or pulses. In the Akan and Ewe ensembles, the bells, rattles, hand clapping and supporting drums such as *kagan* or *aburukuwa* or *petia* provide steady and interlocking patterns that underlie the drumming/performance. A variety of lead drumming patterns are played in dialogue, and in coordination with these patterns to create contrast, interest and harmony. Depending on the drumming style, there may be additional supporting and decorative drums which would engage in dialogue with the lead drum and some other supporting drums, or ornament the drum patterns to create interest. The sounds of the various instruments, vocal melodies, dance movements/rhythms and other contextual elements contribute to the polyrhythmic and polyphonic structure of African drumming/performance. Together, these patterns create the rich texture of the African drumming/music.

Salient features of African Drumming/performance

Whereas in the past, most drumming groups in African traditional societies would specialize in a particular style of drumming (albeit with sub pieces and sections), nowadays, some local and many contemporary drumming/music/dance groups would feature a number of music and dance styles or pieces within a particular performance. For example the local *Dodovi* group in the Aŋlɔ-Ewe traditional area would feature a number of pieces such as *misego, agbadza, kinka, babasiko, gadzo, nyayito* or *leafelegbe*. During major ceremonies or festivals, a number of drumming/performing groups would take turns to perform, or perform simultaneously in the same arena. Such performances usually involve the interaction of performers and audiences and a continuous shifting of the line of demarcation between performers and non-performers. These situations pose a challenge to researchers or scholars who would like to analyze the performance processes. However, the writer attempts to highlight the salient features of the actual drumming/performance processes in the sections below.

Drumming/Performance Settings

African drumming/performance may take place under a tree or a tent, along a pathway or street, in an open field, market, school ground, at indoor location in or in front of a house, religious temple, chiefs/king's palace or court, chapel, studio, school building, physical theater, hotel and conference room. In traditional settings, the drum/musical performances are usually announced by a town crier who would go around beating the gong and making verbal announcements, or nowadays in some communities, speaking through a loud speaker, a few days prior to the performance to inform the community about the upcoming performance/event. Some community members would spread the news about the performance by word of mouth. In contemporary African and African Diaspora societies, performances are also announced by flyers, words of mouth, emails and through Radio and TV. Among the Aŋlɔ-Ewe, the lead drummers of a performing group who reside at different locations of the community would play specific drum signals and excerpts from the drumming repertoire at certain times of the day: early in the morning, and about 10:00 AM and noon hour to remind the community about the day's performance.

Drumming/Performance Procession

Many performances in African traditional societies usually begin with a procession. For example, processions are held during the inaugural ceremonies of new performing groups, religious and political ceremonies, festivals, wrestling and other sporting events and funeral rites of prominent members of communities and groups. The procession may be held through the main routes or streets, communities or areas occupied by those to whom the performance is directed, towards the main performance setting. Nketia notes that, processions form an important part of the many Akan state festivals. They are held for the display of regalia, for the renewal and consolidation of loyalty, and for the purpose of visiting some sacred locations, such as the burial place of the ancestral chiefs, a historical cave, abode of a national God, etc. where some rites have to be performed (Nketia, pp. 141-142). On special occasions, newly formed Ewe music and dance groups, the *egungun* masquerade groups of the Yoruba, the *asafo* companies of the Akan and other performing groups would engage in procession through the main routes or streets, pathways and communities towards the main performance settings. The pace of the procession may depend on the musical style, or it may be set

Figure 130. Anlo-Afiadenyigba Gadzo group heralding the movement of traditional leaders during the Hogbetsotso grand durbar at Anloga

Photo: Modesto Amegago, Nov. 5 2011.

by musicians and dancers, cantors and patrons of the performing groups, ceremonial leaders, chiefs, priests, poets, and spectators who cluster around the performers and move along with them. Processions may go on at normal, slower, walking or hurried pace (Nketia, 1974, pp. 232-233).

Some performing groups feature unique processional pieces while others feature sections of their main repertoires during processions. Most integrated Ewe music and dance groups feature relatively slower versions of their main performances in processions. As stated by Nketia, many Akan performances have unique processional pieces that are featured on ceremonial occasions. For example, the *apenten*, a piece of *kete*, is featured in state processions, to herald the movement of traditional leaders, or to usher performers into the main setting. Its main rhythm is interpreted as, *Ohene nam ompe tem* (the chief walks; he is not in a hurry). Another processional piece, titled, *yetumpɔ* (we are digging gold), is featured in Akan state processions as martial music (Nketia, p. 129). The *mpintin* orchestra (composed of short, medium and long neck *donno* drums, *gyamadudu*, double-headed cylindrical drums and *mpintintoa*, gourd vessel drums), is featured in state processions, to herald the movement of a king or chief (akyea), halting after every few paces, and to provide music for carrying the chief/king in a palanquin, particularly where the procession requires to be hurried (aten) (Nketia, p 133). In addition, a piece of *fɔntɔmfrɔm*, called *atɔpre*, is played as the king is carried in a palanquin and dances with a gun in his hand, or as he walks holding a gun, or followed by gunmen at funerals and other distress situations when the king performs ceremonial shooting (trane) in honor of the departed, or to express his allegiance to the predecessor chiefs (Nketia, p. 137).

Almost every Ewe drumming or musical type has its processional section which is generally referred to as *vulɔlɔ*. The *agbadza, adzida, kinka, gohu, agbekɔ* and *gadzo* feature relatively slower versions of their main performances in their processions while *dunekpoe*, an Ewe social music and dance features a relatively slower version of *kinka* drumming/music in its procession. Among the Aŋlɔ-Ewe, the processional piece may also be featured during the main performances of certain groups (just before the final round of the performance), to create contrast and interest. Procession also forms part of the Ewe religious and state ceremonies such as the graduation and final funeral rites of Afa and Yewe priests and priestesses, installation of chiefs, *Hogbetsotso, Godigbe* and *Danyibakaka* festivals (celebrated to commemorate the history of the peoples).

The Dagbamba *lung* or *donno* and the Yoruba *dundun* drumming are essentially processional in nature. Their performances involve the drummers moving from one arena to another and between different arenas, such as compound, religious temple, palace, public performance arena, or festival ground and market. Similarly, the Yoruba drummers may engage in a procession to accompany the devotees of *egungun* masquerades from one temple or household to another, or a bride to the home of her spouse during marriage ceremony. Procession also forms part of the performances of the Hutu drummers of Burundi and other eastern and southern African performing groups.

Drumming/performance processions are also held by students/ youths during arts and cultural festivals, speeches and prize giving days and other school celebrations. They are also held by some African drumming/performing groups in Canada, USA, Europe, Caribbean and other parts of the world during the *Hogbetsotso, Odwira* and Africa Day celebrations (in Toronto), Ghana Fest (in Chicago) Caribana, Carnival (in Toronto), and Winter Soltice (in Vancouver) celebrations across relatively short and long distances. African drumming groups in institutions such as the University of Arizona and York University may engage in processions during their music/dance performances or other celebrations such as an official opening of Accolade East Building at York University in winter 2006. It is worth noting that severe winter or rainy conditions in some of the above mentioned locations may impede lengthy outdoor processions. The drumming/performance processions may also be held in contemporary theaters from backstage, stage left or right unto the stage, or from the main entrance of the theaters through the audience onto the stage.

Instruments used in Drumming/Performance Processions

Due to the limitations posed to the movements of performers in processions, many performing groups usually pay particular attention to the number of instruments used in processions. Some groups would feature a single instrument, such as bell, rattle, drum, or xylophone (and reserve the remaining instruments for the main performance) while others would feature relatively smaller instruments in the ensembles. Some would feature the entire ensemble of small, medium and large instruments on major ceremonial occasions. On festive occasions, one would see multiple drumming/dance groups in processions through the major pathways, streets, village or town leading to the festival settings (covering relatively long distances, ranging from one to five kilometres or more). In such processions, each drummer usually plays a single instrument, but instruments that are played in pairs or set, for example, the male and female *atumpan* drums and a set of *entenga* drums, are played by a single drummer. The procession may begin at dawn, early in the morning or afternoon, depending upon the performance schedule.

Organization of Drummers/Performers in Processions

There is usually an order of precedence in processions. For example, groups composed of only drummers (such as some Dagbamba and Yoruba hourglass drummers, and the Ewe and Akan Asafo groups) may form one to four vertical rows with their leaders in front or behind them as they engage in procession towards the main performance setting. Members of the Yewe religious sect who engage in *agoyiyi* graduation or ceremonial procession would form a vertical row and be followed by *kagan* drummer (playing a steady pattern: to- te de...) (Amegago, p. 183). Similarly, the Hutu drummers of Burundi would organize themselves in a vertical row as they move towards the performance setting. Members of some Ewe social performing groups would form three or four vertical rows, with the dancers/singers, rattle players and clappers in the front, followed by the supporting and master drummers as they engage in procession towards the main performance setting. During the annual *Hogbetsotso* festival (at Aŋlɔga), the *gadzo* and *asafo* drummers would form two or three or four lines and lead a procession of chiefs, followed by *Tegayiwo*, beautifully clad female entourage, *Zizi*, female praise singers, and followed by the leaders and their retinue and other drummers/drumming groups, praise singers and spectators towards the durbar ground.

Nketia notes that a procession during the Adae festival (of the Ashanti Mampong) would be headed by the Advanced guard (*Twafoa*), followed by '*Domakwaa, Kontire,* Court criers (*Nsenee*), spokesmen (*Akyeame*), trumpets, (*ntahera*) and *Ahumhene*. These are followed by the *kete* orchestra, followed by stool carriers and *Nam-asuro* (the fearless guard), followed by *apirede* orchestra, officers of the treasury (*Sannaa*) and Tobacco carriers (*Tawahyefoa*). They are also followed by the *mpebi* and *nkwawiri* drums, and followed by *nsumankwa* (sword bearers), then followed by the king, chiefs, and their retinues (*Sor-me-sisi*). The *fɔntɔmfrɔm* and *mpintim* orchestras now follow according to the order of precedence and depending on the movement of the chief and music appropriate for him (Nketia, pp. 143-144). Similar and unique orders or precedence may be observed by African drum-

Figure 131. An Asafo group performing in a procession during the installation of a chief at Aŋlɔga, Ghana.

Photo: Modesto Amegago, July 2011.

ming/performing group who engage in processions in the Diaspora settings. The audiences may walk alongside the performers, follow them, or stand by the road side and observe or join the performers who engage in a procession.

Handling of Instruments in Processions

The drums may be carried in hands, on the heads, on the shoulders, across the shoulders and arms, around the waist and between the thighs in processions. Burundi drummers, for example, may carry their drums on their heads and play them in a procession. The Akan and Ewe drummers usually enjoy the privilege of not carrying the heavy drums during performances. Among the Ewe, some volunteers; men and women take pride in carrying the *atimevu*, lead drums and supporting *gboba*, *sogo* and *kidi* drums on their heads and shoulders. Players of the *kagan*, *kloboto* and *totodzi* and portable *aflui/asafo* drums may carry their drums in one hand or by means of straps tied through the drum pegs and across their shoulders and chests, leaving the drum hanging around one side

Figure 132. Young musicians and dancers in a procession during the elementary schools students Hogbetsotso durbar celebration at Aŋlɔga.

Photo: Modesto Amegago, Nov. 3 2011.

or waist area in front of them. During a recent visit to Ghana, the writer observed an Ewe procession in which the lead *atimevu* drum and the drummer were carried on *keke*, a truck and pushed around. During the Akan state processions, the heavy *fɔntɔmfrɔm* and *atumpan* drums would be carried by male volunteers on their heads while drummers of the smaller *kete, fɔntɔmfrɔm, mpintin, adowa* and *asaadua* would carry their drums by strapping them through the drum pegs and across their shoulders and necks, leaving the drums hanging in front of them. Players of the *donno* and *dundun, brekete,* and *gyamadudu* and *sabar* would carry their drums by strapping them around their shoulders, leaving the drum resting between an arm and side of the body and the waist area respectively. The *tamalin* frame drum players would carry their instruments by holding the cross bars inside them with one hand, (resulting in the instruments facing right or left) and play them with the other hand. Also, the *djembefola* (*djembe* drummers) would carry their drums with stripes tied through the vertical

Figure 133. Drummers in the midst of a procession of chiefs and people of Odumase-Krobo during the Ngmayem festival.

Photo: Modesto Amegago, Oct. 28, 2011.

strings and around their waists, leaving the drum hanging low in front of them, or between their thighs. In addition, solo or a group of xylophone player(s) who engage in procession may strap the instruments around their waist, leaving it hanging in front of them.

Procession in Progress

Most processional drumming or music/dance performances usually feature a limited variety of drum patterns and movements since the drummers have to move along while playing thus making it difficult for them to vary their drumming patterns. A solo drummer who plays to accompany the movement of wrestlers or members of a religious or political group may play some introductory patterns to draw the peoples' attention, or signal the beginning of the event. S/he may play repetitive beats to usher the wrestlers, or performers unto the main setting. Similarly, a player of *agblɔvu* or *asafo*, royal drum would play short repetitive phrases and appellations of leaders intermittently during a procession toward a ceremonial setting. He or she may play slowly, loudly and softly at certain moments in relation to the tempo and dynamics of the procession.

Figure 134. A group of young drummers playing their instruments in a procession during Ngmayem festival at Odumase-Krobo.

Photo: Modesto Amegago, Oct 28, 2011.

Other processional sections of the *asafo*, *ijala* and *agbekɔ* for example, may begin by a cantor chanting or reviewing an introductory song and signalling the bell player, singers, clappers, supporting and master drummer(s) (with a conducting whisk, stick clapper, or hand) to begin at the appropriate times, sequentially or simultaneously. In some processions, all the drummers may play in unison from the beginning to the end. In others, each supporting drummer would maintain a steady pattern after the introductory section, while the lead drummer(s) would play a variety of patterns and signals in coordination with the various instrumentalists.

When the ensemble is well established, the lead/master drummer would introduce a drum roll or signal (referred to as *vuyoyro* in Ewe and *a break* in many contemporary African performances), followed by a rhythmic pattern. He or she would repeat the pattern a number of times, ornament it with additional beats, and wait for the supporting instrumentalists, singers and dancers to intensify or change their songs and movements before continuing his patterns. He or she would introduce drum rolls at regular intervals to heighten the effect of the procession after

Figure 135. A group of Burundi drummers carrying and playing drums in a procession.

Thomas Brooman CBE: http://heavenlyplanet.com/

exhausting the previous patterns. The processional sections of integrated Ewe music/dance performances such as *agbadza, gohu* and *kinka*) involve dancers/singers playing rattles or clapping, while that of *agbekɔ* and *gadzo*, and *bɔbɔɔbɔ* involve the dancers holding whisks and wooden swords, and handkerchiefs respectively while moving from side to side and forward, swinging, or swaying the whisks, or wooden swords, or rolling the handkerchiefs. The *agbekɔ* and *gadzo* dancers may also move the whisks or wooden swords upward and downward; or forward high and backward low in relation to the movement of their arms and legs/feet. In such processions, the master drummer would play drum rolls/signal, *krebe krebe krebe krebe*, or *tegede tegede tegede tegede* at regular intervals to heighten the effect of the procession and signal a change or intensification of rhythms or movements. Each signal would be heightened by the performers shouting, *ho o o!!*, or *hododio o o o...!!* while shaking their rattles, clappers and hands upwards. The master drummer may introduce a main rhyth-

Figure 136. Drummers carrying their drums on their shoulders in a procession during the annual Hogbetsotso festival, Aŋlɔga.

Photo: Modesto Amegago, November 2011.

mic pattern, such as, *ga-degide ga-degide- ten…*), to which the *sogo* and *kidi* drummers would respond, *kidi sh kidi kitsikitsikitsi*. The group may intensify the performance on approaching a crowd of spectators or the main performance setting. In Akan ceremonial processions, this is the moment when shield bearers would be tossing their shields in the air to the exciting rhythms of the *fͻntͻmfrͻm* and *mpintin* drums. Similarly, the Yoruba *dundun* drummers who play to accompany an *egungun* masquerade and dancers may halt temporally when they come across friends or spectators. The drummers would change the style or tempo of the music, face the dancers and play for them for some time before resorting to the processional drumming. Both the drummers and dancers may move back and forth while facing one another, or towards the same direction at certain moments of the procession (Euba, 1990, pp. 421-423).

As the group arrives at the main performance setting, the drums (that are supposed to be set on the ground or benches or against drum-stands) may be lowered and placed at their appropriate locations, or the performers may position themselves according to an established order and continue to play until a signal is provided by the lead drummer or cantor for ending the performance. A prayer may be said, followed by a song or a short music and dance tribute to the Supreme Being, divinities and ancestors, and the main performance, or the performers may break after the procession in order to rest for some time, and continue with additional rounds, depending on the occasion and arrangement.

Duration of Processions

The duration of a procession may depend on the pace of the processions, the distance to be covered during the procession, motivation of the performers and spectators' reaction to the performance. On the average, inaugural procession of the Aŋlɔ-Ewe performing groups (covering about three kilometres) may last for over an hour while processions during major festivals such as *Egungun*, *Hogbetsotso*, *Adae* and *Homowo* may last between thirty minutes to an hour. Short processions from specific locations towards some performance settings may last between ten to fifteen minutes. Processions during popular festivals such as Caribana and Carrassauga in the African Diaspora setting of Canada may last between thirty minutes to over an hour. Shorter procession in contemporary theaters may last between three to ten minutes.

Drumming/Performing within the Main Setting

Like the processional performances, performances within the main settings usually feature an introduction, continuation and finale sections consisting of sounds of a single or a set of drums and accompanying instruments, songs, chants, dialogues, dance movements and visual imagery. These may be presented as a series of short or long pieces which may be repeated (albeit with variations) or interchanged a number of times and separated by pauses or breaks.

The Setting of instruments within the main performance Arena

Drums and the accompanying instruments may be set in the main performance setting with due consideration of the position of the leaders and audiences, and in relation to the direction of the wind. The instruments are usually set at a place where they can be clearly heard by the performers and audience members (although in some settings, microphones may be used to project the sounds). The drums may be set in horizontal row, at the center, left or right of the setting, circle, or stage, or in horseshoe, semi-circular and circular formation. For example, the Ewe drummers who perform in community settings may set all the drums in a row, with the lead drums placed by the sides of the secondary drums; the lead *atimevu* and *gboba* would be leaned against *vudetsi* or *vuglatsi*, a wooden drum-stand (held together with iron hooks at its lower sides or legs) set behind the secondary drums. The clappers, singers and dancers may sit around the drummers or in front of the drummers in a circle. In *agbekɔ*, the secondary drums may be set in a row besides the lead *atimevu* drum. A player or players of the *atimevu(wo)* would stand on blocks or on the ground by the right or left side, or the outer sides of the drums. In the version of *agbadza* called *adzida*, which is performed by the elderly Aŋlɔ-Ewe, the two *atimevuwo* would be placed in *vuxɔ*, drum house, a specially designed wooden and glass structure. The *sogo* and *kidi* players may stand by their drums raised on benches while the *kloboto*, *totodzi* and *kagan* players would suspend the drums from the ground on their feet or hold them between the knees, causing the drums to lean slightly forward or toward them. Alternatively, the *sogo, kidi, kloboto, totodzi, kagan* and *gankogui* bell players would sit on a wooden bench in front of the master drummers. In addition, the lead and supporting *aflui/ Asafo* drums may be leaned on stands or on a bench or benches, or the supporting drums may be held between the thighs, with the drummers standing and sitting before playing them while the singers would sit behind the drummers.

In Akan drumming, the larger and heavy *fɔntɔmfrɔm* or *bɔmmaa* drums would be leaned forward against young boys or suspended off the ground by sticks placed under the side facing the drummers, to enable the drums to resonate properly. The *atumpan* would be leaned on forked or wooden stand (held by metal hooks on the legs), and the drummers would play them while standing and leaning forward slightly (in a relaxed manner). The conical and semi-cylindrical closed or open-ended supporting drums, such as *petia* and *apentemma* are played while sitting. An ensemble of *kete* drums may be set in a row or horse-shoe formation by the left, centre, or right side of the setting while the drummers would sit facing most of the audience members. Players of the *djembe* may stand, or sit on stools or chairs at the center, left or right side of the setting or stage in a horseshoe formation, semi circle or closed circle.

The *gun-gon* or *brekete* and *lung* or *donno* (of the Dagbamba); the *tama* or *lunka* (of the Mande), *dundun* (of the Yoruba) and *gyamadudu* (of the Akan) drummers may stand in vertical or horizontal rows, or horseshoe formations (and may move from one location to the other to interact with other performers and audience members. In addition, the *lung* or *donno* and *gun-gon* or *brekete* drummers may sit on the ground while playing at certain moments of the *Damba* festival (celebrated to commemorate the birth of Prophet Mohammed). Similarly, the Yoruba *dundun/iyaalu* drummers may sit while performing (*ijire*) for the Timi of Ede (with the secondary *dundun* drummers facing the entrance of the palace and *iyaalu* player facing the Timi's personal quarters situated at the opposite end of the palace courtyard, from where the Timi normally listens to the *ijire*); or they may sit at the entrance of a religious temple while playing (Euba, 1990, pp. 140-141). The Hutu drummers of Burundi would set their drums in a horseshoe formation at the center of the setting and play while standing, facing most of the audience members. In addition, the *bata* drummers in the Diaspora may sit on benches or chairs horizontally or in a horseshoe formation and hold the drums on their laps horizontally as they play both heads with hands.

The *akadinda* and *timbila* xylophones may be set in horizontal rows; the players of the large instruments may sit on the ground/floor, or on short wooden seats behind the instruments at a central location. In the case of the *amadinda*, the three players may sit at the same side of the instrument, or two players may sit abreast at one side while one player would sit in the middle at the opposite side. As many as thirty players may play the *timbila* (which are tuned to treble, alto, tenor, bass and double bass keys. The instruments may be set in three rows: the players of the large *timbila* may perform while standing behind the players of the small instruments who are seated with the instruments placed on the ground. The instruments may be supported by stones or spare gourds, or held in place with a cord from the player's shoulders, or strung to sticks in the ground. Where players sit on each side of the instruments, the bars may be struck on the extreme edges of the instruments instead of the center (Blades, p. 78). Six players may play the *akadinda;* three of the players may sit abreast, horizontally at both sides of the instrument, and each player playing a set of keys and his parts (Nketia, p. 84). Similarly, a set of two *gyile*, xylophones (of the Dagara, Lobi and Sisala) may be set inside the circle, and the players may sit on the ground or stools and be flanked by two accompanied *koi* or *kuor* (gourd vessel) drummers at both sides. The *gyil* may also be played by a soloist who may be accompanied by a player who uses two sticks to play the side-wood of the instrument. They may be surrounded by dancers (usually) in a counter clockwise circle, and spectators who may sit or stand around the performers.

Solo Drumming/Performing within the Main Setting

Drumming within the main performance settings may be presented by a solo or group of drummers without chanting or singing. But, such performances often involve chanting, singing and dancing. Euba notes that although *dundun* is mainly an instrumental performance, it is also played to accompany chants and songs of *ijala* hunters and devotees of Ogun, god of metal works. The *egungun akewi* (chanting masquerades) are also accompanied by the playing of specific *dundun* patterns. In a type of vocal music called *ilu owe* (drumming of proverbs); the singers usually alternate with the *iyaalu* by providing vocal interpretations of the *iyaalu* patterns. Also, a modernized type of *dundun* known as *tatalo* is characterized by a combination of singing, *dundun* and *akuba* (conga derived) drumming. There is also a category of *rara* court singers who accompany their chanting with drums (Euba, 1990, p. 406). Chanting and singing also form part of the *asafo*, military and *aboafɔɔ* or *adevu* the Akan and Ewe hunters' associations and many African performances.

A solo drummer in the main performance setting may play some introductory patterns, *pede pata pata pata pata...* or *tege dege dege dege dege dege...*, He or she may chant or sing to draw the audience's attention, and introduce the main drumming patterns. He or she may repeat the pattern a number of times, improvise some beats and revert to the main pattern. (This would involve the use of appropriate techniques such as relaxed hands, fingers, hand and stick or sticks, and the playing of the various zones of the drum). The drummer may introduce new patterns after exhausting a given pattern; play loudly, softly, slowly, rapidly, and break suddenly, to establish moments of silence, sing and continue drumming. He or she may move closer to the audience and play certain patterns and engage them in dialogue, clapping, singing and dancing, and would play the finale pattern after exhausting the repertoire.

A *sabar* drummer, who accompanies a wrestling event, may play some drum rolls or signals to charge the atmosphere, motivate the wrestlers and usher them into the ring. He or she may play additional patterns to mark the beginning of the wrestling and play steady patterns to provide background music/rhythm for the event, and would relate his drumming to the dynamics of the event by playing repeatedly, loudly and faster as the wrestling intensifies; and playing softly and slowly to mark the ending of the activity.

Drummers of the Akan *atumpan*, the Dagbamba *lung*, the Yoruba *dundun* and the Ewe *atimevu* may begin their drumming with a drum stroke, continue with additional strokes and patterns or texts on a single or pair of drums and repeat them to express tribute to the Supreme Being, divinities, leaders; flora and fauna. They may play certain phrases loudly, softly, rapidly and slowly, pause, play the ending pattern to convey specific cultural messages.

Some master drummers would play two to seven drums together (in relation to a bell pattern provided by a bell player). Notable among these drummers are Gideon Alɔwoyi, Modesto Amegago, Robert Awute, Sylvanus Kuwɔ (of the Ewe); and the

Drums of Mamprobi Performing group: A master drummer of Mamprobi group.
Figure 137. Within the main setting   Figure 138. Standing by the drum.

Photo: Modesto Amegago at Dzelukorfe, July, 2009.

Figure 139. Bell and rattle players of Mamprobi group sitting in front of the Drummers.

Photo: Modesto Amegago at Dzelukorfe, July 2009.

Figure 140. A group of Asafo drummers leaning their drums against a bench.

Photo: Modesto Amegago, July 2011, Aŋlɔga, Ghana.

drummers of *bugarabu* of Sene-Gambia and *entenga* drums of Uganda, and some drummers of African highlife bands. Any of these drummers may play introductory patterns on one or two drums, followed by the main patterns. He or she may try to replicate the structure of an ensemble drumming by playing the lead drum patterns on the lead drum and responsorial patterns on one or two secondary drums. He or she would repeat the patterns, ornament them, and introduce new patterns, pause suddenly and continue to play. In particular, Alɔwoyie would sing and dance in place, or around the drums, or while lying on a chair, raising his legs upward and clapping with his feet as he plays, to show off his talent and skill. There is, however, a difference between the rendition of a group of drummers who perform in an ensemble and that of a solo drummer who attempts to replicate the structure of a group performance. Such a drummer may have to omit certain beats or add new beats to certain patterns. Nevertheless, his/her rendition may be regarded as unique and his/her talent, skills and creativity should be recognized.

Figure 141. *fɔntɔmfrɔm* drummers of the Ghana Dance Ensemble performing at a setting.

Photo: retaken by Modesto Amegago by courtesy of the Artistic Director, Benjamin Aryetey.

Orchestral Drumming/Performances within the Main Setting

Groups of drummers who accompany recreational, economic and ceremonial activities may relate their drumming to the structure of the activities. Such a group may be led by a master drummer who would introduce the performance by playing specific drum signals to alert participants to get ready for the activity. He or she may play additional signals to usher the supporting drummers into the performance (at the appropriate times) in relation to the activity. The supporting and master drummers may play in unison from the beginning to the end, or each drummer would play specific patterns from the beginning to the end. On the contrary, the supporting drummers would play steady patterns (to provide background music for the activity) while the lead drummer would play varied patterns in relation to the tempo and dynamics of the activity. The lead drummer may focus on a particular or small group of workers, play their appellations and praises and urge them to work harder. S/he may sing some melodies on the drum with the workers, break for a while and play specific phrases to

Figure 142. Some drummers of the Ghana Dance Ensemble playing djembe in a performance at the School of performing Arts, University of Ghana

Photo: retaken by Modesto Amegago, December 2011, by courtesy of the Artistic director, Ben Aryetey.

mark the end of the work, and to accompany the workers back to village or town.

Integrated Drumming, Singing and Dancing

A more integrated drumming, singing and dancing usually features small or large drum ensembles, together with supporting instruments such as bells, rattles, clappers, xylophones, flutes, whistles and trumpets, fiddles, lutes and lyres (depending on the style). Each instrumentalist usually plays a single instrument, but in some performances, a drummer would play a set of two or more instruments together. For example, drummers of *bugarabu*, *entenga* and African highlife; *gota* supporting drums, *kpanlogo* and *bɔbɔɔbɔ* lead/supporting drums would play two or more drums together. In some *agbadza* groups, two or three master drummers would take turns to play. Also, in some (Ewe) *gohu* and *adzogbo* groups, two or three master drummers would play in turns or in unison from the beginning to the end, and at climactic moments of the performance. Similarly, the Hutu drummers of Burundi would take turns to play the *inkiranya* drums, dance and sing as well as play certain patterns in unison.

Such integrated performances may be introduced by the lead or master drummer or cantor in the manners discussed under the processions. For example, the *ijala, aboafoɔ* and *adevu,* hunters' performance types (of the Yoruba, Akan and Ewe respectively), would be introduced by a cantor chanting or reviewing an introductory song (*aho* in Akan), followed by the main signal (which may be a song phrase, a hand gesture, or a swinging of a whisk or horsetail forward or downward toward the drummers) to usher the various performers to begin at the appropriate times. Many Ewe social performances (such as *agbadza, gohu, dunekpoe*) may be introduced by the master drummer playing *Ʋuyoyro,* drum roll or signal to alert the performers. The *Ʋuyoyro* may include *ŋkɔfofodo,* the calling of *ahanoŋkɔ,* "drinking names" of leading members of the group, such as, *Duga te fiawo le,* chiefs live under state funds. This may be followed by *Ʋugbexexle,* review of some of the drumming patterns/texts, and followed by a cantor introducing *Ʋuyɔhawo,* performance calling songs (which are sustained melodies, accompanied by a rattle sound). An example of the *Ʋuyɔhawo* is provided below:

> Gohu nyea fɔ za do
> Tsyiahu nyea fɔ za do loo oo
> Miawo Freemania tsi amlima
> Hadzivodua fo ha gawo le amlɔme
> Made yo Totsuwo namea ne miasi kete e kete lo ooo
> Made yo Vidzrowo namea ne miasi kete e kete lo o o

Figure 143. Master drummer Midawo Aḃwoyie playing three *agbl̴vu*,
royal drums during Hogbetsotso festival.

Photo: Modesto Amegago, Nov. 5, 2011, Aŋl̴ga.

**Figure 144. Amegago Gbasa (Divine Union) performing Afa music and
dance at a funeral of a deceased member at Aŋl̴ga, Ghana.**

Photo: Modesto Amegago, Dec. 2, 2011.

Gohunyea fɔ zado
Tsyiahunyea fɔ zado lo o o o o aye eee
Miawo Fremania tsi amlima
Hadzivodua fo ha gawo le amlɔme
(composed by Atifose Amegago, 1970s).

My Gohu has woken up at late night 2x
Our Freeman has performed a miracle
The composing God has found great songs in sleep
Someone should call me Totsu so we perform Kete,
yes, Kete
Someone should call me Vidzro so we perform Kete,
yes, Kete
My Gohu has woken up at late night 2x
Our Freeman has performed a miracle
The composing God has found great songs in sleep
(composed by Atifose Amegago, 1970s).

The *vuyɔhawo* may be followed by *adzo* or *adzokpui*, the playing of short rhythmic patterns or texts which may be accompanied by songs and dramatic movements. This may be followed by *hawuwu*, a review of *vutsɔha*, the main "performance starting song", and a signal provided by the cantor (with *lashi*, horsetail or whisk) to usher the various instrumentalists, singers and dancers into the performance, sequentially or simultaneously. An example of the *agbadza vutsɔha* is as follows:

Gbadza le mɔ de nu 'me ade le sɔ dzi ne ʋu agbo
Miʋu agbo he e e
Gbadza le mɔ de nu 'me ade le sɔ dzi ne ʋu agbo
Mi ʋu agbo he mɔ de nu mɔ de nu me ade le sɔ dzi ne
ʋu agbo
Gbadza ʋu agbo he e:

Agbadza is on a certain gate one on a horse back
should open the gate
Open the gate yes
Agbadza is on a certain gate one on a horse back
should open the gate
Open the gate yes

On a certain gate on a certain gate one on a horse back
should open the gate
Agbadza open the gate yes (Amegago, p. 126).

In the Aŋlɔga Dɔnɔgbɔ *gohu* style, almost all the instruments would be ushered into the performance simultaneously to create an attacking effect. In other Ewe performances such as *agbadza* and *adzida*, players of the bell, clappers, rattles and *kagan* supporting drums would be ushered into the performance, sequentially or simultaneously while a lead drummer would wait until the ensemble is well established before s/he introduces a main signal to usher in the supporting *sogo* and *kidi* drummers. The lead drummer would again wait for some time before introducing a drum roll/signal, to which the various performers would shout, hoo!! or hododio!! while shaking their rattles, clappers, and waving their handkerchiefs and hands upward, to heighten the main beginning of the performance.

In *kinka*, signal for starting the performance may be provided by a cantor, who after reviewing the introductory song, would usher the bell, rattle players, *kagan* supporting drummer and singers into the performance, followed by the *gboba*, bass and ornamental drummer, who would play lengthy introductory patterns, followed by drum rolls (*gbo ge ge gbo ge ge gbo ge gegedegedegedegedegede…*), to usher the *kidi* and *sogo* drummers into the performance simultaneously. Here, the master drummers would be playing *vukɔgo*, drum-side or shell until the ensemble is well established before they introduce drum rolls in turns. (*krebekrebekrebekrebekrebe*) which the various performers would heighten (hododioo!!) in a manner stated above.

In *agbekɔ*, the introductory drum roll/signal may be followed by a lead drummer playing phrases such as *to ten*, followed by a response *wo d'abɔ* from the dancers/chorus, and followed by other phrases; *gagide tototo teto te gaga,* to which the dancers/ singers would respond, *adzesɔ.* This may be followed by another dialogue between the master drummer and dancers/chorus, which may begin with, *kiniwoe* and a response, *yaa,* or *ziwoe,* from the dancers/chorus. The dialogue which is intended to alert the performers and arouse their emotions, feelings and thoughts, would be followed by a cantor reviewing *vutsɔha,* the main introductory song, and signalling the dancers/singers, bell and other supporting instrumentalists to begin simultaneously or sequentially. Alternatively, the master drummer may begin by playing some rhythmic patterns, to which the dancers would respond with verbal dialogue; and then introduce the main signal to usher the dancers, bell and other instruments into the performance.

In the Akan *kete, adowa* and *fɔntɔmfrɔm* performances, the master drummer may begin by playing introductory rhythmic texts or proverbs in tribute to the Supreme Being, divinities, neighboring creatures, or by a priest saying a libation prayer, interjected with short drum phrases and voices. This may be followed by a cantor and chorus reviewing *aho*, introductory songs or chants (sometimes with hand clapping, body movement and drumming interjections), and followed by the master drummer calling the bell: *Adewura Kofi Ma woho mresu, Adewura Kofi*, cause your self to rise, to usher the bell, rattle and supporting drums into the performance at the appropriate times. After setting the tempo, the master drummer would continue by playing the main patterns in an established order or according to his or her arrangement.

Integrated performances such as *sinte, sɔsɔne*, and *yankadi*, of the Baga, Susu, Mendenyi, Termine and Malinke ethnic groups of Guinea, Mali and Burkina Faso may be introduced by a cantor singing or chanting, or by the xylophonist or master drummer playing some introductory patterns, *pe pata pata pre pede pede*, or melody often in dialogue with the *dundun, sangban* and *kenkeni* drummers, and followed by another drum or song signal, to usher all the drummers/singers and dancers into the performance simultaneously, or at specific times. Also, the Hutus drummers (of Burundi) would begin their performance by chanting or singing, followed by a signal provided by the cantor or lead drummer, to usher the various drummers into the performance simultaneously or sequentially.

Further, a player of the *gyil*, xylophone may begin by playing ("a run through") musical phrases) (called *chob*) from the lowest key to the highest in ascending order, and back from the highest to the lowest key in descending order, followed by the introduction of the main song and ushering the singers and dancers into the performance in the appropriate order (sequentially or simultaneously)(Woma,www. http://jumbierecords.comwomaensemble/womalive.html).

Drumming/Performance in Progress

In some performances, such as *agbadza, gohu, atsyia, adzida* and *kinka* (of the Ewe) players of the *gakogui*, double bell, *axatsewo*, rattles, *akpe*, clappers and *kaganu* or *vuvi* smaller supporting drum, would maintain steady rhythmic patterns while the lead *atimevu* drummer would play a variety of patterns in dialogue with the complementary *kidi* and *sogo* drummers, dancers and singers, to create interest and harmony. A similar arangement may be seen in the *apenten* and *akwadum* drumming of the Akan *kete* suite where players of the bell, rattle and *aburukuwa* drums would maintain steady patterns and the *apentemma* player would engage in dialogue with the *kwadum*, lead drum. This arrangement would also be observed in *fɔntɔmfrɔm akantam* suite, in which players of the *dawuro* bell, *adukrogya, paso, brenko* and *donno* would maintain steady rhythms while the *atumpan* drummer would engage in dialogue with the *frɔm* or *bɔmmaa* drummers and a dancer.

In other performances, the bell and rattles would maintain steady rhythms while two supporting drums would engage in criss cross, and another supporting drum would engage in close communication with the lead/master drum at certain times or throughout the performance. This arrangement would be seen in the *kete aboafoɔ* piece in which the two *aburukuwa* would engage in criss cross, while the *apentemma* would be corresponding with the master drum patterns.

Also, in the *sɔsɔne, sinte* and *yankadi* performances, players of the *kenkeni, sangban (*which have bells attached to them) and the supporting *djembe* drums would maintain steady patterns while the master drummer would play a variety of rhythms to signal the dancers to intensify, change or end their movements. In *agbekɔ*, all the supporting instruments (bell, rattle, clappers, *kagan, kidi, kloboto* and *totodzi*) would maintain steady patterns while the master drummer would play a variety of patterns to engage in dialogue with the dancers/singers.

Some performances require the master drummer to play the standard patterns in a sequential order, from beginning to the end. Others require the master drummer to play the initial patterns in sequential order, and play certain patterns at will, and again play specific patterns according to an established order at the climax or near the end of the performance. Also, in most performances, every main rhythmic pattern, song and movement, and moments of intensification and change of activities would be announced by drum roll or signal or break (as may be observed in the Ewe *agbadza, adzida, kinka, gohu* and *dunekpoe*; and the Mande *sinte* and *sɔsɔne*). In some other performances, signal for changing or intensifying the performance may be played occasionally.

As the performance progresses, the master drummer would introduce a rhythmic pattern, or text, repeat and ornament (by using various drumming techniques), and leave room for supporting instrumentalists, singers and dancers to feature. He or she would introduce a new pattern at a time when a particular song is about to end, or when a dancer or group of dancers are ready to intensify their movements. After playing for some time (about ten to fifteen minutes), the master drummer would signal his co-master drummer to take his/her turn. The co-master drummer may begin by playing drumming patterns that have not been played earlier in order to complement the rendition of his/her colleague. He would later repeat some of the patterns played by his or her colleague after playing other patterns. It is a common knowledge that no two drummers play exactly the same way. Hence, some community members can easily identify the rendition of a particular drummer upon hearing the music from afar.

Performance styles such as *agbadza* and *gohu*, require groups of two to about four dancers to step into the circle at will (provided the arena is not over crowded). Such performances require little and indirect collaboration between drummers and dancers, and the lead drummer may intensify the drumming to introduce rhythmic directions and emphasize particular drum phrases or texts as the dance grows in intensity.

In Bawa (of the Dagara), the musicians and dancers may collaborate on various levels: the dancers may form a circle around the musicians (usually, two xylophonists, two drummers and a bell player). The player of the *gyilmwiere,* xylophone may introduce a melody or signal for the dancers to execute slow and relaxed, walking movements/steps in a circle. He or she may also play another song or signal for the drummers to intensify their patterns

Figure 145. The Klikɔ Kpegisu group performing for a group of Canadian students at the Dagbe Cultural Centre, Kɔfeyia, Ghana.

Photo: Modesto Amegago, July 2011.

and the lead drummer would intensify the drumming to signal the dancers to execute the main dance movement(s), to introduce rhythmic direction. This alternation between the songs, xylophone and dance section may last for hours (Woma, http://jumbierecords. comwomaensemble/womalive.html).

Other performances such as *adowa, fɔntɔmfrɔm* of the Akan; *asafo/aflui* or *kufade* of the Ewe and *sabar* and some other Wolof, Mande/Mandinka or Malinke and Jola performances require an individual or small group of dancers to dance at a time. Here the dancers would be required to relate their movements to the timing and master drum patterns at certain times, as well as express themselves freely at other times in relation to the timing of the music. As noted by Nketia, in *fɔntɔmfrɔm*, while the drums are playing, the master drummer would call a dancer by his name and by-names and praise, or thank him/her and then join in the music, for example:

> Osei
> The watery shrub that thrives on hard ground,
> Noble Osei that lays men low

Osei, true and of pure blood, take it easy take it easy...
Adane: Okuru kari kari

The palm wine pot soiled by froth, Okuru Gyasi Apire
You are brave, you are a man of valour (Nketia, p.
159).

Similar appellations are played in many Ewe and other African
performances. Nketia notes further that, the master drummer
would drum directions for the dancer: move outward, take it
easy, do it gracefully, etc. He watches the dancer as he throws
his hands about appropriately, strides along and kicks here and
there. He regulates the style of the music for the preliminary part
of the dance called *akita* or *nkunta* (hold up). When at the appropriate moment, the dancer stretches his hands sideways, jumps
and crosses his legs in the landing position, the master drummer
begins the main piece and the part that corresponds to the crossing
of the legs and the vigorous part of the dance, and the end posture
and gesture (breaking the cord and cutting through downwards)
(Nketia, 1954, p.42). In *adowa*, various changes in the rhythms
played by the master drummer correspond to changes in the dance
routine. But a dancer would execute certain movements at will
and the master drummer may change the style of the drumming, or
play new patterns as the dancer changes his/her movement.

Other performances, such as *agbekɔ*, *adzogbo* and *atsyia*
require close collaboration between the musicians and dancers.
In *Agbekɔ*, the master drummer would play specific rhythms or
texts such as *toto kre kren*..., to urge the dancers to be alert (to
which the dancers would respond, *aye aye* while hopping backward); *gide gagin,(mibla go dzi)* to tell the dancers to tighten their
belts; *gazegede kren ga*, to which the dancers would respond, *oo
yiwoe*, while moving from side to side; *ton te ga gi den- ten to
ten to dza*..., to tell the dancers to step on the left and right feet
forward, turn through the left and execute *yedudu*, the basic Ewe
movement characterized by contraction and release of the torso
in relation to the oppositional upward downward movement of
the feet and arms. Specific drumming patterns would be played to
tell the dancers to advance, retreat, or enact the tilling of land and
planting of crops; roll of arms through forward and backward (as

Figure 146 and 147. The Dagbe Cultural Troupe performing *Atsyiagbekor* **for a group of Canadian students at Kɔfeyia.**

Photo: Modesto Amegago, July 2011.

Figure 148. The Ghana Dance Ensemble performing Adowa at the University of Ghana, Accra.

Photo: retaken by Modesto Amegago, Dec. 2011, by courtesy of the Artistic Director Benjamin Aryetey.

a form of physical exercise), play games, write or perform class assignment, etc. Also, in *adzogbo* or *adzohu* the master drummer would play specific melo-rhythms, texts or songs (eg. *'Me ade yi vodu yɔ ge nade nu do*, one who goes to call upon God must bow) to urge the dancers to kneel and bow their heads in tribute to the Supreme Being; and pay tribute to master drummer and cantor. The drummer, together with the dancers/singers would communicate themes of allegiance, prayer, perseverance, revelation, beauty, sanctity, etc. (Amegago, pp. 175-180).

A similar mode of collaboration between musicians and dancers can be observed in some Yoruba music and dance (as documented by Euba (1990). For example, in Obatala music, when an *iyaalu* drummer plays the phrase, *Obatala nka wo ja leri*, meaning Obatala is throwing his fighting hand above his head (or is in a fighting mood), the dancer responds by arching his/her arm above his/her head. In addition, during the performance of *yagbayagba* masquerade dance, the *iyaalu* drummer would solo while one of the dancers would move spirally away from the drummers. As he moves backward towards the drummers, the *iyaalu* drummer would stop hitting the drum head and instead, keep squeezing and releasing the tensioning strings, producing the typical sounds of leather when it is alternately tensed and untensed, and at the same time intermittently shaking the jingles up and down, which is described as "dancing to the jingles. Next, the dancer would spiral away from the drummer this time to *gudugudu* solo, and finally he dances to *isaju* solo before the whole ensemble resumes playing (Euba, p. 424).

Ending a Drumming/Performance Section

After exhausting the repertoire, or at the appropriate time, a lead/master drummer(s) may play the ending drum pattern, text, song or signal, or the cantor may raise the ending song or signal, to bring the performance to an end. Examples of the performance ending songs are as follows:

1.

Evua mu lo evua mu:	The drum/performance has fallen, the drum has fallen,
Kaloso Evua mu:	Kaloso the drum/performance has fallen

2.

Ago mado na mi loo ayee:	I am knocking (or asking for excuse), yes
Ago mado na mi loo ee:	I am knocking or asking for excuse), yes
Hesino Visiku be	Composer Visiku says
Medo ago na dumegawo:	I am asking for the elders' excuse
Ago mado na mi loo hee:	I am knocking/asking for an excuse, yes.

Continuing the Drumming/performance

At the end of a performance section, the drummers/performers may take a short break, or sing, or chant, recite poetry or feature some dramatic elements before beginning another round. For example, most Ewe social drumming, singing and dancing sections are followed by *hatsyiatsyia*, chorus section during which the main songs belonging to the repertoire are sung. The *hatsyiatsyia* is led by *henɔwo*, cantors some of whom are drummers. For example, the *hatsyiatsyia* in Agbadza and its sub-styles is characterised by the performers moving rhythmically forward, opening their lower arms sideways and closing them in front of the body in a counter clockwise circle, accompanied by two *atoke*, boat-shaped bells and one or more *gankogui*, double bells patterns, which regulate the singing and provide contrasting background to the performance. During the *hatsyiatyia*, two or three cantors may face the audience and dramatize the song, and move to another location to dramatize the songs for other audience members. In *gohu hatsyiatsyia*, a bigger rattle (*ego*) may be used to emphasize the ending phrases of the songs, or provide ostinati patterns to the concluding sections of the songs. A singer may inteject the *hatsyiatysia* with the word, *ehrihrihri...* and a response, *eshia* from the chorus, or s/he may express, *mino breakim*, to which the chorus would respond, *miano fayam*, (meaning, keep breaking and firing it) to motivate the singers and create excitement. In the Ewe *adzida* drumming/performance, the lead/master drummer may play specific rhythms in postlude to some songs to create interest, and heighten the singing. When enough rounds of the songs have been sung, or at the appropriate time, a cantor would signal for the section to be brought to an end. This may be followed by announcements, or prayer and/or music/dance tribute to the ancestors and Supreme Being, and short dramatic sketches, followed by another round of integrated drumming, singing and dancing in the manner discussed above. Additional rounds of the performance may be presented until the entire performance is brought to an end. A similar arrangement may be seen in some other African performances.

The Climax of Drumming/Performance

There are heightening moments of every performance when participants would intensify their parts and charge the atmosphere. In the traditional settings, the major climax may occur around the ending or during the last round of the performance. In *gohu*, this is the moment when two or three master drummers would play some melo-rhythmic texts together, to engage in dialgoue with the chorus/dancers. The master drummers may play, *tototo krebe gide gazento*, which the chorus/dancers would interpret, *Tsyielele Dzigba le mɔ dzi gbɔ na*, meaning, *Tsyielele Dzigba* is on the way approaching. The drummers would repeat the text, to which the chorus would again respond: *Tsyielele Dzigba le mɔ dzi gbɔna, 'mega, 'megawo va sɔ di koto, tsyielele Dzigba le mɔ dzi gbɔ na*, meaning, *tsyielele Dzigba* is on the way approaching, many elders have gathered *tsyielele* Dzigba is on the way approaching. (The text announces the arrival of the patrons in the performance circle). Also, at the height of *adzogbo* performance, the chorus may sing a song such as:

> Eya do me
> Eee eya do me
> Eya do me
> Ya ya yaa eya do me
>
> The performance has become lively
> Yes, the performance has become lively
> The performance has become lively,
> Yes, yes, yes, it has become lively.

The *adzogbo* cantor and chorus may also chant the following text in a call and response manner to heighten the performance:

> L: Ayiwoele yiwoele yiwoele yi (2x)
> C: Ayiwoele yiwoele yiwoele yi (2x)
> L/C: adzohu ne dze to madu to de me (2x)
> Kpoto lizo iye iye.
>
> Ayiwoele yiwoele yiwoele yi (two times)
> adzohu should enter a certain circle and I will dance it.

Figure 149. The Ghana Dance Ensemble climaxing Atsyia performance at the University of Ghana, Accra.

Photo: retaken by Modesto Amegago, Dec. 2011, by courtesy of the artistic Director Aryetey.

At these climactic moments, some lead drummers in *agbadza* and *djembe* ensembles may carry their drums into the center of the circle and intensify the drumming, move from one part of the circle to the other and play for particular or group of dancers, who would also intensify their dancing, singing and clapping. Other performers and audience members would be moved to intensify their drumming, singing and dancing. This is the moment when a Yoruba *dundun* or *iyaalu* drummer would play *ijalu*, non textual rhythmic punctuations characterized by rapid hand and stick strokes, to which the dancers would respond by kicking their legs outward (Euba, 1990, 143). The *iyaalu* drummer would also play a variety of rhythms, signals or texts to display his wealth of artistic knowledge and elicit appropriate response from the dancer. In turn, the dancer would exhibit a variety of movements to demonstrate his/her mastery of the dance routine and skills, in trying to out do the drummer. In the process, both the drummers and dancers inspire one another (Euba, pp. 424-425). Some audience members who are moved by the performance would sing along with *iyaalu* drummer, or raise a familiar song, which the *iyaalu* drummer may sing on the drum with them from the beginning to the end, or up to a point and digress to another song or rhythmic pattern. Sculptural images (*dufozi* in Ewe) representing divinities and ancestors would be brought into the performance circle at this time.

The Drumming/Performance Finale

There is usually a fall in the dynamics of the drumming/performance after the drummers/performers have expended much energy, during which time a master drummer would play the ending signal or song, or a cantor would raise the ending song, or signal the participants to bring the performance to an end. Some *djembe* drummers may end their performance with phrases such as *tigi takatakatakatakatakataka...pre-pedem pe-pede pede pa...* A Wolof *sabar* drummer may end his/her drumming with phrases such as, gide gide gin ta!. The concluding patterns of the Ewe youths' *bɔbɔɔbɔ* may include *den gada gada gada dedegren*. In addition, the concluding phrases of the Ewe *agbadza* may include *gaden gaden gaden gaden*, or *gatsya gatsya gatsya...kplogba gide-ga gblo*. The ending patterns of *adowa* drumming may include *ke-ken-ke-ken- ke-ken- ken-gen- kedegedegedegedegede.-ke ken*. The *kete* master drummer may play a lengthy finale such as, *tege gre-gre-gre, tege tege tege gre-gre, tege gre-gre-gre, tege-tege tetegedege dege, tege tete gedege tege- tege gregregregregre, gregregre tege gregre, gren- gren...* The finale patterns of *gohu* may include ... *dzadzin dzadzin dzadzin dzadzin dzadzadzadzin, dzadzadzadzin...*, *toto teto teto teton, gazegide ga den to-to kidega*.

It is usual for the chorus to prolong or repeat the last few lines or phrases of the finale song or the whole finale song in integrated drumming, singing and dancing, after the main performance has been brought to an end. Some drummers may play additional drum rolls or patterns at the very end of the performance (to cool it down). Some performing groups may engage in another procession from the performance setting to a designated location where they would end the procession before dispersing to their various destinations. For example, at the end of the Hutu's performance, the drummers would balance their drums on their heads and play them in procession to exit the main performance setting. Similarly, the Akan, Ewe, Dagbamba and Yoruba drummers/performers would engage in a final procession from the performance setting, or ceremonial grounds to designated places, where they would end the procession and disperse to their various destinations. Members of some Ewe performing groups at home and in the Diaspora may gather in their patrons' houses at the end of the performance, to evaluate the performance and conducts of the members, review their financial contributions, spendings and account balances, share drinks or food before dispersing to their various homes.

Duration of the main drumming/performance

The duration of the main performance depends upon the style, occasion, purpose and schedule of the performance, the duration of activity with which the performance is associated, the number of times the performance is repeated and audience reactions to the performance. Some repertoires are relatively short while others such as *agbekɔ*, *adzogbo*, *gohu* and *Adowa* feature a wide variety of movements, songs and drumming patterns. Other performances such as Yewe, Akom and *kete* feature a variety of pieces that form a suite. Regardless of the length of a performance type, it may be repeated over and over again. An afternoon performance (in African traditional society) may last between three to five hours; a morning performances may last between two to three hours while a wake keeping performance may last (for several hours) till the next morning. Performances during inaugural ceremonies may last for about eight hours (morning and afternoon) in the first day, and four to five hours in the afternoons of the remaining two or six days. About three or four rounds of integrated drumming, singing and dancing would be featured during an afternoon performance. Where various performing groups take turns to perform during a festival or ceremony, each group may be allotted between 10 to 30 minutes (depending on the number of performing groups).

A full length performance in contemporary theaters may last for about two hours and may condense different pieces or scenes within the over all performance. Some school presentations may last between thirty minutes to an hour. The audience may prolong the performance by requesting another song or a repeat of a particular piece.

Factors that Contribute to Good or Successful Drumming/Performance

Good drumming is judged or appreciated by those who are familiar with its purpose or know what to look for in a given context. An evaluator may be a drummer, a dancer, singer, child, an adult female or male; farmer, fisherman, hunter, a member or leader of a religious group; a chief/king, queen or a student, or a teacher, or a contemporary cultural critic. The various African societies have ways of determining the factors that contribute to good and successful drumming/performance. Good drumming/ performance may be observed on how well a drummer articulates the drum sounds: rhythmic and melo-rhythmic patterns, tones and pitches and the dynamics of the drumming to communicate the intended message and arouse the feelings, emotions and thoughts of the performers and listeners in specific and various contexts. In addition, good drumming would be seen in the drummer's mastery of skills, knowledge of the drumming/musical repertoire and ability to play the various rhythms or texts in conformity with the musical structure. It would further be seen in the drummer's ability to conform to the timing of the performance.

Good drumming also manifests in the blending of the various instrumental sounds, songs and movements, determined by the tuning of the instruments to create contrast, interest and harmony. It further manifests in the collaboration between the various drummers; the ability of the supporting and complementary instrumentalists to maintain steady patterns, conform to the timeline, articulate their patterns in relation to the master drum patterns, play certain patterns softly as the master drummer articulates and improvises his patterns. Good drumming would also be seen in the ways the master drummer repeats, varies and ornaments his patterns, pauses and leaves room for the supporting instruments to feature. The drummers' ability to coordinate the drumming patterns with songs, dance movements, and related elements also contribute to good drumming. A lead drummer has to ensure that a particular song is about to end before he or she introduces a new rhythmic pattern, and that certain drum patterns correspond with specific dance movements and songs.

The versatility of a drummer, his ability to play sequences of rhythmic patterns in the repertoire also contributes to good drumming.

Good drumming also depends on mutual relations among the drummers, singers and dancers and their conformity to the performance ethics. Nketia notes that, among the Akan, a drummer is considered a sacred person and is immune from assaults and annoyances. Society expects drummers to focus and play very well when a dancer steps into the ring. They are not expected to stop abruptly when a dancer is in the middle of the dance or in the dancing ring, particularly if she or he is an elder and a respectable member of the community. However tired they may be, the drummers must continue until the dancer has left the ring. If the drummers are too tired to continue, the master drummer must communicate this with the dancers through the appropriate drum signal so that the dancer(s) would end the dance or leave the ring before the drumming is ended. Likewise, dancers are expected to comport themselves and avoid stepping into the ring towards the end of the performance, to round of their dancing in a timely manner and not to over tax the patience and endurance of the drummers. If they go contrary to these expectations, the drummers may react to them in a negative way (Nketia, p. 161).

In addition, the wearing of shoes and sandals is usually prohibited in many performances in African traditional setting (although the royal Damba drummers/dancers among the Dagbamba of Northern Ghana and gumboot dancers of South Africa may be allowed to wear boots). Nketia also states that, in *fɔntɔmfrɔm* and *kete*, a commoner must strip his cloth to his waist, dance bear feet and with nothing in his hand. In addition, the use of certain gestures and handkerchief is the privilege of chiefs and noblemen (*aberempɔn*) (Nketia, pp. 160-161). Similarly, the wearing of shoes and sandals are prohibited in many Ewe performances. However, in the present days, one may observe some members of Ewe performing groups wearing sandals and shoes. For example, during a recent visit to Ghana in 2010 and 2011, the writer observed all the members of *Mamprobi* performing group at Dzelukɔfe-Keta wearing sandals during a performance; and another participant in a performance at Dalive-Agave wearing a pair of canvas. One

Figure 150. A spectator raising his hands and fore fingers and middle fingers in appreciation of a performance at a funeral at Dalive, V/R. Ghana.

Photo: Modesto Amegago, July 2011

may also see some professional dancers expressing gestures that were originally reserved for kings/chiefs. Such practices may give an indication of change or flexibility in the enforcement of certain performance ethics, or the violation of such ethics.

Nketia notes further that traditionally, when an *adowa* or *fɔntɔmfrɔm* or *kete* dancer steps into the ring, she or he greets the master drummer and offers him a sum of money (about four shillings in the past) for a drink (of palm wine). Sometimes, a dancer's gift is anticipated by a drummer who praises him as soon as she or he enters the ring in order that she or he might give freely. When the atmosphere of goodwill has been established, the drummers will keep drumming for a reasonably long period of time to enable the dancer to express himself (Nketia, p. 160). When another dancer or commoner steps without first establishing an atmosphere of goodwill, the drummers may not play in full force, or they may play with one hand instead of two hands, or keep playing the prelude to the piece and ignore the dancer's communication, or stop before the end of the piece. If the dancer understands the drum language, the master drummer might say to him, "you are not playing the game" (*wore agorɔ pɔtɔpɔtɔ*), or "a person becomes a drummer that he might get something to eat" (*ɔkyerema yeye o ye adea di*). Master drummers may get impatient with dancers who keep ignoring the music and make rude remarks to them on the drum (I am seeing foul things). Society gives drummers the privilege of making such remarks and of saying similar things to the chief if his presents of drinks to the drummers are not forth coming (Nketia, p. 161). In extreme cases, some Ewe drummers may throw a drumming stick at a dancer who persistently ignores specific drumming/dancing patterns.

Audience reactions to the performance also contribute to its success. For example, the audience may actively participate, comment, critique and motivate the drummers/performers. Audience members may comment on how well the drummers articulate, ornament, and improvise their patterns, or on their skills and knowledge of the repertoire, their coordination of the various artistic elements and the relationship among the various performers. Regardless of the tastes and preferences of the various participants and observers, good drumming may appeal to the young and old, leaders and the led, and members of various socio, economic and cultural groups on some level. It implies that when the drumming or performance fails to conform to all or most of the above mentioned values, it would be judged as unsatisfactory, unpleasant or not good enough.

Difficulty of Determining Good or Successful Drumming within Cross Cultural Settings

It may be difficult for cross cultural audiences and participants to determine the factors that contribute to good or successful drumming/performance unless they have become familiar with the artistic and cultural values. Some cross cultural observers may find it difficult to understand or relate to the polyrhythmic sounds of African drums. Some may try to evaluate the performance on the basis of their own cultural sounds or values. Others may find African instrumental sounds that are similar to the sounds they usually hear in their own music/environment appealing to their tastes and preferences. These problems often compel some African drummers to adapt the quantity and sounds of their instruments to satisfy the tastes and preferences of the new audiences. However, in the process of adapting the African drumming to the new environments, the drummers continue to lose some essential qualities of African performances. In this situation, it is imperative for the African drummers to educate the cross cultural observers/listeners about the values that shape their performances and form the basis of their evaluation. It is also important for the drummers to engage in constant reflections on their performances in the process of negotiating between the various cultures, and in order to determine the limits of such adaptations.

Appreciating Drumming

Individuals or group of performers, observers or listeners may show their appreciation for African drumming on many levels. This may take the form of audience members taking active part in the performance by singing, dancing and playing rattles. It also takes the form of the audience members wiping the faces of drummers, wrapping cloths around their necks, pouring talcum powder on the drummers' necks, fixing coins or paper money on their foreheads, or by throwing money into the performance setting. Some performers or audience members may raise their fore-fingers and middle fingers towards the performers, fan them and spread cloths in front of them to walk on in appreciation of African drumming. Appreciation of African drumming also takes the form of spectators and dancers kneeling down, or bowing in front of the drummers, touching the ground, their chests and foreheads with their hands. Spectators may nod their heads, smile, move their bodies, imitate performers, comment positively, cry, remain silent, or express surprise, or give standing ovation in appreciation of African drumming. They may also shake hands with the drummers, share drinks or food with them after the performance in appreciation of the performance. The audience may show their disapproval by shouting, frowning faces, covering or plugging their ears, remaining silent and leaving the performance arena.

This chapter has elucidated the techniques, structure and processes of African drumming/performance, the values that contribute

Figure 151. A leader/dancer appreciating drumming by fixing money on the foreheads of the drummers of Dagomba donno and gungun

Photo: Modesto Amegago, Oct. 28 2011.

to good drumming and modes of appreciating African drumming/ performances. In conclusion, the writer would like to reiterate that the acquisition of the drumming skills and awareness of the structure, processes and factors that constitute good drumming would enhance people's participation, understanding, evaluation and appreciation of African drumming/performances. The following chapter will shed light on the linguistic or textual basis of African Drumming.

Chapter Eight

Linguistic or Textual Basis of African Drumming

Included in the functions of African drumming is its use as a medium of communication on the basis of language or text. The textual basis of African drumming has been investigated by scholars such as A. M. Jones (1959), Kwabena. Nketia (1963), David Locke and Godwin Agbeli (1980), David Locke (1990), Akin Euba (1990) and Patricia Tang (2007).

In some of the previous chapters, we have learned that some drums have been specifically designed to represent the voices of individuals and social groups, and the sounds of other environmental creatures and features. Language is defined as a body of words and a system for their use, common to a community, nation, or people living within the same geographical area, or having a common cultural tradition. Language is also defined as a mode of communication by voice, using arbitrary auditory symbols in conventional ways with conventional meanings (The Random House College Dictionary, Revised Edition, 1988, p. 753). However, the definition of language in the African context should include human movements, gestures and other environmental sounds that communicate something meaningful to group of people and individuals. The speech or textual mode of drumming is a deliberate attempt by drummers to "speak with their drums", or to articulate or imitate human utterances: speech tones and phrases and vocal melodies on the drums. As Nketia notes, words, phrases and sentences may be transformed into drums sounds, and reinterpreted in verbal terms by the drummer and listener (Nketia, p. 32). He further states that in considering drumming, one must recognize on one level, drum sounds which are organized into rhythms and tones patterns and on the other hand, the verbal correlates in terms of which the drum sounds may be produced or interpreted (ibid, 32).

In his book, *Drumming in Akan Communities*, Nketia refers to signal mode of drumming, speech mode of drumming and dance mode of drumming. He also states that the association of drum sounds with texts finds its greatest expression in speech mode of drumming where texts are used solely for their communicative value, but it is to be found in some measure in the other modes of drumming (ibid. p. 32). Here, Nketia is referring to the use of the Akan male and female *atumpan* and other drums in communication on textual basis in social, ceremonial and other performance contexts. The Akan male and female *atumpan* drums have been adopted by many Ghanaian groups and institutions for use in communication on speech basis and in music and dance performances. However, the various African groups also use some of their own instruments to communicate on linguistic or textual basis. The Ewe, particularly, would employ the *atimevu*, lead drum (which has a relatively wider tonal range) and supporting drums such as *sogo*, *kidi*, *kloboto*, *totodzi* and *kagan* (in *agbekɔ*) and *vuga* and *vuvi* (in *bɔbɔɔbɔ*) to communicate on linguistic or textual basis while the Dagbamba of northern Ghana would use the *donno* and *brekete* for the same purpose.

Although, the textual basis of drumming is no longer emphasized by drummers in many contemporary African societies, there is much empirical evidence on the use of drums in communication on linguistic or textual basis in many African traditional societies. The textual mode of drumming would still be observed among some Wolof, Yoruba, Dagbamba, Akan, Ewe, Ga and some other African drummers. Akin Euba notes that almost all the Yoruba drums may be used to communicate on textual basis, but *iyaalu* or *dundun* ensembles are mostly used in linguistic communication.

The *iyaalu*, functions both as a musical and speech instrument. He notes further that of the various parameters of human speech, only rhythm and intonation are produced on *iyaalu* (Euba, p. 191).

The textual mode of drumming involves the playing of both rhythmic texts and melodies (or melo-rhythms), sometimes in combination with non-textual rhythms/patterns, especially in integrated music and dance performances. In such performances, the drum texts, other instrumental sounds, songs and dance movements are interwoven. Thus, an Ewe *adzogbo* drummer may be speaking, singing and articulating the dance/narratives at a given time. This implies that, in integrated performances, the drum texts, songs and dance movements are intertwined and constitute a holistic performance.

Characteristics of African Drum Texts

Drum texts that feature in African performances vary in lengths: there are short texts that form the main patterns of a supporting drum or signal drum or an introductory pattern of a lead drum. These include the patterns played on the single royal drums of chiefs/kings. An example of such texts (played on the Ewe *Agblɔvu* drum of Tɔgbui Zewu, a divisional chief of Aŋlɔ state) is interpreted as Zewu zea tɔgbɔe wokpɔne le na"; " The pot that is greater than another pot is along a river bank". There are also lengthy texts that range from a few phrases to long drumming patterns and highlight sub-divisions of phrases and statements. Examples of these texts are those played in *fɔntɔmfrɔm, akantam* suite, (which according to Nketia, are over seventy-seven in number), as well as texts that are played on some Yoruba and Ewe lead and secondary drums (Nketia, p. 138). Drum texts are usually composed in the languages and dialects spoken by the drummers and their communities but some new texts reflect a fusion of local languages, English and French. The texts are usually cast in ordinary or colloquial languages, proverbs and allusions.

There may or may not be a one to one correspondence between speech syllables or phrases and drum strokes or phrases. For example, a single drum stroke may represent one or more speech syllables; and two or more drum strokes may represent one speech syllable. The drums texts do not exactly mimic human voices but their close association with human sounds enables people familiar with the performance and culture to understand them.

Euba states further that different sentences may have the same tonal structure and in order to be able to interpret any of the sentences (played on the drum), it is necessary to have adequate knowledge of the context in which they are expressed and of the general train of thought preceding the expression, so that possible alternatives can be judged in term of their logicality, or in relation to the context. Hence, colloquial usage often facilitates the interpretation of the drum texts. For when two different sentences are otherwise undifferentiated in their rendition in the drumming, the more colloquial of the two could be the correct one (Euba, p. 198). For these reasons, proverbs and sayings already well known to people are more easily decipherable when played on drum than the totality of unfamiliar texts (Euba, p. 199).

Variations occur when drummers in different localities continue to reinterpret the texts in their own ways (on the basis of their subjective experiences). Other performers and listeners may give their own interpretations to some of the texts (including drum patterns that were not originally intended to communicate on textual basis). Some of these interpretations/meanings may become accepted by members of a performing group or community over time. All these may lead to varied interpretations of some of the drum texts.

Drum Mnemonic, Vocables or Syllables

In addition to the textual basis of African drumming, many drummers would express their drumming patterns on the basis of what some writers refer to as mnemonics, vocables, and what Nketia refers to as nonsense syllables. The Ewe refer to these vocables or syllables as *vugbe* (lit. meaning, drum sound or language) while the Akan call them *wɔpɔtɔ*. Examples of syllables that are expressed by Ewe drummers are: *ga* (used to express a bouncing hand stroke at the center of the drum head), *gi* (used to express a pressed hand stroke at the edge of the drum head), *de,* (used to express a bouncing stroke near the edge of the drum head), and *to,* (used to express a high pitch stroke at the center of the drum head while pressing the membrane with the other hand/ stick). Similarly, the syllables such as *pe, de, pa, ta* may be heard in some Akan, Ga and Mande drumming. These syllables may be viewed as an abstraction of drum sounds, or the uttering of drum sounds according to the ways they resonate in the ears of the drummers/listeners. Nketia notes (in his discussion of the Akan drumming) that these syllables are an extension of the common phono-aesthetic habit of imitating, non speech sounds, such as mechanical noises, animals' cries, songs of birds, by means of speech sounds (Nketia, p. 33). They are also used when one wishes to speak out the musical rhythms of a particular drum or the inte-grated rhythms of a complete ensemble, in such a way as to bring out the duration of the drum beats and the tone contrast on which the particular piece is built (Nketia, p. 33). Thus, instead of giving the meaningful translation of series of drum beats, the drummer may choose to speak the rhythm in vocables or syllables; she or he may speak them where a proper translation of a section of drum patterns is forgotten, or obscure, or where the drummer is unwill-ing either to give out secrets or to say what is better conveyed by drums than by word of mouth (Nketia, p. 33). They also form part of juvenile texts sung by some parents to their children, to develop their consciousness of rhythm, and enhance their language learn-ing. An example of the juvenile text sung by the Ewe parents to children is: *tigidi gidi, tigidi gidi, dada yi tsilefe gbɔgbɔ ge fia,* meaning, tigidi gidi tigidi gidi, mother is gone to take a bath and will return soon. The syllables are also used in story telling to imitate the sounds of certain instruments, and to accompany or interject actions and speeches of certain characters and enliven the story.

A syllable may be short or long, and may correspond with the duration of the drum beat it expresses. In some cases, one syllable may be used to express more than one stroke; or more than two syllables may represent fewer strokes. An impression of shortness or rapidity is usually conveyed by "r" sound in sequence of vocables/syllables; the syllable before the rolled consonant is comparatively shorter than the one which begins with it. As noted by Nketia, some syllables are open; others are closed by *m, n, sh, tsi* sounds (to indicate softness or muting) Syllables are usually of a plosive type (*p*, *b*, *t*, *d*, *k*, *g*), except for the "r", which is often used to convey a sense of rapidity, and occasionally, "h" in weakly accented high drum beats (Nketia, p.33).

Nketia further notes that, the vowels used depend on the sonority of the drum, or the quality of the drum beat. Front vowels are commoner than back vowels though the latter will be found to occur rather frequently in verbal imitation of hourglass drums (Nketia. p. 34). Slight differences in weight, pitch, or rhythmic grouping of drum beats may be reflected in the sequence of syllables (and in the choice of initial consonant). In Akan drumming, consonants, such as k and g, may be used to represent heavy beats, while others such as t and d, represents light beats, as in, *pe te pete pete*, and *gede gede gede* (Nketia, p. 34). Similarly, in Ewe drumming, consonants such as g and d, may represent heavy beats (such as ga, de, gre). For successive short beats, open syllables are rarely repeated for example, *pepepepe*, or *tetetete*, whereas successive long beats may be represented by the same syllables, for example, *pen pen pen pen*, *ten ten ten ten*, or *kon kon kon kon kon* (Nketia, p. 35).

Similar and differing syllables may be used by players of the Wolof, Mande/Susu, Malinke, Baga, Dagbamba, Ga and Lala drums such as the *sabar, lung* and *brekete*, *djembe* and *djundjun*, *bugarabou*, *kpanlogo* and *icibitucu*. These vocables or syllables are shaped by the languages and dialects spoken by the drummers, the size and sounds of the instruments, weight and speed of the drum beats and individual idiosyncrasies. New syllables may emerge during performance processes and add to the existing ones. With time, some drums came to derive their names from some of the syllables that are used in expressing their sounds. Examples of these are the *gudugudu*, bowl-shaped drum and *dundun* hourglass drum of the Yoruba; *donno*, hourglass drum of the Dagbamba; *dundun* and *kenkeni* of Mande and sub cultures, *gugutegu*, ritual drum of the Ewe of Notsie, Togo; *kidi*, (also called *asivui* and *kpetsi*) supporting drum of the Ewe. These names in turn provide clues for remembering the sounds of the instruments. The drum syllables are now popularly used by drumming instructors/educators and students in some African and North American performing arts institutions. Despite the popularity of the vocables or syllables, some drummers would readily express their drumming patterns on speech/textual basis. I will now provide examples of the drum texts and vocables or syllables used in the various performance contexts.

Drum Texts in Context

Judging from the analysis of the empirical data, the texts that are played in various contexts of African drumming, express multifaceted themes such as tribute to the spirits of the trees, and animals whose products are used in making the drums; the cock and clock bird that awake people at dawn and alert them during the day, and the ancestor drummers, divinities and God who are the originators and custodians of the performances. The Akan call such texts "the awakening". Some of the texts express greetings, appellations, praises, commendation of peoples. Others recount the genealogies and histories of states, chiefs, kings, queens, ordinary individuals and their activities while some relate to the experiences of the age, sex, gender, military, occupational and religious groups. Texts that are played in traditional military contexts express themes of toughness, bravery, greatness, alertness, readiness for combat, communication with divinities and the Supreme Being for guidance and protection; perseverance, victory, defeat and psychological state of the militants, etc.

The texts that are featured in religious contexts express themes such as a call to duty, tribute to drummers, singers/cantors; ancestors, divinities and the Supreme Being; indigenous African, Moslem and Christian's prayer; some in the form of jubilation over happy occasions, such as marriage, wedding, completion of apprenticeship; sympathy over misfortune, revelations; warning about imminent danger, desire for goodness, God's guidance and protection; love relations, sanctity, beauty, perseverance and hope.

In addition, the texts that manifest in drumming associated with socialization express themes of patience, commendation, beauty, social relations, feelings of love, arrival of loved ones, jealousy, patience, social vices, punishment, forgiveness; hailing of leaders, advice and warning to community members; and topical themes.

Texts that are featured in youths' performances express the youths' yearning for the return of their mothers, their comparison of mothers to young ladies, physical appearances of peers, beauty, youths' desire for drink and food; and desire to compete with one another; youths cautioning of peers; their feelings of pains in certain parts of the body, reference to political leaders, the consequences of certain social vices as well as some socially repressed themes.

Within the context of funerals, some of the drum texts express a wish to be surrounded by family members in the after life, a wish to depart without leaving any debt behind; sorrow, sympathy, condolences, a wish for the return of the deceased to life and the fate that awaits the body after life.

Some drum texts express provocative and socially repressed or immoral themes because of the critical roles of African drummers. Such texts may reflect the social realism and may be aesthetically pleasing when played on the drums. Below are some of the drum texts and their contextual functions:

Excerpts from African drum Texts

The following examples are drawn from the Akan "Awakening" text as documented by Nketia. In the first example, the drummer evokes the spirit of the tree which is used in making the drum:

> Tweneboa Akwa
> Tweneboa Kodua
> Kodua Tweneduro
> Tweneduro, wokɔ, baabi a
> Merefre wo, yese bra
> Meresua, momma menhu.
>
> Wood of the drum Tweneboa Akwa,
> Wood of the drum Tweneboa Kodua
> Wood of the drum Tweneboa Kodua, tweneduro
> Cedar wood if you have been away,
> I am calling you, they say come,
> I am learning, let me succeed (Nketia, p. 6; 183).

In the second text, the drummer evokes the spirit of the drum pegs:

Obua Maniampon Akyerema repoma no
Obua, wokɔ baabi a
Merefre wo; yese bra
Meresua, moma menhu

Drum pegs knocked in by drummers,
Drum pegs if you have been away,
I am calling you; they say come,
I am learning, let me succeed (Nketia, p. 10; 183).

A drummer would address the string that is used in making the drum as follows:

Obofunu Ampasakyi,
Obofunu ɔkaa akyire
Obofunu wokɔ baabi a,
Merefre wo; yese bra
Meresua, momma menhu.

Ampasakyi, drum string of the bark of obofunu,
Obofunu, the last born,
Drum string, if you have been away
I am calling you, they say come
I am learning let me succeed (Nketia, p. 11; 183).

A drummer would also address the animal whose skin is used in making the drum as follows:

Kotomirefi Gyaa kɔtɔkɔ,
Kɔtɔkɔ so no me ne sono,
Esono Wokɔ baabia
Merefre wo; yese bra
Dee ohunuu won nyinsene,
Wanhunu w'owosee,
Yenkɔ ye nim, yereko,
Yenkɔ ye nim yeredwane,
Dabere esono abefere,
Esono ebu akuma,
Okokuroko-bedi-atuo e,

Esono wokɔ baabi a,
Merefre wo; yese bra,
Meresua moma menhu

Elephant Kotomrefi that frees Kotoko
Elephant that swallows other elephants
Elephant, if you have been away,
I am calling you they say come
He that saw your birth never apprehend your begin-
ning
He that knew of your formation
Never saw how you were born.
Shall we go forward, we shall find men fighting
Shall we press on we shall find men fleeing...
Let us go forward in great haste
Treading the path beaten by the elephant
The elephant that shatters the axe
The monstrous one, unmindful of bullets
Elephant if you have been away,
I am calling you, they say come,
I am learning, let me succeed (Nketia, p. 11; 183).

A drummer would also address the drum sticks as follows:

ɔfema duo nkonta
Nkonta kɔtɔkɔrɔ
Woakɔ baabi a
Merefrewo; yese bra,
Meresua momma menhu

Drum stick of ɔfema wood
Curved drum stick,
Drum stick of ɔfema wood,
If you have been away,
I am calling you; they say come
I am learning, let me succeed (Nketia, p.13; 183).

A drummer would also pay tribute to the cock and clock-bird that
awaken people at dawn as follows:

Aboa Kokotsinaka Asamoa,

Yegye wo Deeben?
Yegye wo Anyaado
Yegye wo kyerema ba
Kyerema ba da nanye anɔpatutuutu
Meresua moma menhu

Kokokyinaka Asamoa the clock bird
How do we greet you?
We greet you with Anyaado.
We hail you as the drummer's child
The drummer's child sleeps and awakes with the dawn
I am learning, let me succeed (Nketia, p. 44; 184).

He or she would pay tribute to heavens and earth and the creator as follows:

The heavens are wide, exceedingly wide,
The earth is wide, very very wide
We have lifted it and taken it away
We have lifted it and brought it back
From time immemorial
The God of old bids us all
Abide by his injunctions
Then shall we get whatever we want
Be it white or red
It is God, the creator, the gracious one
Good morning to you God, good morning
I am learning let me succeed (Nketia, p. 44).

Similarly, a Yoruba *dundun* drummer would play an awakening text for Timi (king) of Ode as (documented by Euba) follows:

Ola ojire	Man of prestige, you have woken well.
Timi Ojire	Timi, you have woken well (Euba, p. 205).

A *dundun* drummer would greet Shango (a divinity of thunder and lightning) with the following texts (as played to Euba by Ayankule):

N'Olukoso to to   Olukoso I address you
with great respect.

He or she would greet the female leader of Eleriko masquerade group with the following text (as played by Ayanbunmi):

Iya egbe oku oku   Mother of the group,
I greet you I greet you
Obinrin ju obinrin lo oku Women are greater than
women (Euba, p. 206).

The following examples are drawn from the appellations and
tributes played in honor of kings, queens and chiefs of certain
states. For example, the appellations played by an Ewe *atompani*
drummer to the state may include the following:

Aŋlɔ Kotsiklolo naketsi deka nɔ dzome bi nu
Aŋlɔ gɔdɔlifi
Du nɔ eme mase emenya
Xedzra kata ebe yede azi de wɔtete gbe.

Aŋlɔ Kotsiklolo, single firewood has cooked a whole
meal
Aŋlɔ circumventing,
A state in which you would reside without hearing it
secrets
A brave bird, that lays eggs in the desert/wilderness.

An Ewe atumpan drummer may address a chief as follows:

Tameklo tsitsi xoxo
Ebe yemenya mi na ʋɔga ʋɔgawo o
Ne ʋɔga ʋɔgawo mi ye ha
Wo adzɔ ye de tavi ade to

An aged riverine-turtle
That could not be swallowed by great pythons
Even if great pythons swallowed him
They would vomit him along a small river/pond
(cited from the Ewe oral literature).

Also, a Yoruba *dundun* drummer may play *oriki* (appellation) for his highness Oni of Ife (as documented by Euba) as follows:

> Erin lami soba jeje jeje

> Elephant that thrives on prestige, reign peacefully, peacefully (Euba, p. 200).

The following examples are drawn from texts that are integrated with the activities in the life of traditional rulers. Most of them are drawn from the work of Nketia among the Akan in 1963. If a chief is delaying in coming to a gathering, the drummer would address him as follows:

> Chief dress up and let us go
> Osei Asibe (the name of the chief of Kokofu), dress up and let us go
> Otiprape, foremost among his mates
> Chief dress up and let us go
> Osei the last born,
> Do you hear my message?
> Excerpt the heaven except the earth (two times) (pp. 146-147).

If a king is carried in a procession towards a gathering *mpintin* drum ensemble may play specific rhythms that are translated as follows:

> Meso agya mesoagya mentumi: I carry father, he is too heavy for me:

To this the bass drum responds:

> Dwa ho enwa: Can't cut bits off him to make him lighter (Nketia, p.135).

When the leader is approaching the gathering, an *atumpan* drummer may play the following text:

> Come chief come chief come chief,

> If he has been away, he is coming; sure he is
> Chief, walk in majesty
> Chief, take short strides
> Chief, do not hurry, lest you stumble
> Chief, slowly, chief, slowly.
> The leopard, the mighty one, slowly (Nketia, p. 147).

The chief/king/queen may be ushered unto his/her seat as follows:

> Chief you are about to sit down
> Sit down great one
> Sit down gracious one
> Chief you have plenty of sitting space
> Like the great branch, you have spread all over this
> place
> Let us crouch before him with swords of state
> Ruler, the mention of whose name causes great stir,
> Chief, you are like the moon about to emerge
> Noble ruler to whom we are indebted,
> You are like the moon;
> Your appearance disperses famine (Nketia, p. 147).

When an Ewe chief/king is about to speak, a royal (*agblɔvu*) drummer would announce it as follows:

> Kaba gbe dege Kaba gbe de ge: Akaba will command,
> Akaba will command (cited from the Ewe oral litera-
> ture).

As the chief/king or queen rises in preparation to depart from an assembly, a master drummer may play the following text:

> Arise arise, arise, arise,
> Arise, arise, arise, arise,
> The ruler of Sekyere has bestirred himself.
> The great toucan has bestirred himself
> Let the little ones lie low
> He has bestirred himself
> The chief has bestirred himself
> He has bestirred himself the gracious one
> He has bestirred himself the mighty one

Walk in majesty chief
Walk in majesty noble ruler
The leopard emerges from its lair under the tree.
It emerges from its lair and walks in majesty
Walk slowly in majesty, chief
Do not hurry lest you stumble (Nketia, p. 148-149).

In addition, the *mpintin* drummers may play the following texts during the closing dance of the (Akan) Adae ceremony:

Akwadaa mo: Well done young one
Yaa nua mo: Thank you brother: well done
                (Nketia, p. 40).

Examples of texts featured in Traditional Political and Military Contexts

The following are examples of texts/proverbs that are played within African traditional military and political contexts. They may be played by a master drummer, intermediary drummers or by the master drummer and accompanied drummers in dialogue or unison.

The first example is an excerpt from the Ewe *agbekɔ* music/ dance:

Gide gagin dzadzadzadza dzadzadzadzadza giden gagin...

Mibla godzi koko ko ko kokokokoko mibla godzi

Gird up your loin surely surely surely gird up your loin.

The second example is taken from the supporting drum patterns of *agbekɔ*:

Kagan: Mitso mitso: Get up, get up
Kidi: Kpɔ afe go dzi or Mi tso midzo: Look towards home, or let's get up and go
Totodzi: Dzogbe dzi dzi dzi: In the wilderness/desert

Gbedzi ko madɔ: I shall sleep in the desert/wilderness
(cited from the Ewe oral tradition).

The third example which is taken from the texts of a signal drum
of the (Akim Kotoku) *asafo* company is interpreted as follows:

Petepire woahyia petepire: Tough one you have met a
tough one (Nketia, p. 36).

The fourth example is taken from the Akan *Asafo* drumming as
follows:

Bodyguard as strong as iron
Fire that devors nations
Curved sticks of iron
We have leaped across the sea,
How much more the lagoon?
If any river is big, is it bigger than the sea
Come bodyguard, come bodyguard
Come in thick numbers
Locust in myriads
When we climb a rock, it gives way under our feet
Locust in myriads
When we climb a rock, it breaks into two
Come bodyguard, come bodyguard
In thick numbers (Nketia, p. 112).

The following examples are taken from the proverbial texts played
in unison by the heavy drums in the middle portion of *fɔntɔmfrɔm,
akantam* (which are said to be over seventy-seven in number):

1.

Okwan atware asuo
Asuo atware kwan
Ka Opanin ne hwan?
Okwan atware nsuo
Osuo atware kwan
Ka Opanin nehwan?
Ye boa kwan yi kotoo asuo yi 2x
Asuo yi firi titi

Woboa Asuo yi firi
ɔdomankoma ɔboadee
ɔtwe Adawurampong Kwamena
Hwan na ɔkesee ɔtwe se
Sɔ w'o akofena mu
ɔtwie dua tia
ɔde saa na epra ne ho (Nketia, p 139)

The path has crossed the river
The river has crossed the path
Which is the elder? (repeat from the beginning)
We made the path and found the river,
The river is from long ago
Truly the river is from
The creator of the universe
Duiker Adaurapon Kwamena
Who told the duiker to get hold of his sword
The tail of the duiker is short
But he is able to brush himself with it (Nketia, p. 139).

2.

ɔsakani Akuampɔn
Eye dee na Ofusuo da homa mu?
Efiri n'ano,
Akyereko Kwagyan
ɔtware Nwabe Aduru Ohwinm,

Wild bear Akuampɔn
How did it happen that the water buck got tied up in cords?
It is because he could not hold his tongue
Akyereko Kwagyan
He crosses the Nwabe river and gets to Ohwim (Nketia, p. 140).

Examples of texts featured within the Context of Religion

The following examples are drawn from drum texts that feature in African religious contexts. The first two examples are drawn from Ogun drumming (as narrated by a Yoruba drummer Ayansola and documented by Euba (1990)):

Ogun gbe rere ko mi-	May Ogun bless me with goodness
Orisa gbe te mi ko mi	Orisa bless me with what is my due (Euba, p. 208).

The ensuing examples are drawn from *adzohu/adzogbo*, (a sacred drumming/music/dance of the Fɔn-Ewe of southern Benin, Togo and Ghana.

The first text is usually played by the master drummer and sung by the dancers who move across the performance setting, holding mirrors in their hands to display their beauty). (The text was played and narrated by the master drummer Foli Adade, 1997; 1999).

    1. Drum language: Gazete gide gazete gide gadete ga zetega tedegide gadetega...

Eʋe:	Ewɔ ze atsyiadosi wɔ zebodza atsyiado legbasi wɔ zebodza
Meaning:	The stylists are ready to display (Foli Adade, 1997; 1999).

The second example is a tribute which is usually narrated by a lead dancer, played by the master drummer and re-enacted by the dancers. (The text was played and narrated by the master drummer Foli Adade, 1997; 1999; and by Emmanuel Agbeli, 2010):

Lead drum:	*Dzadza dzadza dzadza dzadza gadegi tegi krebe gi*
Eʋe:	*Dzadza dzadza dzadza dzadza avalu koe le kɔ na mi*
Meaning:	*Dzadza dzadza dzadza dzadza* tribute lies on our neck
Lead Drum	*gitsi gide gin gitsi kre gidega gadegitegi krebegi*
Eʋe:	*Minye avalu vutɔ minya avalu hasinɔ, avalu koe le kɔ na mi*

Meaning: We pay tribute to the drummer and
                composer/cantor, tribute lies on our
                neck (narrated by Foli Adade,
                1997; 1999; Emmanuel Agbeli,
                2010).

The third example is a melo-rhythm played by a master
drummer, sung by the chorus and danced by the dancers (in unison):
The text reflects a way of consulting a divinity or Supreme Being.

Lead drum: Gagren tototo gaden ga
                Gazetegiden tote dzadza dzin
                Gagren to to to gaden ga

Eʋe: Made yi vodu yɔge nade nu do
                Nugbeyila megbea go mado o
                M'ade yi vodu yɔ ge nade nu o.

One who calls upon God must bow (and touch the
ground with fore-head and chin)
One who calls upon God must bow
                One going on a journey does not
                refuse to knock
                One who calls upon God must bow
                (cited from the Ewe oral tradition).

In the fourth example, the lead drummer and dancers express
tribute to the Supreme Being in the Muslim's way: (The text
reflects a fusion of the Fon, Ewe and Yoruba languages.

Drum language: (begins with toto dzadza dzadza
dzadza...)
Gidegin tegi krebegin dzadzadzin dzadzadzin,
Gide gin tegi krebe gin gagi krebegin tegi krebe gin
detegagin gagide gagin gagiden gin gagide gagi,
gi to to to te, gi to to to ten (ga) gidegin tegi krebe gin

Eʋe:
Atsyiado megbɔna 'tsyia loloe
Dzadzadzin dzadzadzin
'guze atsyiado megbɔna tsyia loloe

Mafa lomboe mafa lomboe
Ka fe len ji Oluwa
Oluwa da da ani,
Oluwa da da ni, Allah
Oluwa da da ni
Atsyiado megborna Atsyia loloe.

The stylist, I am coming to display 2x.
The stylist, I am coming to display
Aguze, the stylist (says) I am coming to display,
I will pay tribute (give the land) to God,
God is a good God
God is a good God, Allah
God is a good God
The stylist, I am coming to display (narrated by
Emmanuel Agbeli, 2010).

In the following text, the lead drummer and dancers recount a
revelation that the past performers claimed to have received:

Drum language: Gidegadegi tegin tegiden gin to
Dzadzadzin dzadzadzin (2x)
Gidegadegi tegi tegiden gin
Vlo gadegi tegi tegiden gin
Vlo dagegin tegin tegiden gin (to)
Ga to-to degidega- ga to-to degidega
Gadegide gadento degide ga
Gagidegin- didegagin
Gatoto degidega gide (gren) gito- kren ga dzi tsi dzi
tsi dzi.

Eʋe: Dzosohu zu vodu bo do asi na dawoe
dzadzadzi dzadzadzin (2x)
Kpɔwoe zu vodu fo nu na gbetɔ
Hɔwoe zu vodu bo yɔ hubonɔ
Oyekple dɔ su nu mi, Oyekple dɔ su nu mi
Ata kudo viwoe dɔ sunu mi,
Aoo legba masi kpele,
Oyekple dɔ su nu mi dzidahutɔ kplokplo adza 'xɔlu mi.

Meaning:
Dzosohu became God and spoke to the brave ones,

> Dzadzadzin dzadza dzin
> Leopards became God and spoke to human,
> Eagles became God and spoke to the priest
> Oyekple revealed these to us, Oyekple revealed these
> to us
> Ata and vi revealed all these to us
> Our God would never fail us
> Master drummer, play (loudly)
> And make us strong (narrated by Foli Adade 1997; see
> also Locke and Agbeli, 1980, pp. 44-45).

In the past, *adzohu* performers would be secluded in the forest for many months where they would undergo rigorous training in communication with the divine. While in seclusion, they would claim to have received revelations from the Supreme Being, sometimes through neighboring creatures and divinities. Such revelations were composed into the drum texts, song and dance movements. (Ata and vi are special fruits that grow in Yorubaland: vi resembles kola nut; they are used by the Yoruba, Fɔn and Ewe religious leaders in rituals).

In the following example, the master drummer, complementary drummers and dancers narrate a story of an elderly man who was led by a young man into a dance circle, and knowing very well that the elderly man did not know how to dance the routine, the young man left him in the dancing circle. This act was considered by the elders a serious violation of the social ethics:

> Drum: Ga gi den-ga gi den- gigi te dzi gadegren-gite
> Dzadzadza dzadzadza gito
> Gito gide gin de ga gito gito gide gidega gi to
> Gito ga to to tegi krebe gin
> Ga gi den ga gi den gigi tegren gadegren gi te
> dzadzadzadza gito.

> Eʋe: Ovitse Ovitse wo di mi va gu me
> Bo zɔ hayahaya hayahaya muyɔ o.
> Ete na sɔm sɔ wua muyɔ wo
> Gbetɔ na sɔm sɔ wua muyɔ wo.
> Nku mɔ sude ma mɔ di di te 2x
> Ovitse ovitse wo di mi va gume

Bo zɔ hayahaya haya haya muyɔ wo.

Oh young boy young boy
You have brought me into the dancing circle
and walked away roughly I call you
Because of this would somebody kill me?
I call you.
A person to kill me, I call you
Remember what you have done to me
Young boy young boy
You have brought me into the dancing circle
And walked away roughly roughly I call you (narrated
by Foli Adade 1997; Emmanuel Agbeli, 1999; 2010;
see also Locke and Agbeli, 1980).

In the following example, the master drummer and dancers
express socially unacceptable behaviour or action and its consequences:

Eʋe: Ye wonye looo ye wonye fiafitɔ ame bada ye
wonye 2x
Wo fi fi tsya wom lɔ na gbe de o
Wowu ame tsya wom lɔ na gbe de o
Xoxoa lɔa? Devia ha nalɔ?
Wo kata ame dekae wonye
O ge mtuna xo na adaba o daba li xoxoxo ge va do 2x.
Fiafitɔ ku tsi agba ngɔ, oo ku tsi agba ngɔ oo (2x).

Such are the people they are 2x
They are thieves and bad people,
They steal and would not admit it
They kill and would not admit it
Would the elder admit for the younger to admit?
They are the same people
Beard does not narrate an old story to the eye lash
The eye lash was living long before the beard came
into being
There lies the thief dead in front of the stolen good
Ooh dead in front of the stolen good… (narrated by
Emmanuel Agbeli, 1999; 2010).

Texts featured in the context of socialization

The following are examples of texts that feature within social contexts. The first example is an excerpt from the *dundun/iyaalu* text played during Ikomo, child-naming ceremony:

Omo tuntun	New born baby
Enikan ii moro	No one fails to rejoice at the sight of
Tuntun ko ma yo	A new born baby
Omo tuntun	New born baby
	(Euba, 1990, p. 412).

The second example is an excerpt from Wolof *sabar* drumming piece called *Ceebujen* (as played by Tala Faye). The text was composed in honour of Lenge, a woman who used to cook delicious rice and fish.

Lenge, Ceebu Lenge, akadai sor ne: Lenge always prepares delicious rice and fish

The following text and song are played by two or three *gohu* lead drummers in dialogue with the chorus, to express a historical incident that led to the punishment of a citizen of Anexɔ or Little Popo (a town near the Benin boarder in Togo) by Kundo, a Dahumean king, also known as Gbehanzin, (a son of Glele) who reigned between 1889 and 1894, and people's desire for good or healthy life.

Lead drum: *Gahrebegite gin dzadza* (two times).
Eve: *Kpɔ gbale dzie Kundo la zɔ.*
Chorus: *Dzawutɔ be mele tɔgbuiwo fe zikpuia dzi*
Wobe ame ade laxɔ miawo srɔ le Wɔkedzi, adze sɔ sɔ sɔe
'Nexɔ tɔwoe wo nua Kundo wu ame le Wɔkedzi
'Meawo na da Kpe ne mianɔ sesie.

Gahrebegiten dzindzadza
Kundo will walk on leopard skin
Dzawutɔ says, I am on the ancestral stool

They say who will take our wife/husband at *Wɔkedzi*
It is all lies
The *Anexɔ* people have done it
Kundo murdered at *Wɔkedzi.*
People should give thanks for good health (cited from
the Ewe oral Gohu; Amegago, p. 163).

In addition a lead *gohu* drummer would express tribute to a
leader with the following text:

Lead drum: *Gadegre tento krebekrebe gadegren tento.*
Eʋe: Gbanake tatɔ krebekrebe, gbanake tatɔ.
English: *Gbanake* is our leader *krebekrebe Gbanake* is
our leader (Amegago, p.165).

In addition, the lead and complementary drum texts of *nyayito*
or *leafelegbe* (a musical style for the elderly Ewe) caution the performers as follows:

Lead drum: detega detega dzadzidzidzidzadzi... dza-
dzadzadza
Ewe: Gbasi nagbeagble kliya kliya
Complementary drums: shkidigish kri...
kitsikitsikitsikitsi...
Ewe: Godui vuvu nado kliyakliya

English: Refuse to trade, refuse to farm
You would wear worn out cloths
(See Amegago, p. 168).

An example of the lead and supporting drum texts of *dunekpoe* or *adzro* are interpreted as follows:

Lead drum: De ten-ga te di ge ga ga den ga
Responsorial drum: kidigin kitsi shkrikitsi...

Ewe: Tsoe kee ko, eya ha agblɔ nya woave woa
Meaning: Forgive him/her; would you be offended by
his/her utterances?

Texts featured in Youth Performances

The following examples are drawn from the Ewe and Ga youths' *gota, bɔbɔɔbɔ* and *kpanlogo* drumming. In the first example, the *gota* lead drummer expresses the youths' yearning for their mother:

Lead drum: Ga*zegitetegi Gazegitete gigiga.*
Eʋe: *Dada gbɔgbɔge dada*
               gbɔgbɔge namea.
English: Mother will return, mother will
               return to me (Amegago, p. 165).

In the second example, the lead drummer of *bɔbɔɔbɔ* refers to a West African leader and his country as follows:

Lead drum: Gadaga gadenga   gadegren gaden
English: Thomas Sankara, Burkina Faso

Another *bɔbɔɔbɔ* drum text is interpreted as follows:

Ge metua xo na daba o, daba o, daba o (two times).
Daba li xoxo hafi ge va dzɔ,
Gake kpekpe le ge ŋu wu adaba

Beard does not narrate an ancient story to the eye lash,
eye lash, eye lash (two times)
The eye lash was living long before the beard was born
But beard is heavier than the eye lash.

The following *kpanlogo* lead drum text compares a young lady to a mother:

Fine fine baby ino go fine pass your mother.

A student *atumpan* drummer in Ghanaian elementary and secondary school may play the following text during a change of lesson period, drum recital and school performances:

Wɔ dɔ za dodo ge

Work for the night is falling

Kuviatɔ fe agbleme ye da dzia vi do
Snakes breed on a lazy person's farm

Kutrikuku dua nugawo dzi
Perseverance overcomes difficulties
Dikeke afe gbegble
Unhealthy competition destroys households.

An example of texts featured on African Radios

An example of drum texts that are played during the Ghanaian news broadcast is as follows:

Ghana muntiee Ghana muntiee....Ghana listen, Ghana listen...

Drum Texts featured in the Context of Funerals

The following are examples of texts that are featured within the context of funerals.

Examples of drum texts that feature in the funeral music played by Ayanbunmi (as documented by Euba, 1990) are as follows:

Airin ono ni no sun bi:
May God grant that when I die, I will sleep surrounded by my children.

Emi naao ni je:
May I also not leave behind unsettled debts (Euba, p. 208).

The drum texts that are played by *atumpan, mpebi* and *nkwawiri* drummers during the Akan funeral rites include the following:

Damirifua due damirifua due damirifua due.
Condolences, condolences, condolences.

Another text which is played on the Kɔrabra signal drum of the Akan during the funerary rites of a chief of Akim Abuakwa is interpreted as:

Kɔrabra: When you go, return (Nketia, p. 36).

The above text also forms part of the lyrics of the dirge that is sung in the funeral context.

The texts played by the Ewe *atimevu* or *agblɔvu* or *atompani* drummer on funeral occasions may include:

Ewe: Ku nye nuxoxo dzɔ kple gbetɔ: Death originated
with human
Gake nɔvi tɔ wɔ nublanui: But death of a fellow is
pathetic
Babanawo: Condolences
Dzudzɔ… le nutifafa me. Rest… in peace

The discussion above has elucidated the textual basis of African drumming. It also points to the interconnection of human beings and other environmental creatures and features; the attributes of leaders, relationship between leaders and the led; and African socio-economic, educational, religious, ethical, political and aesthetic values. In view of the fact that much of these texts remain within the oral traditions, the researcher has to establish rapport with the cultural bearers and cross examine the data in order to check the veracity or authenticity of the texts. It has been noted that some of the texts express provocative and socially repressed themes because of the critical role of drummers in African societies. However, a researcher who sets out to investigate such themes may have to engage in dialogue with the cultural custodians (leaders) in order to solicit their views about representing such themes within public domain.

In this contemporary era, there has been a continuing shift from textual to text-less basis of drumming. As noted by Nketia, knowledge of the drum text in growing less and less widespread even among drummers themselves (Nketia, 1963, p. 42). This phenomenon is due to the emergence of new modes of documentation, communication, the generational gap and censorship of some of the texts (especially those that express socially repressed themes). However, there is much empirical evidence that most of the traditional forms of dance drumming which are now text free originally had verbal bases, which helped to preserve unwritten scores from generation to generation (Nketia, p. 42). Despite the contemporary challenges, the drums texts form part of the African epistemological system, and can be used to complement other modes of documentation, communication, creativity and education in this era. A study of the drum texts would enhance people's understanding of the Africans' historical and cultural experiences.

Some arts educators in Africa and African Diaspora settings of North America and Europe have been exploring some of the texts in teaching students about the communicative and documentary functions of African drumming thus creating awareness about the socio-cultural functions of the drums. However, the preservation and dissemination of the drum texts would require creating more communities of participants and listeners, and educating the people about the cultural significance and meaning of the texts, as well as encouraging them to use them in performances, creativity and education. These endeavors may involve the modification of some of the older instruments and sounds and the invention of new instruments that best facilitate the preservation and dissemination of this significant cultural heritage for the benefit of humanity.

I will now provide examples of the syllables that are used in expressing the African drum beats, drawing from my own experiences and research, and the works of my predecessors such as A. M. Jones, David Locke, Godwin Agbeli, Kwabena Nketia and other researchers.

Examples of the Vocables or Syllables expressing African drum beats, strokes, or sounds

doumbek *hand drumming syllables*

The syllables that are used in expressing the doumbek drumming patterns include:

Doum: a low bass sound produced by hitting the center of the drum with bare hand.
Ka: a high sound produced by hitting the outer edge part of the drum
Tek: a higher sharp sound produced by hitting near the rim of the drum (Balagula Ltd website, 1996).

The following examples are syllables used in expressing the various sounds played on the *djembe* drum. Of the many sounds that can be produced on the *djembe*. Many *djembe* drummers/ instructors usually focus on three main sounds that are referred to as bass, tone and slap or bass, bass, tone, tone and slap, slap (when doubling the sounds or playing each zone of the drum with the alternate (stronger and weaker) hands. The bass sounds are played at the center of the drum; the tone or open sounds are played in a zone closer to the rim or edge of the drum while the slaps are produced in the same zone near the rim or the edge of the drum. It is worth noting that various drummers may express their drumming patterns with slightly different syllables, but the following are syllables that may often be heard among many *jembefola*.

djembe *hand drumming patterns and syllables*

Go/gun: a bouncing (bass) sound produced by hitting the center of the drum with relaxed hand.

Do/dun: another bouncing (bass) sound produced by hitting the center of the drum with the alternate hand, usually after go/gun.

Pe: a high tone produced by playing the area near the rim or edge of the drum-wood with a hand or fingers.

De: another high tone (sound) produced by playing the area near the rim or edge of the drum-wood with an alternate hand or fingers, usually after pe.

Pa: a higher sound produced by slapping the area near the rim or edge of the drum with the hand/fingers.

Ta: another higher sound produced by slapping the area near the rim or edge of the drum with the alternate hand (using mostly the fingers), usually after "pa".

Prem: higher sound produced by hitting the area near the edge of the drum with hands almost simultaneously.

It should be noted that some drummers or drum instructors may express the bass sound as poom (see Isaak, 2006, pp. 7-8); some may also pronounce it as *ko* (in a lower tone) instead of *go*. Other drummers may produce some higher sounds by slapping the area around the center of the drum-head. Some may employ two or three fingers in producing some sounds around the area near the rim or edge of the drum, which they may express as ti, gi, ta, ka....

Thus, a combination of *djembe* sounds may be expressed as godo pata godo, godo kata godo, pede pata pata pata pata... or tigi taka taka taka, pre pedem pe pede bede pa.

Kpanlogo *hand drumming patterns and syllables*

The following are some of the syllables that are used by players of the Ga *kpanlogo* drums in expressing their main drum beats or strokes: (The drummers employ hand techniques in playing three main areas or zones: the center and near the rim or edge).

Ga/Go: a bouncing tone/sound produced with relaxed hand at the center of the drum-head

Do: a bouncing sound produced by hitting the center of the drum with alternate hand, usually after "go".

Pe/po: a mid tonal sound produced by hitting the area near the edge of the drum with relaxed hand or fingers.

De/do: another mid tonal sound produced by hitting the area near the edge of the drum with alternate hand/fingers, usually after "pe".

Pi: a soft or muting sound produced by pressing the fingers slightly at the center, or edge of the drum.

Ti: another muting sound produced by pressing the fingers at the area around the center, or edge of the drum, usually after "pi".

Pa: a higher pitch sound produced by slapping the area around the center or edge of the drum-head with slanted part of the three fingers.

Ta: another high pitch sound produced by slapping the area around the center or edge of the drum-head with slanted hand/fingers.

Prem/prom: a sound produced by hitting the area near the center or edge of the drum with a hand followed immediately by the other hand.

A combination of some of these sounds may be expressed as prem pede prem pede gadege-dege (patun); pem pede pitipiti pedebede pitipiti, pedem pata- pedem pata... in *kpanlogo* drumming.

Syllables expressing Akan hand drum beats

The following are some of the syllables that are used to express *apentemma/agyegyewa* hand drum beats:

Pe: a clear sound produced by hitting the area around the edge of the drum with relaxed hand/fingers.

De: a relatively clear and soft sound produced by hitting the area near the edge of the drum with alternate hand/fingers, usually after pe.

Pi: a soft/muting sound produced by pressing the fingers/hand on the center of the membrane.

Ti: another muting sound produced by pressing the fingers/ hand at the center of the drum, usually after pi.

A combination of the *apentemma* and *agyegyewa* sounds may be expressed as pede pede pata pata or pedem pedem piti piti.

Syllables expressing lung *or* donno *sounds*

Traditionally, *lung* or *donno* drummers explore three main pitches: low, middle and high. Locke maintains that the melodic intervals between these pitches can be compared with diatonic values. According to him, the interval between low and medium pitch tones is about a minor third; that between mid and high pitch tone is a major second and between low and high pitch tones is a perfect fourth (Locke, 1990, p. 37). The sound of the hourglass drum varies in relation to the amount of pressure exerted on the strings; the greater the pressure, the higher the sound.

The following are some of the syllables used by the Dagbamba players and some drummers of the Ghanaian School of Performing Arts, as documented by Locke (1990).

Zan: low pitch open tone (initial tone in a phrase)

Dan/don: low pitch open tone

Den: mid pitch open tone

Din/*dun*: high pitch open stroke

Ti: grace note;

Keren: ornament

Hi: portamento effect in which a low pitch is struck and the tension cords quickly are squeezed and released; the sound is low-high-low with the second and third strokes produced entirely by squeezing (Locke, p. 38).

These syllables may be expressed by players of the *dundun or iyaalu* of the Yoruba and *tama* of the Mande and sub groups. Thus, a combination of the *lung* or *donno* sounds may be expressed as dan dididin da didin, don dududun do dudun, etc.

Syllables expressing gungon sounds

The following are some of the vocables or syllables that are used by players of *gungon* or *brekete* double-headed cylindrical snare drum in expressing the drum beats, as noted by Locke (1990), and as can be heard among the players. The *gungon* players use four basic strokes. These include:

1. Open stick stroke played at the center of the drum skin
2. Closed stick strokes played at the center of the drum skin,
3. Open stick stroke played above the snare.
4. Open hand bare stroke played above the snare (Locke 1990, p. 28).

Examples from a Dagbamba master drummer, Zablong Abdallah, 2010.

Ka: a low sound produced with a stick at the center of the drum.
Ki: a relatively mid tonal sound produced by pressing the stick at the center of the drum head.
Gn/ng: decorative sounds produced by brushing the drum skin gently with a hand while playing or muting softly with the drum stick.

It should be noted that some drummers and students of the Ghanaian School of performing arts may express the open and closed center strokes with the syllables: ga and gi.

A version of the *gungon* vocables as expressed by Abubakari and documented by David Locke among the Dagbamba in 1990 is provided below:

Ka or *bip*: open center stick strokes.
Kek: *bep*: closed center stick strokes
Ti or *di*: open above the snare stick strokes
Gi: open above the snare hand stroke (Locke, 1990, p. 29).

A combination of the *gungon* sounds may be expressed as ka-ki-ka- ki- ng ng ng-, ka-ka- ki- ng ng ng; kaki ka ki tidi tidi, kakakaki tidi tidi tidi; ga-gi.ga-gin (ng ng ng), ga ga-gin ng ng ng.

Syllables expressing djundjun, sagban and kenkeni beats

The following are some of the syllables used by the *djundjun*, *sangban* and *kenkeni*) drummers in expressing their drum beats. Most of the sounds are produced by hitting the center of the drum. The drummer usually hits the drum-head with a stick held in one hand while hitting a bell tied to the drum shell with a metal rod held in the other hand. The result would be an interweaving of drum and bell sounds. For the sake of simplicity, only the sounds produced on the drums are provided below:

Dundun *stick drumming syllables*

Ba(m)/ga: a bouncing stroke produced with a stick at the center of the drum-head

Bim/gin: a relatively higher sound produced by pressing a stick at the center of the drum-head.

Ka: a high pitch sound produced by hitting the drum shell.

A combination of the *djundjun* sounds may be expressed as bam bim- bam ba ba-bim; or bam bi bim- bam bi bim- ba bi bim-; or ga-gin- ga-ga-ga gin-. Some drummers may use additional syllables such as don and dun in expressing the *djundjun* beats (relative to its name).

Sangban and *kenkeni* stick drumming syllables

Ga/ge/ke/te: a bouncing stroke/sound produced by hitting the center of the drum-head

Gin/kin/di: a relatively higher or muting sound produced by pressing the stick at the center of the drum-head.

A combination of the above syllables may be expressed as ge gi gi, ge gi gi…; gigi gan gigi- ga ga ga-gan-gi gin; kegen-ki- ki--, kege kegen-ki-ki-ki…

Syllables expressing sabar *beats*

The following are some of the syllables used in expressing the *sabar* drum beats, as expressed by a *sabar* drummer and instructor Tala Faye (2006; 2007): The sounds are played on the supporting *col* and m'beng m'beng drums:

The *col,* secondary *sabar* drum, hand and stick drumming syllables

Gin/gun: a bouncing sound produced by hitting the center of the drum-head with relaxed (slightly scooped) hand.

Ta: a bouncing stroke/sound produced by pressing the drum-head (near the edge) while hitting the center with a stick.

Da/ra: a bouncing stroke/sound produced by hitting the center of the drum-head just after removing the pressed hand (usually after ta). This sound sometimes begins with the consonant "t" but it is expressed in a lower tonal range. The "ra" usually denotes rapidity of a beat.

Ba: a medium sound produced by hitting the area near the edge of the drum-head with a hand usually after ta.

A combination of these sounds may be expressed as gi-gin ta.ta, gi-gi-gin--gin- ta.ra ta-ta.ra, gi ta.ba.ta gi.ta bata gi gi ta.ba.ta gi; and gi.gi.ta-gi.gi.ta- gigita-ta-ta gi; ta ta- ta-ta- ta- tara tara- gin gin gin…

A more elaborate version of the *sabar* vocables is provided by Patricia Tang (2007)) in her recent study of *sabar* drumming. Most of the syllables used in expressing the sounds of the *col* (supporting drum) correspond with the ones provided above.

Tang provides three basic hand strokes in *sabar* such as *gin*, *pin* and *pax*. She further provides various hand and stick strokes and their vocables or syllables (based on the rendition of right handed drummers) as follows:

Gin: left hand strikes the center of the drum, creating the resonant bass sound.

(on the *col* (secondary drum), left hand strikes the edge of the drum; like pin on m'beng m'beng).

Pin: Left hand open stroke (struck near the edge of the drum head) hand bounces off.

Pax: Left hand strikes the edge of the drum head, primarily with the finger tips pads, and the hand is left there instead of bouncing off (creating a sharp slap-like sound (in contrast to the pin (which is allowed to resonate).

(on the *col*, hand sometimes with thumb stuck under hits the center of the skin: also known as pa, bax and ba).

Ja: stick strokes played with the right hand; the stick hits the skin and bounces off freely. Also known as jan, tan ten, ta, tas sa, ya, ra and dam.

Ca: stick stroke similar to ja but hits flat against the stick so
that the length of the skin has contact with the skin (also
known as cex).

Tet: stick stroke; left hand dampens the edge of the drum
before and during the stroke, creating a higher pitch,
sharper sound, also known as te or tek.

Cek: stick stroke; stick taps the edge of the drum head, creating a non resonant clicking sound.

Na: stick stroke; hit at tip of stick and stays on the skin.

Rwan: pin or pax immediately followed by ja. This combination occurs frequently enough to be notated as a unit (also
known as rwa, ram). For example, rwan followed by *pax*
can be notated as ram- bax (Tang, 2007, 100-101).

Syllables expressing Ewe Drum beats

Below are some of the syllables that are used in expressing
Ewe drum beats. They are drawn from the writer's experiences
and the works of Jones (1959), Locke and Agbeli (1980).

atimevu *hand and stick drumming syllables*

Ga: a bouncing sound produced by hitting the center of the
drum with relaxed hand.

Gi: a bouncing sound produced by pressing the hand/fingers
near the edge of the drum-head.

De: a bouncing sound produced by hitting the center of the
drum-head with a stick.

Dzi: a high sound produced by pressing the drum-head with
hand/fingers while hitting the drum-wood with a stick
held in the other hand.

Tsi: a higher sound produced by pressing the area around the
center of the drum-head with a hand while pressing the
stick at the center or sliding it (slightly) forward on the
drum-head.

To: a higher sound produced by pressing the drum-head with
a hand while hitting the center with a stick.

Dza: the simultaneous sounding of *ga* and *kpa*.

Kre: de followed by *ge or gi.*

Vle: ga followed by *de.*

Vlo: playing *gi* and *de* in a very rapid succession.

Ka: a high pitch sound produced by hitting the drum shell with a stick.

Tu: the *ka* followed by another high pitch stroke.

Kpa: a high pitch sound produced by hitting the side of the drum shell with two sticks simultaneously.

Kpla: a high pitch sound produced by hitting the drum shell with sticks at closed interval.

Additional syllables such as *be,* ze and *ten* may be used in expressing the Ewe lead drum sounds. For example, when played faster, the pattern, *degide* or *tegide* may be expressed *krebekrebe…* Also, a slight pressing of the skin with the other hand and hitting it just after releasing the hand off the skin, may be expressed *ze(n)* or *te(n).* In addition, the syllable *ta* may be heard in instrumental and speech surrogated pattern of the *atimevu* as in the phrases, *magba hrebe gita,* or *ehua d'aridzaridza hrebe gita.* The *"ta"* sound may be produced by pressing one hand at the edge of the drum and hitting the area with a stick held in the other hand.

A combination of the *atimevu* sounds may be expressed as *gadige gigi te gi krebe gi; giden to to krebe ga; to krebe gide tote giden; toto dzadza dzadza dzadza , kren to kren totega; vlo vlo tevlote gadegi, te-gidegide to.to- kide to.to ga degren tega toto gazegide gitegi.*

gboba *hand drum syllables*

Gbo: a bouncing sound produced by hitting the area around the center of the drum-head with relaxed hand

Do: a bouncing sound produced by hitting the center of the drum-head with relaxed hand (usually after *gbo*).

Ge: a mid tonal sound produced by hitting an area around the edge or near the center of the drum-head with relaxed hand

De: another mid tonal sound produced by hitting around the edge or near the center of the drum-head with relaxed hand (usually after or before "ge")

Hin: a relatively higher sound produced by hitting an area around the edge of the drum-head with relaxed hand.

Gin: a relatively higher sound produced by hitting an area around the edge of the drum-head with relaxed hand (usually after *hin*).

Tsya: a higher (sharp) sound produced by hitting or slapping an area near the edge/rim of the drum-head with slanted hand at the edge.

Additional sounds such as *kpo* which is close to *gbo*; *go*; and *be*, which is close to "*de*" may be used by some drummers in expressing some *gboba* drum beats, depending upon the timbre and tuning of the drum, and individuals' auditory systems. Similar syllables may be expressed by the drummers of *gudugudu*, kettle drum of the Yoruba. A combination of these syllables may be expressed as *gbodo gbodo gbo hi gin, gbodogbodogbodogbodo hi gin; kpogo belebele; gedegede gbodo-gbo gbodo*...

sogo *hand drumming syllables*

Ga/da: a bouncing sound produced by hitting the center of the drum-head with relaxed hand.

Gin: a higher sound produced by pressing a hand on an area near the edge of the drum-head

Te: a sound produced by hitting an area near the edge of the drum with relaxed hand, usually after gin

Ge/de: a mid tonal sound produced by hitting the area between the center and edge of the drum with relaxed hand.

Tsya: a higher sound produced by hitting (slapping) the area near the edge of the drum with a slanted hand (around the knuckles and three fingers).

Here too, related syllables may be expressed such as *gba* which is close to *ga*; *gbo* instead of *gi*, and *to*, instead of *te*, depending on the tuning and timbre of the drum, manipulation of the hands, intensity of the strokes, speed and structure of the drumming. A combination of syllables may be heard such as *ga gite, ga ga ten, ga-krebe ga-krebe ga-ga-te; ga-hrebe ga-hrebe ga ga te, gite gite gada gada, or gbotogboto gbadagbada, zete gede zete gede te higin...* .

sogo *stick drumming syllables*

Te: a bouncing sound produced by hitting the center of the drum-head with a stick

Ge/de/ke: an alternate bouncing sound produced by hitting the center of the drum-head with a stick.

Kre: a sound produced by hitting the center of the drum-head with one stick, followed immediately by another.

Ki: a muting sound produced by pressing a stick at the center of the drum-head.

Tsi: a muting sound produced by hitting the center of the drum-head with a stick, immediately after *ki*.

Sh: a muting sound produced by pressing a stick at the center of the drum-head.

A combination of these syllables may be expressed as *tegeden tegeden, tedigen tegiden; tegedege-kitsi; sh kede kitsi kede kitsi kede-gedege...* .

Kidi *stick drumming syllables*

Ki/ke: a high sound produced by hitting the center of the drum-head with a stick.

Di/de: another high sound produced by hitting the center of the drum with a stick, usually after ki or ke.

Gi/ge: another high sound produced by hitting the center of the drum-head with a stick, usually after de or ge.

Ki/tsi a muting sound produced by pressing the stick on the drum-head.

Kre/kri: closed strokes produced by hitting the center of the drum-head with sticks in rapid succession or almost simultaneously.

Sh: a muting sound produced by pressing a stick at the center of the drum-head, immediately after *kri.*

A combination of some of these syllables may be expressed as *kidikitsikitsi; kidigidi shkrish krikitsikitsi, kidikitsi sh krin kitsi kidikitsi.*

kagan *stick drumming syllables*

Ka: a high pitch sound produced by hitting the center of the drum-head.

Ga/da: a high pitch sound produced by hitting the center of the drum-head with a stick, usually after ka.

Ke/de/ge: a high pitch sound produced by hitting the center of the drum-head.

Ta/to: a higher pitch sound produced by hitting the center of the drum-head while pressing a stick or hand on the membrane.

ŋu: a muted sound produced by pressing a stick on the drum-head (to punctuate a beat).

Additional sounds, such as *Kre/gre/gra:* denote closeness or rapidity of strokes. A combination of these syllables may be expressed as *kaga kaga, kagan kagan, kre- kedege.., kadagra...,* *teden ta...*

kroboto *stick drumming syllables*

To/te: a low tonal sound produced by hitting the center of the drum-head with a stick.

Gi/dzi: a relatively higher sound produced by pressing the stick at the center of the drum-head.

Re: a sound produce by hitting the center of the drum-head in rapid succession.

Ge/de/be: a mid tonal sound produced by hitting the stick at the center of the drum-head.

Additional sounds such as *gren, kre* and *kro* may be expressed to denote closeness or rapidity of certain strokes. A combination of the syllables may be expressed as *to to gin-gin-gin..; tegi-krebegi...* in *agbekɔ*; or *regedegedegede-tegi, gi- gi- gin tegi, gi tegi tegi tegi* (in *kpegisu).*

axatse or akaye rattle syllables (fist hand, palm and thigh and shaking techniques

Tsya: a high pitch sound produced by hitting the rattle on a thigh or in a hand or by shaking it (round).

Ku: a high pitch sound produced by hitting the rattle against a palm or fixed hand upward.

A combination of these sounds may be expressed as, tsyakutsyatsya, tsyakutsyatsya kutsyakutsya kutsyatsya...

Akpe hand or stick clapping syllables

Kpa: a high pitch sound produced by handclapping or by hitting two sticks or clappers against one another.

gankogui *Ewe double bell and* atoke *boat-shaped bell syllables*

Tiŋ: a high pitch sound produced by hitting the lower bell.

Ko/go: a relatively high pitch sound produced by hitting the upper bell

Ke: a relatively higher pitch sound produced by hitting *atoke,* boat-shaped bell with metal rod at slanted angle.

Kreŋ: close or double strokes produced by hitting the *atoke* boat-shaped bell with metal at slanted angle.

These syllables may form phrases such as *tin ko. ko-ko...; tin go-go; tin- ko- ko.ko-ko-ko- kotin; tin.go, tin go-go.go-go-go-goti...; ke keren,* etc.

During an interview with the elementary and secondary school students at Aŋlɔga and Keta (November 1997) on the modes of expressing Ewe drum patterns, some student-respondents usually confused sounds such as *ga* with *gba, te* with *de, gbo* with *kpo.* This ambiguity was due partly to the tuning, tonality and the closeness of these sounds and the students' inability to differentiate between some of the sounds. It is worth noting that drummers in the various African Diaspora setting may express some of the above syllables and others that emerge in their performance processes (depending on the timbre of the instruments, tuning systems, spoken languages, playing techniques, and other environmental factors).

Cross Cultural Comparison and a Guide to Expressing African Drumming Patterns

The above discussion has elucidated the syllables used in expressing some of the African drum beats and patterns. It has also shed light on the similarities and differences between the syllables across cultures. One would observe similarities between some of the syllables used in expressing the beats of the Akan *agyegyewa* and *apentemma* and the Ga *kpanlogo.* In both contexts, the syllables, *pe* and *de* are used to express mid tonal sounds. The syllables *pa* and *ta* are used to express the soft or muting sounds of the *agyegyewa* and *apentemma* while the syllables, *pi ti pi ti* may be used in expressing the soft and muting sounds of the *kpanlogo* drums. Further comparison can be made between the syllables used in expressing the Ga *kpanlogo* and Mande *djembe* hand drumming patterns. For example, the syllables *go* and *do* are used in expressing the bass sounds of both *kpanlogo* and *djembe* while the syllables such as *pe, de, pa, ta, pra, prem, prom* are used in expressing the mid tonal and higher tonal (slap) sounds of both drums. Also, the syllables, *ta, da, ra* as used by *sabar* drummers in expressing some of their stick drumming patterns on the supporting *col* drum, are similar to some of the syllables; *te, den, ta,* used in expressing some Ewe *kagan* strokes. It can be deduced from the above analysis that similar syllables may be used to express the sounds of drums that are similar in size, shape, pitch and timbre and which involve the use of similar techniques. These can be seen in the syllables used in expressing the sounds of the *djembe*, *kpanlogo*, *agyegyewa* and *apentemma* which have similar pitches and whose players employ similar hand techniques. Further comparisons would elucidate similarities and differences between the various cultural syllables and their strokes.

It can be inferred from the above analysis and comparisons that, syllables that are used in expressing hand drum beats or strokes include: *ga, da, gba, go, do, gbo, kpo, hre, be, hin, gin, pe de, te, ti, be, pem, poom, pra, pre(m), pro, pa, ta, gin* and *tsya*. Syllables that are commonly used in expressing stick drumming and drum wood beats or strokes include, *ga, de, te, ke, de, ki, di, ka, da, gran, ta, to, dzi, tsi, re, kpa, kpla and tu.* Syllables that are used in expressing low tonal sounds include, *ga, da, dza, go, do, gun, dun, ba, gba, kpo, pi,* and *ti.* In addition, syllables that are used in expressing mid tonal sounds include *de, ge, te, be, re, kre, hin, gin, dzin.* Syllables that are used in expressing high tonal or pitch sounds include; *gi, pe de ka, pa ta, ki, te, tin to, ton, tsya, tsi, kpa, kpla, kra, kre, da, gran, vlo.* Syllables such as, *sh, ki, tsi, pi, ti*; and consonants such as *n, m,* may mute some drum beats, strokes, or patterns. Other syllables such as *ga, de, te, ta, to, dza, gblo, tsya, ken, gren, gen, den, pa,* may end the overall performance (2000, pp. 228-229; 2011, p. 164).

I have indicated variations that are due to the size, tuning and timbre of the instruments, drumming techniques, weight, pitch, speed of the drum strokes; the drumming structure, differences in languages spoken by the drummers and individual differences. In view of the tonal nature of many African languages, the various syllables may be transposed to a higher or lower tonal range, but such transpositions or variations may be held in check by the contextual factors and knowledge of the music/dance and cultural values. With the above factors notwithstanding, the analysis provides a basis for understanding syllables used in expressing African drum beats/ strokes and serve as a basis for further cross cultural comparison, education, creativity, performance and research.

Summary and Conclusion

This book has elucidated the origins of African drums and the environmental factors that inspired the construction of the various drums. It has also discussed the uses and functions of drums in African and African Diaspora settings, thereby illuminating the musical, social, communicative, historical, documentary, philosophical, educational, therapeutic and entertaining functions of African drums/music/dance. It further shed light on the roles of drummers in African cultures, categories of drummers; the acquisition of the drumming talent, skills and knowledge; societal perceptions of female drummers and the emergence of female drummers in African and African Diaspora settings. The book also re-examined the training of drummers in traditional and contemporary African societies, the drummers' remuneration and socioeconomic status; the effects of contemporary changes on drummers' socioeconomic status, and suggested the need for a reconsideration of the drummers' roles in societies. Also included in the book is a discussion on the organization of drumming groups; the rationale for forming such groups; groups' repertoires and rehearsals and the drum making processes. The book also reviewed the techniques, structure of African drumming; performance processes: the values that contribute to good and successful drumming, as well as the modes of appreciating African drumming. It further discussed the textual bases of African drumming, drum texts and their contextual references as well as provided a cross cultural comparison of syllables used in expressing African drumming patterns.

In these ways, the book has contributed to the preservation and dissemination of African and world music/dance thereby providing a basis for further creativity, performance, education and research. It is obvious that the ongoing intercultural contacts and developments in technology and transportation have facilitated the movement of African drummers, drums and drum making resources from the continent, to and from the Diaspora and other parts of the world. The phenomena have made available new materials and techniques for constructing African drums at home and abroad, and have provided more opportunities for drum makers and drummers to share their arts with the global community. However, these developments are taking place alongside the gradual decline of the traditional contexts of African drumming. In these situations, it is imperative to preserve and perpetuate the traditional contexts of drumming which would serve as educational avenues and a solid foundation for new generations of African drummers and newly emerging contexts. There is also the need for recognition and protection of the rights of the originators of the drums, drum makers, drummers and drumming custodians in order to do justice to them. The writer also reiterates the need for societies to re-examine the role of drummers in order to deliberate on ways of sustaining the drumming traditions as well as the need for constant training of drum makers, drummers, drumming educators and researchers to serve the various contexts. Moreover, opportunities should be created for people of various ages, sex, gender, ethnic or racial groups, to learn, perform and perpetuate the African and world drumming traditions. Above all, the environment should be protected to ensure regular supply of the drum making resources.

Glossary of
African Terms

Aaleru	A town leader of drummers among the Yoruba
Ablɔme	A communal gathering or performance space among the Aŋlɔ-Ewe
Aburukuwa	A small closed-ended supporting drum used in the Akan Kete music
Adae	A festival celebrated by the Ashanti to commemorate and offer gratitude to their ancestors
Adakagoʋu	See Adakawu
Adakaʋu	A box resonator used by the Ewe drummers during a period of banning drumming
Adedemma	One of the smaller drums of the Fɔntɔmfrɔm orchestra
Adeʋu	hunters' music and dance of the Ewe
Ado	An old musical type performed in the kingdom of Dahomey
Adowa	Social drumming/music and dance of the Akan
Adzida	Aŋlɔ-Ewe sub musical/dance style of Agbadza usually performed by adults in which the tall lead drums are used
Adzo	A short dramatic display of rhythms/songs or movements in some Ewe performance styles

Adzohu	Sacred music and dance that originated among the Fon of the Republic of Benin during the 17th century and spread among the Ewe
Adzɔkli	An Aŋlɔ-Ewe music and dance style usually performed by adults by some groups at Anloga
Adzro	An Ewe music and dance genre, also known as Dunekpoe
Afa	An Ewe and Yoruba God of divination and wisdom
Aflui	An Akan influenced music/dance type associated with the Aŋlɔ-Ewe military system
Agbadza	A popular music and dance of the Ewe of West Africa
Agbekɔ	A historically hunters', military and now a recreational and theatrical music and dance of the Ewe
Agoyiyi	A musical procession of the Yewe priests and priestesses usually performed during the graduation ceremony, and final funeral rites of the deceased members of the Yewe sect.
Aho	A sung prelude in Akan Adowa and Kete music and dance
Ajogan	A musical style played by women in the palaces of Agbome and Port Novo in Dahomey
Akamba	An ethnic group in the Ukumba region of Kenya
Akantam	A suite of Fɔntɔmfrɔm music and dance composed of a cycle of proverbs played by the drum orchestra
Ako	An old musical orchestral performed in the kingdom of Dahomey
Akpese	See Borboorbor
Akukua	See Aburukuwa
Akukuadwo	See Aburukuwa
Akyerema	An Akan name for a drummer
Alaafin	The king of Oyo state of Western Nigeria

Anake	A name of male youths in Kikamba
Apa	A shoulder strap attached to a Yoruba dance
Apentemma	A bottle-shaped intermediary drum used in many Akan ensembles
Apinti	A ritual drum played for Obatala, the Yoruba God of creation
Aro	A pair of metallophones used by Yoruba musicians
Asaadua	A recreational dance/drumming of the Akan
Asiko	A straight-sided open-ended drum which is narrower at the bottom, also called Boku
Atompani	The Ewe male and female drums that had been adopted from the Akan
Atsyia	A social music and dance style performed mostly by the Ewe women of southern Togo and southern Ghana
Atumpan	The male and female talking drums of the Akan
Ayan	An ancestral drummer of the Yoruba also regarded as God or spirit of drumming
Azaguno	An Ewe name for a drummer
Azagunoga	An Ewe name for a senior drummer
Azagunokpe	An Ewe name for junior drummer
Bale ilu	See Aaleru
Bata	A double-headed, fixed pitch conical drum of the Yoruba and Yoruba descendants in Cuba.
Blatso	A binding and unbinding or liberating ritual performed for the leading members of Aŋlɔ-Ewe performing group
Bloukpete	An old musical type of the kingdom of Dahomey
Bommodu	
Bɔbɔɔbɔ	A recreational music and dance of northern Ewe youths of Ghana
Bragorɔ	Puberty rites performed for Brong-Ahafo female youths of Ghana

Brenko	One of the secondary drums of the Fontɔmfrɔm orchestra
Bugarabu	A set of three of four Jola drums
Bugum	A fire festival celebrated by the Dagbamba in Dagbon
Col	An oval shaped closed ended secondary Sabar drum
Damba	A festival celebrated by the Dagbamba to commemorate the birth of Prophet Mohammed
Dimba	Bush Mango tree
Dipo	Puberty rites/music of the Ga-Adamgbe and Krobo of Ghana
Djembe	An open-ended goblet drum traditionally used by the Mande, Malinke, Susu and sub-groups which is gaining popularity around the world
Egungun	A type of Yoruba masquerade
Entenga	A set of 16 Uganda drums
Etui	A name of the male youths in Kikamba
Etwie	A snarl drum of the Akan designed to imitate a leopard
Igbin	A drum associated with Obatala, a Yoruba God of creation
Fontɔmfrɔm	A drum/music and dance orchestra, traditionally performed in the court of the Akan kings
Frɔm	A set of large drums used by the Akan, also referred to as twenekese or bɔmma drum
Gahu	Yoruba influenced Ewe-youth social music and dance style
Gbedziyiyi	A practice whereby members of newly formed or revived Aŋlɔ-Ewe performing group wake up at the dawn of the inaugural day and walk to *gbedzi*, an outskirt of the town, and begin strolling though neighboring wards, showcasing excerpts from their musical compositions

Gohoun	A social music/dance which is reported to have existed in Dahomey during the 18th century and is still performed in some Ewe communities of Benin, Togo and Ghana
Gyamadudu	A double-headed cylindrical drum of the Akan
Gye Nyame	An Akan anchor symbolizing the omnipotence of God
Gorong yeguel	A closed-ended secondary Sabar drum
Gota	An Ewe youth's music and dance style
Gudugudu	A kettle-shaped drum of the Yoruba
Gugutegu	An ancient ritual drum of the Ewe at ŋɔtsie in Togo
Hanye gokoe	An old musical type performed in the kingdom of Dahomey
Hogbetsotso	An annual festival of the Aŋlɔ-Ewes that commemorates the exodus of their ancestors from ŋɔtsie, Togo
Homowo	An annual harvest festival of the Ga of southern Ghana
Hounvla	An old musical type of the Fɔn of Dahomey
Ijala	Yoruba hunters' chant
Ikehin	Yoruba secondary tension drum
Ikomo	Yoruba child-naming ceremony
Indlamu	A contemporary Zulu dance
Ipese	A set of Ifa drums.
Iyere	Ifa chants
Jeli/jali	Malinke musical verbal artisans
Jembefola	Mande or Mandinka name for a drummer
Kaloso	One of the divinities in the Ewe Afa religious system
Karyenda	Royal drums of Burundi
Kebero	A large double-headed drum used in Ethiopia, Sudan and Egypt
Kerikeri	A Yoruba secondary tension drum

Kete	A court music and dance orchestra of the Akan performed on other occasions as a form of cultural presentation
Kori	A gourd vessel drum of the Kasena Nankani
Kpanliga	A double iron bell used by the Fon musicians of Dahomey
Kufade	A music/dance style associated with the Aŋlɔ-Ewe military system
Kutiridingo	A mall open-ended supporting drum of the Mandinka of Senegambia used in the Tantango or Saruba ensemble
Kutiriba	The smallest supporting drum used in the Tantango ensemble
Kwadum	A lead or master drum in the Akan kete orchestra
Kyaa	One of the drums used by the Akamba of Kenya
Laklevu	An open-ended snarl drum of the Like clan of the Aŋlɔ-Ewe designed to imitate the sound of a wolf
Lamb	Senegalese wrestling competition
Logo Azagu	Silk cotton tree used in carving some Ewe drums
Lokele	An ethnic group in central Africa
Lawbe	A caste of carvers among the Wolof of Senegambia
Lundaa	A term used to refer to lead drumming part among the Dagbamba
Lung	Dagbamba name for an hourglass drum, commonly called Donno
Lunga	Dagbamba name for a drummer
Lunga paga	Dagbamba female drummer or drummer's wife
Lung doli	Dagbamba drum stick
Lungkpahira	Responsorial part in Dagbamba drumming
Lung Naa	Dagbamba chief drummer
Lunsi	An association or group of Dagbamba drummers
Letemedzi	One of the main divinities in Afa divination corpus

Mamprobi	The name of a suburb of Accra, the capital city of Ghana, and a style of Gohu music and dance performed by the Aŋlɔ-Ewe of Dzelukɔfe
M'beng m'beng	A secondary Sabar drum
Nmani	Percussive gourd and songs musical style performed by Dagbamba women usually during weddings and marriage celebrations
Mpebi	A drum orchestra associated with the Akan political system
Mpintin	A drum orchestra performed at the court of the Akan chiefs. It consists of hourglass drum and gourd vessel drums and cylindrical double-headed bass drums
Mpintintoa	Gourd vessel drums played to accompany the movement of the Asante king.
Mutula	A type of tree used for carving some of the Akamba drums of Kenya
Nama-suro	The fearless guard in the Akan procession
Nder	An open-ended lead Sabar drum
Ngoma	A generic name for drums found in Congo, east, central and southern part of Africa
Ngui	A composer among the Akamba
Nguni	An Akamba solo singer
Nkrawiri	One of the drum orchestras associated with the Akan political system
Nsenee	Court criers in the Akan procession
Ntahera	Elephant tusk trumpet traditionally blown in the court of the Akan kings and chiefs
Nthele	The elders/leaders of an Akamba dance group
Nyamalaka	A hereditary caste of musicians among the Mandinka
Nyamalao	See Nyamalaka

Nyayito	An Aŋlɔ-Ewe music and dance style usually performed during the funeral rites of the elderly people; it is also called Leafelegbe, Dekɔnyanu and Akpaluwu
Nyikɔʋu	Sacred male and female drums used by the Aŋlɔ-Ewe in the past to announce the capital punishment of state criminals at midnight at Aŋlɔga, the traditional capital of the Aŋlɔ state
ŋkɔfofodo	An Ewe modes of calling someone with the prolonged name or playing such a name on a drum
Oba	A Yoruba chief
Obatala	A Yoruba God of creation
Obuku Ware	Yoruba name for billy goat
Ode	Yoruba name for a hunter
Okyeame	A spokes person in the Akan political system
Oriki	Yoruba praise poems
Osan	Tension strings on Yoruba dundun drums
Osekye	A musical type played with double-headed drums and ensembles of bamboo pipes
Paso	A high-pitched drum used in the Fɔntɔmfrɔm orchestra
Petia	A secondary drum used in the Akan Adowa music
Premprensua	A type of lamellaphone used by the Akan of Ghana
Sambani	An outer compound of a Dagbamba house
Sampahi Naa	A deputy chief drummer among the Dagbamba
Sanga	A double-headed cylindrical drum, and social music and dance of the Akan of Ghana
Shango	Yoruba divinity of thunder and lightning
Saworo	Jingles attached to the Yoruba Iyaalu hourglass tension drums
Seprewa/Sikyi	An Akan youth music and dance style
Talmbat	A small closed-ended secondary Sabar drum, also called gorong

Tamalin	A square-framed drum used by the Ewe and Akan youths
Tantango	An open-ended drum of the Mandinka of Senegambia
Taushi	A conical drum of the Hausa
Tawahyefoa	Tobacco carriers in the Akan procession
Twafoa	Advanced guard in the Akan procession
Tweneboa	A type of cedar wood used for carving some of the Akan drums
Tweneduro	See tweneboa
Tungune	A short open-ended Sabar drum
Udu	A pot drum of the Igbo of Nigeria
Wɔpɔtɔ	An Akan word for the drum language
ʋu	An Ewe word for drum or vehicle
ʋublala	An Ewe drum-maker who utilizes staves of wood in constructing drums
ʋuga	lead Ewe drum
ʋugbegbexexle	A review of rhythmic patterns by the Ewe drummers at the beginning of a performance
ʋulɔlɔ	A drum/music and dance procession
ʋukpala	A drum carver among the Ewe
ʋutsɔhawo	Performance starting songs of the Ewe
ʋuvi	A secondary drum in an Ewe instrumental ensemble
ʋuyɔha	An Aŋlɔ-Ewe introductory song genre sung in free rhythms accompanied by a rattling sound to "call" the performance
Yeʋe	An Ewe divinity of lightning and thunder
Zenli:	An earthen ware drum played by women in the palaces of Dahomey
Zeri Tobu	A drum recitative assessment of a Dagbamba student-drummer

Bibliography

Abdallah, Z. (edited by Locke, D.) 2010. *The Lunsi Drummers of Dagbon*. Accra, Ghana: Institute of African Studies, University of Ghana.

Agawu, K. 1995. *African Rhythm: A Northern Ewe Perspective*. New York: Cambridge University Press. 1995.

_____. 2003. *Representing African Music. Postcolonial Notes, Queries and Positions*. New York and London: Routledge

_____. 2006. "Structural Analysis or Cultural Analysis? Competing Perspectives On the Standard patterns of West African Rhythms" In *Journal of the American Musicological Society* 59 (1): 1-46.

Akpabot, S. E. 1995. *Music in Nigerian Culture*. Michigan: Michigan State University Press.

Amegago, M. 2011. *An African Music and Dance Curriculum Model: Performing Arts Education.*Durham, North Carolina: Carolina Academic Press.

_____. (ed.). 2009. *Review of Human Factor Studies*. Volume 15, No. 1 June

_____. (2009). "Zizi A Forum for African Women's Expression of Sociocultural Values: A Case of Anlo-Ewe Women". In *Review of Human Factor Studies Volume 15, No.1*, June.

_____. 2009. "Aesthetics of African Music and Dance Revisited: A Case of the Ewe Music and Dance". In *African Journal For Physical, Health Education, Recreation and Dance*. Volume 15, November-December.

_____. 2007. *"Dance Elements of Ewe Music and Dance"*. In African Journal For Physical, Health Education, Recreation and Dance. Volume 13, November – December.

_____. (2000) *An Holistic Approach to African Performing Arts Music and Dance Curriculum Development and Implementation*. Unpublished Ph. D. Thesis, Simon Fraser University Burnaby, B.C.

_____. (1995). *Mid-Lane: Some Western Influences on Ghanaian Music and Dance*. Unpublished Masters Thesis. Simon Fraser University.

_____. 1988. *The Role of Misego Dance in Anlos Migration and the Hogbetsotso Festival*. Unpublished Diploma Thesis.

Ames, D.W., and Anthony V.K. 1973. *"Igbo and Hausa Musicians: Comparative Examination"* Ethnomusicology 17 (2): 250-78.

Amira, J. and Steven, C. 1992. *The Music of Santaria: Traditional Rhythms of the Bata Drums*. Tempe, Arizona: White Cliff Media Company.

Anderson, R. 1990. *Calliope's Sisters: A Comparative Study of Philosophies of Art*. Englewood Cliff, New Jersey: Prentice Hall.

Anku, William. 1986. *Rhythmic Procedures in Akan Adowa Drumming*. Unpublished M. A. Thesis

_____. 1988. *Procedure in African Drumming: A Case of Akan/Ewe Traditions and African Drumming in Pittsburgh*. Unpublished Ph. D. Thesis.

_____. 1996. "Holistic Considerations for West African Drum Music Analysis". In *Journal of Performing Arts*. 1996/7. pp. 12-16.

_____. 1997. "Principles of Rhythmic Integration in African Drumming" *Black Music Research Journal 17 (2):* 211-38.

Anyidoho, K. 1997. "Ewe Verbal Art" In *A Handbook of Eweland, vol. 1, The Ewes of Southern Ghana*, edited by Francis Agbodeka, pp. 123-52, Accra: Woeli Publication.

Avorgbedor. D. 1986. *Modes of Musical Continuity among the Anlo-Ewe of Accra: A Study In Urban Musicology*. Michigan: A Bell and Howell Information Company.

Barz, G. 2004. *Music in East Africa: Experiencing Music, Express-ing Culture*. New York and Oxford: Oxford University Press.

Battin, M., Fisher, J., Moore, P., & Silvers, A. 1989. *Puzzles About Art: An Aesthetic Case Book*. New York: St. Martin's Press.

Bebey, F. 1975. *African Music: A People's Art*. Translated by Jose-phine Bennett. New York: L. Hill.

Blades, J. 1970. *Percussion Instruments and their History*. New York and Washington: Frederick A. Praeger, Publishers.

Charry, E. 1996. *"A Guide to the Jembe"*. In Percussion Notes 34, no.2 (April 1996).

Chernoff, J. M. 1979. *African Rhythm and African Sensibility*. Chicago: The University of Chicago Press.

Cooper, D. E. (ed.). 1992. *A Companion to Aesthetics*. Cambridge, Massachusetts: Blackwell Publishers Limited.

Diallo, Y. & Hall, M. 1989. *The Healing Drum: African Wisdom Teachings*. Rochester, Vermont: Destiny Books.

Dor, G & Omojola, B. 2005. *Multiple Interpretations of Dynam-ics of Creativity and Knowledge in African Music Traditions*. Point Richmond, California: MRI Press.

Doumbia, A &Wirzbicki, M. 2005. *"Anke Dje Anke Be"*. In 3idesign, p. 86.

Ebron, P. 2002. *Performing Africa*. Princeton and Oxford: Princ-eton University Press.

Epega, A. A. and Phillip, J. N. 1995. *The Sacred Ifa Oracle*. San Francisco: Harper San Francisco.

Euba, Akin.1988. *Essays on Music in Africa*. West Germany: Iwalewa-Haus.

_____. 1990. *Yoruba Drumming: The Dundun Tradition*. Lagos and Bareuth: Elekoto Music Centre.

Fiagbedzi, N. 1977. *The Music of the Anlo-Ewe: Its Historical Background, Cultural Matrix and Style*. (Unpublished Doc-toral Dissertation). Los Angeles: University of California.

_____. 2005. *An Essay on the Nature of the Aesthetics in African Musical Arts*. Ghana: Royal Crown Press Limited.

Floyd, M. 1999. *Composing the Music of Africa: Composition, Interpretation and Realisation.* Aldeshot and Brookfield: Ashgate.

Friedson, S. 1996. *Dancing Prophets: Musical Experience in Tumbuka Healing.* Chicago: University of Chicago Press.

_____. 2009. *Northern Gods in a Southern Land: Remains of Rituals.* Chicago & London. The University of Chicago Press.

Gavua, K., ed. 2000. *A Handbook of Eweland, vol. 2, The Northern Ewes in Ghana.* Accra, Woeli Publication.

Greenberg, J. H. 1948. *"The Classification of African languages".* American Anthropologist, n.s. 50 (1):24-30.

Hornbostel, E.M. V. (1928). *"African Negro Music".* In *Africa, vol. I, no. I.* Roodepoort,Transvaal, South Africa: African Music Society.

Isaak, C. 2006. *African Rhythms and Beats: Bringing African Traditions to the Classroom.* Burlington, USA: JPMC Books Inc.

Jackson, I. (ed.) 1985. *More Than Drumming: Essay on African and Afro-Latin American Music and Musicians.* Wesport & Connecticut.: Greenwood Press.

Jones, A. M. & Nkombe, L. 1952. *The Icila Dance Old Style: a Study in African Music and Dance of the Northern Tribe of Northern Rhodesia.* Roodepoort, South Africa: African Music Society.

Jones A. M. 1959. *Studies in African Music.* London: Oxford University Press.

_____. 1965). *"An Experiment with the xylophone Key"* In African Music, vol. III, no 2, 1965. Roodepoort, South Africa: African Music Society.

Kaptain, L. 1992. *"The Wood That Sings":* The Marimba in Chiapas, Mexico. Everett and Pennsylvania: Honey Rock.

Kavyu, P. N. 1986. *Drum Music of the Akamba.* Hohenschaftlarn: Klaus Renner.

Kebede, A. 1995. Roots of Black Music. *The Vocal Instrumental and Dance Heritage of Africa and Black America.* Trenton, New Jersey: African World Press, Inc.

Koetting, J. T. 1970. *"Analysis and notation of West African drum Ensemble Music,"* Selected Reports. 1/3, pp. 116-136. 1970.

Kubik, Gerhard. 1965. *"Discovery of a Through Xylophone in Northern Mozambique"* In African Music, vol. III. Roodepoort, Transvaal, South Africa: African Music Society.

Ladzekpo, K. 1971. *"The Social Mechanics of Good Music: A Description of Dance Clubs Among The Anlo-Ewe-speaking People of Ghana"*. In Journal of Ethnomusicology 5 (1) 6-22.

Ladzekpo K. and Ladzekpo, A. K. 1980. *"Anlo-Ewe Music in Anyako Volta Region, Ghana"*, pp. 216-231. In May, Elizabeth (ed.). Music of Many Cultures. Berkeley: University of California Press.

Ladzekpo, K. and Pantaleoni, H. 1970. *"Takada Drumming"* In African Music Journal 4 (4).

Lemuel, J. (ed.) 1982. *Toward Defining the African Aesthetics.* Washington: Three Continent Press Inc.

Locke, D. and Agbeli, G. 1980. *"A Study of the Drum Language in Adzogbo"*. In Journal of International Library of African Music. Grahamstown: Rhodes University.

Locke, D. 1987. *Drum Gahu: A Systematic Method for an African Percussion Piece by David Locke.* Crown Point: White Cliffs Media Company.

_____. 1990. *Drum Damba: Talking Drum Lessons.* Crown Point, Indiana: White Cliffs Media Company.

Merriam, A. P. 1964. *The Anthropology of Music.* Evanston: Northwestern University Press.

Mensah, A. A. "1982". *"Gyil, The Dagara-Lobi Xylophone"* In Journal of African Studies, 9 (3), 139-154.

Monson, I. (ed.) 2000. *The African Diaspora: A Musical Perspective.* New York and London: Garland Publishing Incorporated.

Nettl, Bruno. 1972. *Music in Primitive Culture.* Cambridge. University of Harvard Press.

New Grove Dictionary of Music and Musicians. Macmillan Publishers. 1980.

Nketia, J.H.K.1954. *"The Role of The Drummer in Akan Society"* In African Music Society Journal. Vol. i. No. 1, pp. 34-43.

_____. 1963. *Drumming in Akan Communities.* Accra: Thomas Nelson and Sons Limited.

_____. 1974. *The Music of Africa.* New York: W.W. Norton & Company Inc.

_____. 2004. *African Art Music.* Accra: Afram Publication Ghana Limited.

Omojola, B. 1995. *Nigerian Art Music.* Ibadan: Ifra.

Opoku, Mawere. 1987. *"Asante Dance Art And The Court".* In Anthropological Papers American Museum of Natural History, 65, 192-199.

Ottenberg, S. 1971. *Anthropology and African Aesthetics.* Ghana: Ghana University Press.

_____. 1982. *"Illusion, Communication, and Psychology in West African Masquerades".* In Ethos 10 (2):149-185.

Pantaleoni, H. 1972. *"Toward Understanding the Play of AtimeÙu in Atsyia".* In Journal of Ethnomusicology 5 (2) 64-84.

Sachs, Kurt. (1940). *The History of Musical Instruments.* New York: Norton.

Sieber, Roy. 1971. *"The Aesthetics of Traditional African Art".* In Carol F. Jopling (ed.), Art and Aesthetics in Primitive Societies. New York: Dutton. Pp. 127-131.

Simha, Aron.1991. *African Polyrhythm, Musical Structure and Methodology.* Cambridge: Cambridge University Press.

Strand, J. L. 2009. *The Sambla Xylophone: Tradition and Identity in Burkina Faso.* Ph. D. Dissertation Unpublished. Wesleyan University Connecticut.

Tang, P. 2007. *Masters of the Sabar: Wolof Griot Percussionists of Senegal.* Philadelphia. Temple University Press.

Thompson, R. F. 1968. *"Esthetics in Traditional African Arts".* Art News 66 (9): 44-45, 63-68.

_____. 1971. *"Aesthetic of the Cool: West African Dance".* African Forum 2 (2):85-102.

Tracey, H. 1970. *Chopi Musicians Their Music Poetry and Instruments.* London, New York and Toronto: Oxford University Press.

Wachsmann, C. (ed.) 1971. *Essay on Music and History in Africa.* Evanston: North-western University Press.

Welsh-Asante, K. 1985. *"Commonalities in African Dance: An Aesthetic Foundation".* In Asante Molefi K. & Welsh-Asante, K. (eds.). African Culture: The Rhythm of Unity. pp. 71-81.

Wiggins, T. and Kobom, J. 1992. *Xylophone Music from Ghana.* Crown Point: White Cliff Media Company.

Younge, P. Y. 2011. *Music and Dance Traditions of Ghana: History, Performance and Teaching.* North Carolina: Mcfarland and Company Inc.

Related Audio-visual sources

Abdoulaye, Camara. 2006. *West African Dance Volume 2.* California: Carlsbad SQS Video.

_____. (2004). *West African Dance Volume 1.* California: Carlsbad SQS video, 2004.

Diop, Mapathe. 1992. *Sabar (sound recording) Dance drumming of Senegal.* Seattle, Washington: Village Pulse.

Corke, Benny. 1984. *The Drums of Dagbon: Caribbean Crucible.* England: Third Eye Production.

Dunlop Geoff. 1992. *Dance at Court.* New York: RM Arts (film); WNET (Television Station.

John-Miller, Chernoff. 1985. *Master Drummers of Dagbon* (sound recording). Cambridge, Massachusetts: Rounder Records.

LeBagatae. 2004. *Tinkanyi (1).* Chicago: Quietly Productions.

_____. 2004. *Tinkanyi (2).* Chicago: Quietly Productions.

Ly, Mamadou. 1992. *Mandinka Master Drummer.* Seattle, Washington: Village Pulse.

Younge, Pascal. 2000. *Ghana: Rhythms of the people: Traditional music and dance of the Ewe, Dagbamba, Fante and the Ga people.* Montpelier: Multicultural Media.

Yamamoto, Hiroshi. 1996. *Gambia, Liberia, Ghana and Nigeria.*
Japan: S. I. JVC Victor and Co.

URL

Adeyemi, Oba. *The Alaafin of Oyo.* http://www.africanstyles.com/
culture/talking_drum.html Retrieved May 2 2011.

Africa Alive. *The African Musical Instrument Collections.*http://
www.Africa~alive.com Retrieved April 19 2011.

*African Bongos: Music Mosaic: The Pulse of Global Harmony:
Ngoma Traditional Drums of Zimbabwe.* http://www.
myspace.com/linoswengara/photos/659174#%7b%.22lm
Retrieved April 19 2011.

*African Music Safari. Mystical African drums: Their Origins and
Traditions* http://www.african music.safari.com/udu-drums.
html Retrieved April 19 2011.

Amadinda Artists, Instruments and Recordings from Uganda.
http://amadinda.co.uk/sebi.do Retrieved April 19 2011.

Answers.com. Was the xylophone invented in West Africa? http://
www.wiki.answers.com/q/was_the_xylophone-invented_in_
West_Africa Retrieved January 9 2012.

Art Drum. http://www.com/Ashiko.htm Retrieved April 19 2011.

Balagula Ltd. *Dumbek or Doumbek The Middle Eastern Drum.*
http://www.natashascafe.com/html/drum.html   Retrieved
April 19 2011.

Bischoff, M &Abyhoj, D. *African Musical Instruments.* http://
www.Bischoff.dk/afro~index/htm Retrieved, December 2011.

Bougarabou- Irie Tones. http://www.erietones.com/item/bougara-
bou Retrieved April 19 2011.

Brazabeat: Music of the Congo. http://brazzabeat.org Retrieved
May 4 2011.

Burundi Drummers. Retrieved from http://burundidrummers.
com/aboutus Retrieved April 19 2011.

Charry, E. 1996. *A Guide to the djembe.* http://echarry.web.
wesleyan.edu/djembearticle/article.html Retrieved April 19
2011.

Christo: African Music.com. The History and Overview of African Music. http://www.afgent.com/african_music3.html Retrieved April 19 2011.

Congo Brazaville Art and Music: Voices, Drums, Soukous/Rumba, Urban Art, Sculpture. http://www.congo~brazaville.org/art Retrieved April 19 2011.

Dawson, Daniel. *Treasures in the Terror: The African Cultural Legacy in the Americas.* http://www.nku.edu/~freedomchronicle/oldsitearchive/archive/issues/treasuresintheterror/index.html Retrieved April 19 2011.

Djembe Direct: About the Djembe. http://www.djembedirect.com/about/djembe.html Retrieved April 19 2011.

Destefano, John, *History of Drums*.http://wwwpendz4.tripod.com/historyofdrums.html Retrieved April 2011.

Djembe History.http://www.afrodruming.com/djembe-history.php Retrieved April 19 2011.

Drumdojo: History of Drum. http://artdrum.com/udu.htm Retrieved April 19 2011.

Enjoy Burundi. Drum Sanctuary. http://www.enjoyburundi.info/~do~not~miss/gishora~drum~sanctuary Retrieved April 19 2011.

Genuine Afric: African Drums and Art from Genuine Africa. http://www.genuineAfrica.com/African_drums.htm Retrieved. April 2 2011.

Grosvenor, G and Grosvenor M. *Djembe Art: Fine Drums.* Gavin@djembe~art.de. Retrieved May 20 2011.

Haitian Drumming for Drummers. http://www.Steampunkopera.wordpress.com/2011/07/19/Haitiandrumming-for-drummers/ Retrieved. February 1 2012.

Hamill, Tim. *African Drum Exhibit: Hamill Gallery of Tribal Art.* http://www.hamillgallery.com/STTE/contact.html Retrieved April 19 2011.

Harper, Colter. *Life, Death and Music in West Africa.* http://context.org/articles/winter-/2008/harper/ Retrieved, January 5 2012.

Hartenberger World Music Collection. http://www.hwmconline.com Retrieved April 19 2011.

Heavenly Planet, 2009. *Drummers of Burundi.* http://www.heavenlyplanet.com/featured/dob/html. Retrieved April 19 2011.

Historical Museums of Southern Florida. *Caribbean Percussion Traditions in Miami.* http://www.hmsf.org/collection~caribean~traditionshtm Retrieved April 19 2011.

Hogan, B. *Locating the Chopi Xylophone Ensembles of Southern Mozambique.* http://www.ethnomusic.ucla.edu/pre/vol-11html/Hogan/html Retrieved May 4 2011.

Isigubu Zulu Drum. http://www.kalimba.co.za/product_view/focus/php?product Retrieved January 3 2012.

Kanyinsola, A. *The Talking Drum Orchestra.* http://www.kanyinsola.com Retrieved December 15 2011.

Karyenda Drums. Retrieved from http://karyenda.co.tv/

Kenya Tourist Board. *Music and Dance: Magical Kenya.* http://www.magicalkenya.com/index.php?=com_content%task=viewid=75%temid=196 Retrieved April 19 2011.

Kubiak, Conrad. *Spirit in the Wood.* http://www.spiritinthewood.com/conrad. Retrieved April 19 2011.

Meinl Percussion: Djembe Drums. http://www.x8drums.com/meinl~djembe~182.htm Retrieved April 19 2011.

*Motherland Music.*http://www.motherlandmusic.com/drums.htm Retrieved, April 192011.

Music Around the World: Music of Africa. http://www.cartage.org.lb/en/themes/arts/music/world; http://www.eyenee/.com/world/Af/index Retrieved April 19 2011.

Nasehpour, Peyman. *Peyman and His Tonbak: Tombak, Ghaval and Daf.* http://nasepour.tripod.com/peyman Retrieved April 19 2011.

National Museums Scotland. *Double Naqqara (kettle drums) from Morocco, North Africa.* http://www.scran.ac.uk/database/record.php?usi=000~000~604~486~C Retrieved. April 2011.

National Music Museum. http://org.usd.edu/nmm/africa/3179/ugandadrums.html Retrieved April 19 2011.

Ngoma Drums. http://en.wikipedia.org/wiki/ngoma_drums Retrieved April 19 2011.

Origin of Djembe. Retrieved from http://en.wikipedia.org/wiki/Djembe#origin Retrieved April 19 2011.

Popovic, Mislav. *Drums of Burundi: Tradition and Customs from all over the World.* http://traditionscustoms.com/music~and~dance/drums~of~burundi Retrieved April 19 2011.

Portable Drums Collections: Musical Instruments of Africa. http://www.brooklynkids.org Retrieved April 19 2011.

Raine-Reusch, R. *World Instruments Gallery.* http://asza/udu.shtml Retrieved April 19 2011.

Rebirth African Art Gallery. *African Drum History.* http://www.rebirth.co.za/African_drum_history_djembe_drum.htm Retrieved April 19 2011.

Religious Rhythms: The Afri-Brazilian Music of Candomble Sounds and Colours. http://www.soundsandcolours.com/articles/brazil/religious~rhythms~the~afro~brazilian~indigenous~music~c Retrieved April 19 2011.

Robinson, N. S. 1999. *Frame Drums of North Africa and Eastern Europe,* retrieved from http://www.nscottrobinson.com/framedrums.php. Retrieved April 19 2011.

Robinson, N. Scott. *World Music and Percussion.* http://www.nscottrobinson.com/ Retrieved April 19 2011.

Sabar Drums. http://www.sabardrums.com Retrieved April 19 2011.

Torres, Ezekiel. *Hand-made Afro Cuban Checkeres and other Percussions.* http://www.afrocubanbatadrums.com Retrieved May 11 2011.

Traditional music of the Ugandan People. http://www.face~music.ch/instrum/uganda_instrumen.html. Retrieved November 20 2011.

Ugandan Musical Instrument. http://www.ugandatravelguide.com/musicalinstruments.html Retrieved May 16 2011.

Ten Thousand Villages. http://www.tenthousandvillages.com/catalogue/image.popup? Retrieved May 2 2011.

The Archives of Contemporary Music. http://www.arcmusic.org/features/archives/percpan_Brazil/instrbrazil.html Retrieved April 19 2011.

The Bandir (Bendir): Middle Eastern Musical Instruments. http://
wwwmideastweb.org/culture/bandir.htm Retrieved April
192011.

The Origin of Bata. http://en.wikipedia.org/wiki/bat%C3%A1drum
#The Lukum.C3AD_and_the BatC3A1 Retrieved April 19
2011.

Traditional Instruments of Uganda. http://www.face.ch/instrum/
uganda_instruments.html Retrieved April 19 2011.

Wild Wood instruments. *A Conga Drums and Percussions.* http://
www.wildwoodinstruments.com/ashiko.htm Retrieved, April
19 2011.

Williams Michael. *Mbira/Timbila, Karimba/marimba: A Look at
Some Relationships between African Mbira and Marimba.*
http://www.michaelwilliams.com/PNMbiraTimbila.pdf
Retrieved April 19 2011.

William, Ruth. 2011EzineArticle.com. *Djembe Drums for Music
Therapy.* http://ezinearticles.com. Retrieved April 19 2011.

World Musical Instruments.com: http://www.worldmusicians.
com/c~9~world~drums.aspx Retrieved April 19 2011.

Zanzibar.net. *Zanzibar: Ngoma Music and Culture: Music Styles.*
http://www.zanzibar.net/music_culture_music_styles/ngoma.
Retrieved April 19 2011.

Index